W9-BCS-254

782.13
L25c

79856

DATE DUE			
Apr 25 '74			
Jan 31 '75			
Jul 9, '80			
Dec 12 '80			

WITHDRAWN
L. R. COLLEGE LIBRARY

CRITIC AT THE OPERA

WITHDRAWN
L. R. COLLEGE LIBRARY

Also by Paul Henry Lang

MUSIC IN WESTERN CIVILIZATION

MUSIC AND HISTORY

GEORGE FRIDERIC HANDEL

A PICTORIAL HISTORY OF MUSIC
(WITH OTTO L. BETTMANN)

PROBLEMS OF MODERN MUSIC (EDITOR)

THE CREATIVE WORLD OF MOZART (EDITOR)

STRAVINSKY: A NEW APPRAISAL OF HIS WORK (EDITOR)

ONE HUNDRED YEARS OF MUSIC IN AMERICA (EDITOR)

THE SYMPHONY, 1800–1900 (EDITOR)

THE CONCERTO, 1800–1900 (EDITOR)

CONTEMPORARY MUSIC IN EUROPE
(EDITOR WITH NATHAN BRODER)

Paul Henry Lang

CRITIC AT
THE OPERA

W · W · Norton & Company · Inc ·
New York

CARL A. RUDISILL LIBRARY
LENOIR RHYNE COLLEGE

782.13
L25c
J9856
Sept 1972

Copyright © 1971 by W. W. Norton & Company, Inc.

FIRST EDITION

SBN 393 02163 7
Library of Congress Catalog Card No. 70-77408

ALL RIGHTS RESERVED
Published simultaneously in Canada
by George J. McLeod Limited, Toronto

PRINTED IN THE UNITED STATES OF AMERICA

1 2 3 4 5 6 7 8 9 0

TO THE MEMORY OF
A GREAT NEWSPAPER

The New York Herald Tribune

CONTENTS

CONTENTS

PREFACE

THIS BOOK is not a history nor a dramaturgy nor an esthetics of opera, though it contains something of all three. These chapters are drawn from the reviews and Sunday articles on opera written during my nine years as music critic of *The New York Herald Tribune* (1954–63). They represent responses, not research, and so, even when organized chronologically and by schools, and bound together with connecting tissues, this collection of critiques and essays could not attain the systematic continuity of a work planned from the outset. Still, it does have a plan: to convey the ideas and reactions of a critic at work. To preserve this spontaneous quality, I have resisted the temptation to up-date and have refrained from any additional research beyond a modicum of literary grooming. Nor have I suppressed my share of inconsistencies. The passing of a decade or two brings changes in both views and perspectives, while the ideological battles settle into well-dug trenches. Unless a critic is considered a mere reporting automaton, he must undergo experiences that change his outlook and judgment, and he must take risks and at times abandon his defenses. Finally, proportions have been left largely unaltered; works heard more often are therefore discussed more often and in more detail.

At times I deal with the general problems of opera as exemplified by a work that happened to raise them. I believe that many of these ideas, often spurred by the excitement or disappointment of a particular performance, and expressed under the well-known conditions of high-speed American journalism, may present candid musical pictures that sober reflection in one's study, surrounded by reference books, could not produce. The connecting links are minimal—in most cases space breaks in the text take their place—and the only new material added is the introductory essay, which gives the contents a proper frame, and the chapter on opera buffa, which was needed to bridge the large gap between Gluck and Mozart.

Whoever reads a book about a subject he knows and likes resembles a child listening to a well-known story: he resents omissions; and there are many omissions in this book. The reader will find nothing about early opera. This is not because I am not interested in such operas; on the contrary, I am convinced that the slowly gathering recognition of Baroque opera promises to enrich our enjoyment immensely. However, a newspaper critic is pretty well restricted to the "standard repertory," which encompasses less than two hundred years of the more than three and a half centuries of operatic history. I did not encounter staged performances of opera earlier than Gluck's *Orfeo ed Euridice*, and any additions based on my teaching and research activity would have modified the physiognomy of this book, the avowed object being, as I have said above, to convey views and judgments directly resulting from performances attended in the theater.

As to contemporary opera, I must ruefully admit that while most concert audiences are conservative, a circumstance well understood and exploited by those in control of our public musical life, none are more stubbornly conservative than lovers of opera. The usual lag between audience acceptance and a developing art is considerably larger in opera than in recital music. Those concerned with creating and fostering contemporary art should never play for safety, as may be quite proper for historians, and sometimes for critics—they should indulge in enthusiasm. But for this very reason their operatic endeavors can be put to extensive use only in the subsidized theaters of Europe. With few laudable exceptions, neither the public nor the managers will accept them in this

country, and thus I have met with very little modern opera
in the line of duty.

The critic working for a daily newspaper is considerably
circumscribed in his field of action. On the one hand, the
"entertainment industry," with its box-office-oriented policies
holds him to a narrow horizon; on the other, there is a
widespread notion that the critic's sole duty is to report what
happened and how. The real and proper duty of the critic,
however, is to convey his impressions, to contribute his personal insights, to share his professional knowledge; good
criticism must be alive to the complexities of art and should
enrich the experience of the reader. Certain aspects of the
music critic's work are not open to differing opinions; arbitrary alterations in the score, poor intonation, missed notes,
and so forth are concrete facts. But whether a work is good
or bad, whether a performance is stylistically correct or a
character faithfully portrayed, are matters for individual evalu-
ation, in which the questioner's temperament and professional
equipment play a decisive role. The disagreements among
critics which not infrequently result are often held up with
glee as irrefutable proof of the uselessness of musical criticism.
Such divergences of opinion, more often than being due to
incompetence, are perfectly reasonable, and are simply the
expression of differences among individuals who see things
differently. To be sure, this "seeing" must and can be disciplined, but it should not be depersonalized. Absolute imparti-
ality is beyond the power of man, and would in any case
result in the writing of extremely dull criticism. And, of
course, on the day after, we are always wiser—and the process
goes on until our last day.

Since the *Herald Tribune* had a most enlightened and liberal
policy concerning the treatment of the arts, neither I nor my
colleagues were held to any strict journalistic "code" and
could follow our own bent and style. The good old "Trib"
recognized that in the critic's soul too there is a creative
spark. This freedom permitted me to spend more time and
space in discussing the works than in reporting on the per-

formance, and provided the main justification for this book. By eliminating the critique of the performances from the reviews, and omitting topical references, I was left with a sizable body of writings about opera as a work of art.

An author usually justifies his work by his conviction that it will contribute to the literature of his field. But in reality he writes his book for its own sake, because ideas not collected into a book are like the unburied; they can neither live nor die. I enjoyed shaping these sometimes disparate thoughts into what I hope is a coherent whole; I felt I had something to say, and after all, that is the main justification for any book. As a critic I was like a pasha of old, changing my bed companion every night. I trust, though, that this book will prove to be more than a one-night companion.

I wish to thank Mr. Walter Thayer, executive vice president of the *Herald Tribune* at the time of my retirement from the paper, who gave permission for the use of my reviews, and Mr. George Brockway, my publisher, who conceived the idea of the book and suggested the procedure to be followed; and I am deeply indebted to my wife, Anne, without whose counsel and help I would not publish a Christmas card.

PHL

Chappaqua, New York, 1970–71

CRITIC AT
THE OPERA

INTRODUCTION

WEBSTER defines opera as "a drama of which music forms an essential part." But this is only the beginning of an explanation. The employment of singing as the principal means of theatrical expression is so totally different from the usual procedure in drama that an altogether new set of esthetic criteria is called for. Opera music is a highly special, purely theatrical language which even such great lyricists as Schubert, Schumann, Brahms, and Hugo Wolf were unable to create. What is important in opera is the measure in which the music succeeds in evoking and conveying the inner personality, and in intensifying—even creating—the dramatic situation. As cannot be the case in a spoken play, this evocation is more or less independent even of the words—indeed, opera is not a play *with* music, but a play *in* music. And this is at the core of the misunderstandings that attach to opera.

Music alone cannot create *dramatis personae;* to do so it must ally itself with words. Without them, the music of an opera, no matter how beautiful, remains a thought without a body. Yet once a text has sketched an operatic personage, the music takes over and develops it far beyond what is inherent in the words. No musical genre has ever been the subject of so many theorizing prefaces and exegeses as opera, and in no other genre do we have reform movements proposed and opposed with such frequency and ardor. Musicians, dramatists, and philosophers have all been concerned with it, discussing the relationship between the spoken and the lyric theater, words and music, dramatic poet and composer; the nature of the libretto; the primacy of music or the drama; and so forth. Even Mozart, a composer without literary interests and ambitions, expressed himself at length (in his letters) about operatic music and dramaturgy.

Singing is not merely an enhancement of passionate speech but its transliteration into a different medium. Since, however, the sound of the singing voice is related to emotional speech, it is infused with psychological elements, bringing to music an immediacy of feeling that no other art, not even instrumental music, is able to equal. In opera, where music is assisted by a conceptual text, expressive gestures, and movement, it can call forth a depth of intensity unparalleled on the spoken stage; the changing emotional states of the protagonists are seen through a magnifying glass.

Drama in the theater attempts to render life, to conjure up in a small place, in a short time, with a limited number of figures, the illusion of the whole world. It is in the nature of the spoken drama that its conflicts must be treated with a certain logic, and its construction rests on a chain of causes and effects. Opera is not representation in the manner of the spoken theater; its expressive possibilities are not on the same plane with reality but are stylized abbreviations of it. The plot is merely a sketchy basic frame, for the decisive element must be the constructive, formal, and expressive power of music. Immediate sensuous expression is hampered in the drama by the constant intellectual procedure that must be followed, an inhibition absent from opera. Music in a good opera provides something that at once precedes and surpasses the concrete concept of the drama, for music dissolves feelings into melodies and harmonies, rhythms and counterpoints which in themselves have no conceptual meaning. The painting of character in the spoken drama requires time; in opera it is almost instantaneous. The action in a play demands a certain movement; in opera, the action is constantly suspended by stationary lyric effusion. In the drama, plot and action must be unfolded; opera aims at comprehensive summary, at the dramatic exploitation of the psychological moment.

The relationship between text and music goes far beyond musical declamation of the words, and it is here especially that opera differs so much from the legitimate theater, even from other types of vocal music. In the combination of text and music the latter's role is primary; though moods are more powerful than impressions, and the word is superior to the mood, music transcends them both. The text is not only secondary, moreover; from the point of view of total form it can be negligible. In contrast to the spoken theater, opera does not present a coalesced whole; indeed, at times it even hides the text, and, ironically, we do not miss it. The content of a poem cannot be detached from its rhythm and form; the content is the poem itself, the way it is, from word to word. It is another matter with most operatic lyrics, even those by such consummate craftsmen as Metastasio or Boito: the rhythm of the verse is washed away by the rhythm of the music. Here, in fact, the choice and arrangement of individual words is less important than the content; yet strictly speaking it is not the entire content, only the most important idea, that matters.

In *The Magic Flute*, Tamino falls in love with Pamina when he sees her picture; he sings a superlatively beautiful aria, but we do not watch very closely what he says. Instead of singing "O image angel-like and fair," he could substitute "The new sensation I undergo is so different from all I know" (Cherubino), yet the aria would not change at all, because the music is solely concerned with the sentiments evoked by falling in love and is so breathtakingly beautiful in conveying a young man's yearnings that the details, the actual words, are superfluous beyond the mere "statement" that Tamino is in love. Thus the aria becomes an almost total stylization. What the romantic realists did not realize in their rejection of this stylization was that it can also become a concentrated symbolic expression of a dramatic figure and of his entire fate. This is the power of opera: by this extraordinary ability of music it can rise above the finite world and far beyond the expressive capabilities of words.

One of the objections raised against pre-Classic opera concerns the frequent repetition of lines, even of single words. Such repetition of textual fragments is so alien to the spirit of the spoken drama that it could arise only in a genre not interested in the direct and literal exploitation of the text. The Baroque composer did exploit the text, but he was concerned only with the lyric's main affective statement, and since his musical ideas needed much more space than the text provided for, he returned to the principal affective words and repeated them, not infrequently a dozen times or more.

Then there is opera's most characteristic and unique possession, the ensemble, in which several protagonists sing together, each one of them pouring out his innermost thoughts. Even with the best enunciation, the several texts sung simultaneously can be comprehended only in snippets, yet the ensembles are often the high points in operas and usually carry the strongest dramatic impact. There is no parallel to this in literature, for the ensemble is both theme and elaboration presented together. Victor Hugo, who had no feeling for opera, nevertheless exclaimed when he first heard the quartet in *Rigoletto:* "This is marvelous, simply marvelous! Ah, if I only could in my play make four people talk simultaneously in a way that the public would understand the words and the varying sentiments." But he could not, because the operatic ensemble is determined largely by its musical material rather than by the import of its text. The ultimate in ensembles, the compound finale, with the whole cast on the stage, is altogether governed by a musical logic to which action and plot must be reconciled. Indeed, the purely musical considerations that are not readily perceived by the untrained ear are staggering. An aria may be superfluous and dispensable from the point of view of dramatic structure but may have considerable relevance to tonal balance; the concordance of keys in a Handel or Mozart opera is as important structurally as it is magnificent aurally. The public may not know about this but subconsciously feels its unifying force.

Perhaps the chief stumbling block for the layman used to the spoken theater, however, is the prevalence of unnatural situations in opera. On the operatic stage an aria must be properly developed and ended, a purely musical requirement that can create moments which from the point of view of the legitimate theater verge on the ludicrous. The hero, mortally wounded, manages to sing a lengthy aria, with ringing top notes, before he succumbs. Instead of coming to his aid, the others on the stage all gather around him to hear the aria. It is such incongruities that have prompted literary critics—and not a few modern musicians—to heap scorn on opera. However, all such objections were—and still are—based on the mistaken belief that an opera should have the same reasonable continuity, the same logic of cause and effect, as the spoken play. But, as we have said, opera is more than a play with music. It would have little *raison d'être* if what it conveys to us could be rendered just as well in words. Music in an opera has a more than illustrative role; it is more than an ornament that enhances the effect of the drama. Indeed, it arrogates the primacy to itself. These are large claims, but were the pretensions of opera without esthetic justification it is improbable that a host of geniuses, from Monteverdi to Wagner, would have addressed their talents to it.

At just about the time when the modern theater of Lope de Vega and Shakespeare had completely emancipated itself from the liturgic and mystery plays, a learned academy in Florence, the Camerata, endeavored to recreate the Attic drama. Their creation had respectable parents—music and drama—but the progeny, which they called opera, proved to be misbegotten.

Since the Florentines were ignorant of the music of antiquity, they obtained their bearings from literary sources, from the extant plays and theoretical writings. There can be no question that there was incidental music in the theater of antiquity, both solo and choral, but the Florentines incorrectly envisioned the Greek theater as sung drama. From that assumption they concluded that in the Attic tragedy the purpose of music was to underline and heighten the dramatic dialogue (a play *with* music); they therefore saw the most important requirement in their "operas" as the intelligibility

of the text. This inviolability of the play being the alpha and
omega of Florentine musico-dramatic esthetics, the great new
invention, the recitative, was a simple declamation supported
by a self-effacing accompaniment. Frequent cadencing imped-
ing the free flow of even this meager music was compulsory,
because in their declared dependence on the text the composers had to follow the verbal punctuation. But the learned
antiquarians soon had to surrender to superior creative forces,
and within a few years the new art form became a musical,
rather than literary, genre.

The history of opera really begins in 1607, when the first
overwhelming genius, Monteverdi, appeared with his *Orfeo;*
a drama was created in music, profoundly expressive, truly
dramatic music. To be sure, there was music in the medieval
jeux, in the mystery and miracle plays, which are usually
cited as the ancestors of opera, but neither they nor the mad-
rigal comedy has really anything to do with it. Opera came
about when music took possession of the theater. And we
must remember that the use of ancient myths notwithstanding, we are in the presence of a genuinely Baroque phenomenon, not a reconstruction of antiquity or even of the Renaissance; this was contemporary art. Yet opera cherished the
humanistic dream and, unlike the spoken theater, clung to
the stories of the gods and heroes of antiquity. In no other
form of the theater did the old humanistic spirit last so long
as in opera; the Orpheuses and Daphnes, the Oedipuses and
Electras lived and remained popular from Monteverdi to Stravinsky. It goes without saying that the "facts of history"
(*fatti storici*) upon which the librettists insisted were only a
thin veneer to hide a world of fantasy, for this opera (as Romantic opera was later to do) avoids the nearness of life by
relying on a distant, quasi-historical milieu. The distance did
not exclude, however, what the Baroque called *accidenti veris-
simi;* the operatic stage was generously strewn with the
corpses of the slain. Nevertheless, Monteverdi, Cavalli, Cesti,
and other great composers of the earlier part of the seventeenth century wrote real music dramas. The characterizations
and the passions unleashed in a work like *L'Incoronazione di*

Poppea are starkly dramatic and every bit as convincing and powerful as those in Verdi's *Otello*.

The second half of the seventeenth century brought the first decisive change in the construction of opera: the separation of the action-carrying recitative from the reflective, lyrical aria. Thereafter, and for a long time to come, we are dealing with a musical theater based on closed forms, "numbers." These closed operatic forms, and their distinctive idiom, became the principal carriers of the new Baroque musical thought, and they decisively influenced everything far into the eighteenth century, whether sonata or symphony, Passion or Mass. Now the point of gravity gradually shifted from the rational interpretation of the words, which the humanistic tradition demanded, to the purely musical; music became self-serving, not an adjunct of the drama. This was a concept of the lyric theater in which song dominated not so much as dramatic expression but as a purely musical manifestation. (The Germans very aptly call this opera *Musikoper*, a term which unfortunately does not come off in English.) With the victory of music, the libretto was reduced to a schematic frame, using either thrice-familiar historical or mythological subjects, or allegorical fantasies. The artistic value of the libretto, its versification, its poetic lyricism are all virtually lost, as the musical construction, determined by a rigorously enforced system, governs the number and position of the arias. Furthermore, this late-Baroque musical "tragedy" had a fatal undramatic twist: the happy ending at all costs, which became the chief concern of librettist, composer, and public. Thus the aria is no longer a dramatic element. It lives its own life, almost independent of the play; at best it had some relevance to the momentary situation. This bel canto opera became the national genre, and if there was anything that could unite the many warring city states and kingdoms of Italy, it was opera, their very own creation. It did not take very long before the rest of Europe was conquered by it.

The extent of this operatic activity in Italy seems to us unbelievable. So many opera houses in so many cities were active that the rush of production exceeded creative control. The demand for new operas was so great that the local composers could not satisfy it, and there arose the institution of the *compositore scritturato*, who traveled from theater to theater, was given a ready-made libretto (the *scrittura*), and composed an opera on the spot, though not before carefully taking the measure of the available forces. He had to be careful about his custom-made vocal parts, because the singer's voice was all-important, transcending dramatic and even overall musical consideration—it had to scintillate for its own sake.

Posterity has judged this Baroque opera harshly, denouncing it as interested neither in true drama nor in true theater but solely in the singer. The adverse opinion rests on a good deal of ignorance; we simply do not know enough about this long-forgotten kind of opera. Of the thousands of Baroque operas, only a handful is available, and whenever one or the other is resurrected, it is likely to be killed off by well-meant but mistaken antiquarianism. For while the "music opera," "singer's opera," or "concert opera" (all derogatory epithets originating in the Wagnerian era) has certain features hard to reconcile with our present-day musical concepts, it also boasts great qualities. In Baroque opera was created the azure Mediterranean melody that enthralled generation upon generation of music lovers and permeated every corner of the domain of music, including church music. This rapprochement between stage and church constitutes, for the northern Protestant, one of the most difficult obstacles to the appreciation of both eighteenth-century opera and Italo-Austrian church music. The northerner feels, not without reason, that there is something essentially Catholic—and pagan—in this music, and senses that, next to Catholicism, the ancient classical and pagan world is closest to the Mediterranean Latin, in whose heart these two worlds get along quite well together. However, without an Alessandro Scarlatti and his school, the entire future history of music would have been totally different. While the currently derided da capo aria ruled opera (and is present in its operatic form—and never objected to—in Bach's Passions and cantatas), it was by no means always a mechanical structure; the inventiveness of the composers often endowed it with remarkable and subtle variants. It was Baroque opera, too, that introduced the so-called accompanied recitative, the most powerful means of dramatic expression in stage music. Unlike the aria, it is a free form in which every word is set carefully as the text unfolds, while the orchestra accompanies with great flexibility. Indeed, contemporary writers, among them Metastasio, warned against the too-frequent use of the accompanied recitative lest it make the aria anticlimactic. Finally, in the large *scena* the composers of the late Baroque combined all these elements; here, especially in Handel or Jommelli, secco, accompagnato, arioso, and aria are interdependent and respond to the exigencies of the drama. Nevertheless, the obstacles to the revival of this infinitely rich musical treasure are considerable, and many problems, among them that created by the castrato roles, remain to be solved.

The French *tragédie lyrique* was the only important independent offshoot of the Italian Baroque opera. Eventually it had to make peace with its ancestor, but not before contributing some valuable new elements to the internationalized Italian opera.

In French opera the participation of the orchestra was much more important than in the contemporary Venetian theater; the ensemble was larger and more colorful, using a variety of instruments in contrast to the simple accompanying orchestra of the Italians. This aspect of French opera, as well as its elaborate use of the chorus, exerted considerable influence on the future history of the genre. It was with Lully that descriptive mood pictures—storm, dawn, night, and so forth—originated; they continued to live all the way to *The Flying Dutchman* and *Otello*. By the time of Mozart the orchestra had become an integral part of the musical drama, a full-fledged partner with the stage. In one of his letters to his son, Leopold Mozart writes: "Your style of composition requires unusually close attention from the players of every type of instrument, and to keep the whole orchestra at such a pitch of industry and alertness for at least three hours is no joke." The overture also underwent changes. In the older opera there was no rapport between overture and the opera itself; there is none, for instance, in Gluck's *Orfeo ed Euridice*. Neither the composers nor the public wanted more than a curtain-raiser, during which the latecomers might be seated. It was only toward the middle of the eighteenth century that the idea of an organic connection between overture and opera began to gain acceptance. The critics now demanded an "analogy" with the contents of the drama. However, there seems for some time to have been disagreement whether this relationship should encompass the whole opera, in which case the overture would be a sort of symphonic résumé, or whether it should merely lead into the first act.

In its purest form, opera, the most original creation of the Italian Baroque, has always remained Italian. All other opera that developed a distinct national style, like the French or the German, is something different. While all Italy, where the spoken theater could not even remotely compete with the lyric stage, revelled in opera, other countries, with a highly developed and flourishing legitimate stage, greeted the new genre imported from Italy with varying degrees of hostility. The two arts, ostensibly sisters, were rivals and could not live together in comfort. In Venice, more than a dozen opera houses kept librettists and composers busy—but in Madrid, where several dozen playhouses with a thousand actors took care of the incredible productivity of the playwrights, opera was scarcely known. In other countries, such as England, that had also been among the leading musical nations but now were dominated by the stage, there was no national opera for a long time to come. In France, where the literary tradition was very strong, it was an Italian, Lully, who established national opera, which he dominated with dictatorial powers in the face of opposition from the leading literary men.

In Germany the situation was especially awkward. When Schütz's version of *Dafne* was performed in Torgau (1627), Germany suddenly had opera—before it had a developed theater of any sort. The Germans did have their school theaters, and the Jesuit theater in the Catholic south, but the public theater consisted of ragged wandering troupes. There was no dearth of able composers in the country, but there was a dearth of theatrical talent among them, and if such talent arose it was either overwhelmed by the Italians (Keiser) or left the country and joined the Italians (Handel, Hasse). Thus the reason for the tardiness of German opera—*Dafne* was a solitary case—was the inability of the resident German composers to adjust to a foreign cultural trend. And yet it was only in Germany that the Venetian type of public opera theater—as opposed to the strictly court establishments—found a counterpart, in Hamburg, Weissenfels, Bayreuth, and a few other cities. By the seventeenth century there were quite a few stately opera theaters; the Brunswick opera, built in 1690, held an audience of 2500, and there were magnificent buildings in Dresden, Vienna, Prague, and other places where the spoken theater was still in its infancy. But all this was an importation; the modest beginnings of German national opera collapsed completely before the onslaught of the Italians, as one after the other of these institutions yielded to Italian composers and Italian personnel. Thereafter most German composers took to the writing of "Italian" operas, and the official court poets, whether in Vienna, Dresden, or Mannheim, were librettists engaged from Italy. Frederick the Great, who also built a luxurious opera house, said that he would rather have an aria sung by his horse than by a German prima donna, and even Goethe thought Italian far superior for singing to any other language. As is well known, a similar view concerning the superiority of Italian over the French language prompted the famous opera war in Paris. In the face of all this stands the remarkable fact that both Baroque and classical opera were carried to their summit by Germans outside of Italy: Handel in London, and Mozart in Vienna. But of course they composed Italian operas, which reminds us of the importance of the Italian operatic enclaves in Vienna, Dresden—even St. Petersburg—which loom as large in the history of the genre as the achievements of Venice, Naples, and Milan.

The opposition of the literary world to opera was widespread, intense, and powerful. Addison and Steele ridiculed it in England, Swift detested music altogether, but especially opera; St. Evremond and Boileau denied its validity "because music is incapable of rational narration"; Gottsched and Schlegel, the esthetic lawgivers in Germany, opposed it; even in Italy, the Arcadian poets and philosophers, Aristotelians to a man, maintained that "it is not natural to speak in music." Yet nothing could thwart the success of this much-denounced, paradoxical, and hybrid form of art.

Lully had already become aware of the Janus face of opera. He was inspired by the great spoken drama of his age, of the *grand siècle,* but he was also bewitched by that fragrant vapor that envelops the drama the instant music takes possession of it. Though a cool-headed and typically orderly composer in the French manner despite his Italian origin, he well understood that when set to music, a play can rise into regions where the spoken drama can no longer follow.

Literary plays are seldom if ever suitable for musical composition—the tempo of the spoken drama is different from that of opera. In the play the lyric moments are not primary; the action is not constructed for their sake; but in opera they are of supreme importance—even in Gluck and Wagner, who were opposed to musical elements not subservient to the drama. (It had to be so, of course, because despite all their theories they were musicians first.) Here we are faced by a vital trait of opera, highly characteristic of its nature. As we have mentioned earlier, in key situations, where the spoken drama is compact and swift in action, opera's lyricism arrests and seemingly destroys the dramatic proceedings. Dramatic concentration, motion, liveliness are all abandoned for the sake of lyricism. As a matter of fact, opera condenses the dialogue to make room for this lyricism; the action in the recitatives is swift so that the effusive aria, which suspends all normal theatrical activity, can be reached quickly. Obviously, this is so different from the dramaturgy of a recited play that radical changes are needed to make a play suitable for operatic treatment.

In order to adjust the original play for the purposes of the composer, a third person, the librettist, is called upon to join the enterprise. He takes the agreed-upon subject—usually a play—and, with more or less success, converts it into a "book," which the composer then sets to music. The conception of the librettist's role has changed from period to period, but he is always interposed between playwright and composer. Time and again critics make the mistake of discussing, say, *The Marriage of Figaro*, by analyzing Beaumarchais's ideas and intentions, whereas what Mozart set to music was da Ponte's masterly arrangement, made with opera in mind— quite a different thing. The librettist does not and should not approach his task from a purely musical or a purely literary angle, but from a third, very specific point of view: that of the lyric theater. Whether his conception is more musical or more dramatic depends on which of the components he finds more suitable for this third approach. Metastasio, the great librettist, whom the Italians regard as one of their literary giants, receives short shrift from modern literary critics and writers on opera. They fail to realize that the admired dramatic poet, worshipped by generations of musicians, wrote not plays but "dramas *for* music," that is, of the "third genre," which cannot be judged by purely literary-theatrical criteria.

Crises in operatic history are more profound than in instrumental music. Instrumental music could shed Baroque linearity and move from the invisible depths of canon and fugue to the very visible forms of the pre-Classic sonata, symphony, and concerto, but opera first had to resolve the particular contradictions that always exist in the relationship between the stage and the changing modes of life. The first modern reform movements arose against the "pure musicality" of the opera seria. One of them wanted to safeguard the basic operatic ideals but infuse the musical theater with a new dramatic momentum; this was the new heroic-classic opera of Gluck and his disciples. The other wanted to do away altogether with the opera seria by replacing stylization with vivid and exciting episodes taken from ordinary life: the opera buffa. Now we have arrived at a period of operatic history which is visible to the opera-going public and so requires little discussion in this introduction. Gluck, whose reform is described in Chapter One, is the oldest regular tenant in our opera houses. We shall see that aside from his very considerable personal achievement, his influence on future opera was more legendary than actual. Anyway, reform movements usually end in compromise. The other "reform" movement, which created the opera buffa, is the subject of Chapter Two.

At the end of the century, Mozart created a magnificent synthesis between seria and buffa, reaching an ideal balance between drama and music as well as between stage and orchestra, yet without abandoning the primacy of music. While unquestionably he towers over his contemporaries, we should not forget the many fine composers who worked in the same vineyard.

The development of opera in the nineteenth century differs considerably from that in the previous two centuries. As we have seen, in the older opera the course of the drama was subordinated to music; form was the result of an aggregation of more or less independent musical pieces that exploited the basic moods of the text. In contrast, nineteenth-century opera placed music in the service of the drama. More precisely, on the one hand it adjusted the musical form, while on the other, even when it resorted to closed aria forms, the musical matter of the aria obeyed the dramatic situation not only in basic mood but in its entirety. Thus, while the Mozartean opera is formed by the exquisite stylization of broadly planned and smoothly flowing musical units, Romantic opera gathers together smaller, interlocking units of shorter breath but corresponding more closely to the dramatic text. The "numbers" of the older opera characterize by their entirety; the new opera characterizes step by step, in small details. The success of the older opera depended on the composer's ability to reconcile the independent musical forms with the requirements of the drama; the new opera succeeds when despite the constant and detailed dramatic characterization it achieves larger musical units. Thus the problem of Romantic opera is not whether the text permits the creation of broad and unified moods, but whether it is possible to build musical scenes on the basis of the inner dramatic unity of the libretto. The transition between the two eras was led by Cherubini, Beethoven, Weber, Spontini, Spohr, and some lesser composers, while in the works of Rossini, Auber, Meyerbeer, Donizetti, and Bellini the Romantic formal principles and dramaturgy take hold and in many cases dominate. Romantic opera culminated in the works of Verdi and Wagner, who represent two extreme types. Wagner places the point of gravity in form and expression in the orchestra; Verdi's operatic procedure rests on the ago-old Italian tradition of song. The chief ancestor of Wagner's musico-dramatic fabric is the old accompanied recitative, while Verdi reconciles the aria opera with the Romantic urge to create moods, without, however, succumbing to the growing tendency toward extreme theatrical realism. "To copy reality can be a good thing," he said, "but to invent it is better, much better." In general, the Italians remained attached to the centuries-old traditions; they are like distant descendants whose traits are recognizable in their ancestral portraits. Actually, in the nineteenth century most of the tendencies exhibited by the Classic opera of the late eighteenth century continued to be alive in modified form, but the mood changed because Romantic opera was attracted to popular, national, epic, and exotic subjects and elements, though it also cultivated the heroic opera. Wagner represents the really new turn, seemingly in opposition to all contemporary opera and most of what preceded him. For while the concept on which it is based—the *Gesamtkunstwerk*, the "universal art work"—is literary and philosophical, in essence the Wagnerian opera represents an epoch-making new musical language and apparatus. Ever since the inception of opera, the great innovations in music's expressive means—from Monteverdi onward—have come mostly from opera. The literary protestations notwithstanding, the principal feature of opera was still music. Nor was the famous *Gesamtkunstwerk* new. It was present the moment poetry, music, drama, acting, and the dance were joined. The French *ballet de cour* and the

Italian *sacra rappresentazione,* with their elaborate staging, songs, and dancing certainly presented a union of the arts, yet they were no more a *Gesamtkunstwerk* than was Wagner's elaborate concept. There will never be a union of the arts on equal terms, because a real opera contains the entire theater in its score. And it is the score that counts; no matter how distinguished the singers and the dramatic and visual effects, the opera is altogether in the hands of the conductor who interprets the score.

Post-Wagnerian opera variously tried to follow the Bayreuth example, though—except for Strauss—with little success; or it remained faithful to the old Italian precepts; or, again, it experimented with new librettos reflecting new literary tendencies such as *verismo.* There is a notable and most interesting tendency, though, as exemplified by Berg, to return to closed forms. All of these the reader will meet in the following chapters.

We have seen that the Florentines tried to take their departure from the drama of classical antiquity, forming their opera from the spirit of the drama. But opera's cradle was surrounded by musicians who within a short time expropriated this new form of art, turning it into theater dominated by music. From Monteverdi to Dallapiccola, and until very recently, in every opera music has been the master. Opera is indeed a paradox and a hybrid, and will always be a magnificent compromise, but it is also an eternal lesson of the power and scope of music, for, as Kierkegaard said: "Where language ceases, music begins."

One

———————

GLUCK

G LUCK is a great and much-admired composer whose august reputation is still intact nearly two centuries after his death. As anyone who has ever read a book on the history of music knows, Gluck is acclaimed the classical composer par excellence, "to whom is due much of the credit for opera as we know it today." Nevertheless, this contemporary of Kant, himself a philosopher of sorts, lives mostly by dint of his tremendous reputation as the creator of the new, rational theories of opera. Unfortunately, when the theorist is too much emphasized it is at the expense of the illusion created by esthetics. Thus, Romain Rolland, a connoisseur of seventeenth- and eighteenth-century music, surprisingly saw the principal merit of *Orfeo ed Euridice* in its "moral strength." In music, as in life, our virtues are often the obstacles to success. Gluck's was a rich life, yet this great composer commands more respect than popularity. His name is much better known than his music; the musician suffers from the reputation of the reformer. Only two or perhaps three of his many operas are occasionally heard, and these are seldom dusted off for the repertory unless one or the other of the great ladies of opera wants to demonstrate her independence, or take a dignified leave from the stage. During his long period of Olympian entombment, a whole collection of legends has grown up around this austere and dedicated artist, and no theater bill, press release, or review fails to reproduce some of them. The Germans claim Gluck among the founding fathers of their Classical school, yet, though German by birth, he never wrote a German opera and left no particular impression on the so-called Viennese School. Although he was of German stock, his entire orientation as well as his training was Italian, and later French, and if we must place him, he should be considered a French counterpart of the Italo-German Hasse. Even when in Vienna, he lived in an Italian environment, because Vienna had for some time been one of the great outposts of Italian opera, with many resident Italian musicians, and the imperial court poet was none other than Metastasio, the universally admired master and high priest of the Italian lyric stage.

Gluck began his career by writing Italian operas in Italy and ended it writing French operas in Paris. His acquaintance with the French musical stage came early, and he became proficient in it—though at first in its comic variety, well liked in Vienna—long before he set foot in France. In fact, Gluck became the first exponent of comic opera on German soil. It was the "General Director of Spectacles" at the imperial court, Count Giacomo Durazzo—a Genoese enamored of French culture, particularly the theater—who introduced the vaudeville and opéra comique to Vienna. He was a friend and protector of Gluck's and had a hand in the "reform." These comic operas are altogether delightful, and it is a pity that they are unknown. Without them Gluck would never have risen to his revered status in the "serious" opera, for in these charming works he learned to create characters rather than types, human characters free of all stylized grandeur. But there was another French genre with which he became acquainted in Vienna in the 1750s: the tragedies of the *grand siècle*, notably the plays of Racine. The resident French theater in Vienna alternated the frivolous with the serene, vaudeville and opéra comique with classical tragedy; and, as we shall see, the classical theater in general and Racine in particular were to play an important role in the life of the reformer. It is remarkable how readily he was able to leave the Metastasio-Hasse type of highly formal and aristocratic opera and plunge into the carefree, saucy, petit-bourgeois world of French comedy. (It is of course equally remarkable how readily he could find his way back to the formal opera.) But Gluck, the composer of comic operas, is passed over today lest we destroy the image of the noble dramatist who reformed that wanton and frivolous Italian opera, just as Handel, the eminently secular dramatist, must not be permitted to destroy the image of the composer of sacred music.

Gluck was largely self-taught, both as a musician and as a man of letters. Among the great composers, he was one of the slowest in maturing, and technically never in the upper brackets of the age's high craftsmanship. For sheer musical talent and ability, a Jommelli or a Traëtta was undoubtedly his superior, yet his music outlived them. There can be no question that this earnest, devoted, and dedicated artist was a great composer, but he was a child of the Age of Reason, and his undeniable glow was a well-ordered, somewhat subdued glow. He was a composer who worked with cool deliberation, whose every melody and scene was polished and buffed until it had the feel of alabaster. There is also a certain edifying, almost didactic, element in his music, for he used intellect even when inspiration should have had the upper hand. Furthermore, he was a born man of the theater and bound to the words. Though he studied with Giovanni Battista Sammartini, the most forward-looking instrumental composer in Italy, his purely instrumental output, all of it from his youth, is negligible. Even in the operas, the instrumental numbers, unless an integral part of the dramatic situation, are impersonal, conventional, and at times lacking in substance. Most of his overtures are equally conventional opera sinfonias, formal to the point of offering nothing but thrice-familiar formulas, though some of his later operas he prefaced with real overtures that announce the coming theatrical action in mood and theme. But when Gluck allows his heart to beat unencumbered by theory, he can call forth real and moving human passions. We must also consider that into the stereotyped and dying Baroque opera seria he suddenly injected a tone that was not unworthy of the classical subjects he set to music.

Gluck's *Orfeo ed Euridice* is the oldest opera in the standard repertory and is looked upon with respectful admiration. Every operatic establishment prides itself on staging *Orfeo* periodically to demonstrate its attachment to Classicism, for this work is indeed universally acclaimed as the incarnation of the true music drama, the great reform opera that changed the course of musical history and led directly to Wagner. We are dealing here with a historical reconstruction that does not wholly agree with the truth. *Orfeo* is a great work and deservedly famous—but not solely for the above reasons. The trouble with most performances is the presence of an almost ostentatious reverence not so much for the music as for the famous old "classic." This music is indeed noble, but it has a healthy countenance; there is nothing in it that calls for a prayerful attitude and subdued dynamics. On the contrary, Gluck was still close to the Baroque tradition of beautifully chiseled arias requiring expansive bel canto; after all, *Orfeo* is still a "castrato opera." Take for instance the music Orpheus sings when addressing the Furies. This is a melting, sensuous serenade in the purest Neapolitan manner which should be sung with a full-bodied voice and a free and easy delivery so as to envelop the Furies as well as the audience. Regrettably, it is usually delivered in a tame and colorless fashion, like Victorian church music. Or consider the first air, a light and elegant Rococo piece customarily performed in a severely "classical" style, that is, without life. This is probably the worst side of the popular conception of Classicism, for it ignores the very important contribution made by the Rococo to this style. The playful element, coming from the Italian intermezzo and opera buffa, was blended during the transitional era with the fine-grained elegance of French dance music. Although the Rococo was superseded by the Classic style, a good measure of its decorative elegance survived and was absorbed as an integral element of the new style. Gluck, a globe-trotter, was acquainted with every musical practice from Naples to Copenhagen, and as I have remarked above, he not only knew the light French comic opera but composed some examples of it himself. To disregard or minimize the *galant* element in Gluck

—or in any composer of the latter part of the eighteenth century—is to falsify the nature of his music. If the melodic turns
and the rhythm are given a uniformly solemn aura, the elegance and sparkle are lost. This is eighteenth-century music
and not the music of a hypothetical antiquity, and it should
reflect eighteenth-century musical thought. If we take away
the sensuous charm of unabashed bel canto, the aristocratic
gaiety and lilt of the dances, what is left is a historical document rather than a living masterpiece. Safeguarding the elegance is the more necessary because of Gluck's rather restricted sense for counterpoint and even for everyday part-
writing. And while he was capable of harmonic finesse for
dramatic ends, his cursive harmonic writing is unadventurous
and at times downright simpleminded. There is a measure of
stiffness and cerebral orderliness in Gluck, but that is the very
thing that should be minimized in performance. Conductors
should forget about the romantic reverence associated with the
works of the great legendary reformer of opera and simply
play them as good music. They will make a real "classic" out
of *Orfeo* by removing the marmoreal quality into which it has
frozen ever since Wagner appointed Gluck his official forerunner.

"The music should serve," said Gluck, "it should be no
more than an accompaniment to the drama." But is music,
such as the magnificent choral dirge at the opening of *Orfeo*
(inspired by Handel's *Hercules*) and several of the great arias,
"mere accompaniment" to the words? It is music, pure, heartfelt music, and that is why it still lives, not because of any theories. The much-censured Neapolitan opera tradition of unadulterated song is still here and is the chief reason for the enduring popularity of *Orfeo* as compared to Gluck's later—and
perhaps greater—operas which are much more studiedly "classical." It is still the sheer attraction of beautiful music that
largely dominates here. (There is, of course, a gap between
beauty and enjoyment, and the one cannot be easily explained
as a means to the other.) It is the reform element, rather, that
causes certain limitations in this masterpiece, chief among these
being the static quality, the slow-moving pace, due in no small

measure to the absence of lively recitatives, now proscribed. This places a burden on the stage director, who now tries to overcome it by the lavish use of ballet.

But there is another pronounced drawback not, however, attributable to the reform; on the contrary, it is a leftover of the most questionable aspect of Baroque opera, the absence of male voices. When a woman sings the role of a man, there is no theatrical illusion. Whenever this device was successful in post-Baroque times, as in Mozart's *Figaro* and Strauss's *Rosenkavalier*, the role is that of an adolescent well short of twenty. But Orpheus is not an adolescent, and how can a woman in voice and figure persuade us that she loves Eurydice and is willing to brave the Furies in Hades to regain her? Granted that Orpheus, like most gods and heroes in the old opera seria, is an idealized type rather than an individual personality, and that therefore the "neutral" castrato could do justice to the part; nevertheless, much more could be made of this role today than usually is. Gluck himself was conscious of the problem created by the castrato, who was by that time fading from the scene, and himself offered a solution in a version of *Orfeo* made for Paris in 1774, twelve years after the original production in Vienna. To the Italian any means that would make possible extraordinary vocal feats was justified and acceptable, hence the popularity of the artificial *primo uomo*, whose vocal virtuosity was phenomenal. But the French had never accepted the castrato, and a transvestite role was sure to drown a Parisian performance in breezy Gallic pleasantries. Therefore Gluck changed the leading role from alto to tenor. Though the French revision of *Orfeo* into *Orphée* is not so carefully made as the subsequent conversion of the Italian *Alceste* into a French opera, to my mind it is to be preferred to the original Italian because it provides the necessary relief both psychologically and musically, and it leads to much less self-conscious music-making. The changes wrought by the reworking of this score are much more profound than a mere shift in personnel; "Che faro senza Euridice," delivered by a cautious alto, is a piece of an entirely different character from "J'ai perdu mon Eurydice" sung by a confident tenor. The purist should remember that the castrato's alto was not a dark voice but a powerful, "white," male voice of extraordinary range. Those who maintain that the original vocal range must be preserved at all cost lest we falsify Gluck's intentions forget that the dark-hued female alto already falsifies these intentions quite generously. Today we do prefer the French to the Italian *Alceste,* and it seems that the only reason European houses cling to the Italian *Orfeo* is once more because of its codified role as the "first reform opera," though of course the very presence of the castrato belies that. However, the Italian *Orfeo* can also be produced with more satisfying results by using Hermann Abert's excellent edition of the score, in which Orpheus's role is give to a baritone. The changes represented by the transposition are minimal, the gains in theatrical, psychological, and dramatic values considerable. (Of course, in American houses we are still saddled with that curious nineteenth-century compilation wherein the French *Orphée* is transposed into the alto keys and the French text back-translated into Italian, thereby achieving the worst of both worlds.)

Another thing that changes the essential character of this opera is the attempt to present a picture of classical antiquity, a revival of cothurnus and armor, rather than the world of an eighteenth-century opera still predicated on the colorful staging and elaborate machinery of Baroque opera. Gluck has been associated by most historians with the movement led by Winckelmann and Lessing, which banished the frivolous Rococo Cupids and Venuses and the Anacreontic Bacchuses admiringly imitated from the French, and revealed to Germany the true classical Greece, the land, in Winckelmann's pregnant but misleading phrase, of "noble simplicity and serene grandeur." What these writers understood by Greek art was not, however, the great art of Phidias and Praxiteles but the late and less admirable Hellenistic art which swept them off their feet when they first beheld it in Naples and Rome. Neither Winckelmann nor Lessing nor Gluck—not even Goethe after them—ever looked upon Athens or Delphi. It took another century before Schliemann, possessed by the same ideal, revealed the Greece that still lay buried beneath the soil. It was largely a fictitious, ideal vision of ancient Hellas that quickened the imagination of so many a poet, sculptor, musician, and historian, just as the ideal of Rome haunted the dreams of northern rulers.

Some years ago I heard *Orphée et Eurydice* in Aix-en-Provence; it was a thoroughly absorbing, modern, and historically correct performance. What greeted the audience was a typical eighteenth-century spectacle, not pseudo-classical antiquarianism. All the singers wore elaborate costumes with profuse ornaments, Orpheus being particularly resplendent in his colorful robe, plumed hat, and dress sword. We should bear in mind that the eighteenth-century man, dressed in satin, brocade, and lace, wearing an elaborately coiffured and powdered wig, was a gay and fantastic creature who confirmed nature's law that the male of the species is more impressively decorative than the female. The stage machinery, always of paramount importance in old opera, was recreated at Aix-en-Provence with astonishing cleverness. Rocks and gardens appeared and disappeared, but the crowning glory was the final appearance of Amor, riding a chariot on a patch of cloud up in the skies—an eighteenth-century operatic print come alive. The result of this excellent production was not a stuffy "classic" but a warm and graceful opera. This prestigious and long-suffering work, now presented like a fragile Grecian urn, does indeed have life in it and can be made fully enjoyable. With all its limitations it is replete with noble, elegant, and at times poignant music, and if it could be rescued from the old routine, from antiquarianism and abstract theories, it could become a genuine favorite. The clear voice of a tenor, a little less awe, and a more vivid eighteenth-century conception and approach would achieve this.

Gluck's contemporaries called him "the Racine of music," obviously intending to compliment him as the composer of tragedies. But surely *Orfeo-Orphée* is more a *ballet chanté* than a lyric tragedy; the much-praised classical drama is nonexistent because a happy ending, in the best Baroque tradition, thoroughly falsifies it. The dead Eurydice revives and lives ever after in conjugal bliss with Orpheus. The third act, with its *deus ex machina* ending and the completely undramatic figure of Amor, contradicts all the reforms instituted in the first two acts. The artifice of the happy ending, practically mandatory in Baroque opera, violates not only the theories of the drama but often the plain logic of the plot and, in the case of *Orfeo* and several of the other reform operas, the general character of the play from which the libretto was made. The enforced happy ending is an illogical intervention that repudiates the rest of the design. (One of Gluck's colleagues, Johann Gottlob Naumann, an able German composer living in Denmark, composed an *Orfeo* in 1785. He sidestepped the problem by making Eurydice docile; she does not turn back and therefore does not have to die, and the happy ending ensues quite smoothly.) Many a great dramatic work of the Baroque suffers from this lack of credibility, and in accepting the contemporary convention, Gluck certainly ignored the principal tenet of his reform: "dramatic truth." Perhaps that famous reform bears a little scrutiny, and one may reflect that the theories and theses fit together too neatly and arouse a suspicion that too great stress is often laid upon faint indications.

"There is a book to be written," says T. S. Eliot, "on the commonplaces of any great dramatic period, the handling of fate and death, the recurrence of mood, tone, and situation." Such a book on opera, especially on old opera, has not yet been written; more precisely, while we have some excellent studies on the history of opera, the categories Eliot enumerates have scarcely been investigated. Thus in our history books *Orfeo ed Euridice* seems to have appeared on October 5, 1762, from nowhere. The Baroque opera seria was not the freakish nonsense posterity prefers to consider it; the theatrical picture it presented was not materially different from that offered by the highly appreciated spoken theater before the advent of Garrick and modern acting. Tragedy was performed in almost exactly the same way as opera seria, the actors advancing to the footlights and declaiming their parts with dignity, while everything else on the stage remained stock still. As a matter of fact, in the Comédie Française a good deal of the eloquent, statuesque, recitative-like declamation has been retained almost to this day. The decor and the costumes were shared by the spoken and lyric theater, neither of which was concerned with what we today call the utilization of stage space, or with verisimilitude in action and representation. Actually, there was more life in a sumptuously mounted opera than in the spoken theater, and in France, where drama was infinitely more developed than in Italy, the discrepancy between the animation at the Académie Royale de Musique (the "Opéra") and the decorum at the Comédie Française was startling to foreign visitors. A performance of one of Rameau's operas was so colorful that it would shame any nineteenth-century grand opera. Also, until the second half of the eighteenth century part of the audience was seated on the stage of the Comédie Française, as it is today at sold-out piano recitals. True, the intrigues in Baroque opera plots were complicated beyond intelligibility, and the unvarying sequence of recitative—aria was monotonous, but the situation was far from being so dismal as our music histories want us to believe. The intermezzo and the opera buffa had begun to force changes in the seria as early as the 1720s; but the great watershed must be placed at about the middle of the century, when the philosophers and critics began to doubt the esthetic validity of the three unities and were converted to the idea of "natural acting," several of the leading men of letters having observed Garrick in London.

Here a few dates may be noted in relation to 1762, the year of *Orfeo*'s appearance. Rousseau's most influential *Letter on French Music* appeared in 1753, his "operetta" *The Village Soothsayer* in 1752. The important writings on opera, proposing far-reaching reforms, by Quadrio (1752) and Algarotti (1755), made the rounds all over Europe, and Goldoni's modern comedy-librettos were eagerly set by a number of eminent composers. Algarotti advocated an almost Romantic concept of the unity of all the arts, with the proviso, familiar to us from Gluck and Wagner, that in an opera the music should be the servant of dramatic poetry. It is here, too, that we first encounter Gluck's main thesis: "dramatic truth." It was several years after the appearance of Algarotti's work that Calzabigi and Gluck began their reform movement, and a comparison of the famous manifesto-preface in *Alceste* with certain portions of Algarotti's *Saggio sopra l'opera* will show almost verbatim agreement. By 1760 Diderot, Lessing, and others advanced modern theories of dramaturgy, Noverre introduced pathbreaking reforms in ballet and pantomime, and such eminent composers as Jommelli and Traëtta composed advanced and highly dramatic serious operas. The da capo aria was considerably modified, the stereotyped sequence of recitative and aria changed by the agitated accompanied recitative, and the decorative duet transformed into dramatic confrontation. On the other front, Galuppi's and Piccinni's fine, modern comic operas, with ensembles, and, especially in Piccinni's *La buona figliuola* (1760), with extended compound finales, conquered all of Europe.

Looking at the operas composed by Gluck from *Orfeo* onward, one is immediately struck by the fact that he composed so-called reform operas whenever his librettist presented him with a reform libretto. Between the revolutionary new works he was perfectly content to hew to the old style. Even after his sixth and last reform opera, *Iphigénie en Tauride*, the crowning glory of his lifework, Gluck slid back, in *Echo et Narcisse* (which has an atrocious book), to conventional if attractive music. Obviously, the librettist must have had an important role in the "reform."

Ranieri de Calzabigi, the librettist of *Orfeo*, *Alceste*, and *Paride ed Elena*, was a fantastic character, one of those incredible literate adventurers the world unfortunately ceased to produce after the eighteenth century. He strikes one as an elder brother of da Ponte, Mozart's excellent librettist, for both of them were first-class charlatans as well as superbly equipped men of letters. At one point they actually meet: both were friends and boon companions of Casanova. Calzabigi's main field was finance. He was expert in setting up lotteries, which he did in partnership with Casanova, and in devising banking systems. Calzabigi organized the international banking system in Vienna and for a while was the virtual head of the imperial treasury. That in the end these undertakings ended in deficits, shortages, and other contretemps does not concern us here. What interests us is that between these complicated and far-flung operations he also managed to write excellent treatises on opera and some fine librettos. He was an uncommonly versatile man of letters, an archeologist, a translator of Milton, a frequent borrower of ideas (especially from Diderot)—though without ever mentioning his sources. His *Dissertation on the Works of Signor Metastasio* (1755) is a remarkable exposition of operatic dramaturgy, in which Calzabigi clearly perceived the problems of the congealing opera seria. We know that he was the author of the important preface to Gluck's dramatic ballet *Don Juan,* but he was undoubtedly also behind the celebrated preface to *Alceste,* always considered Gluck's own manifesto of the reform.

Now what was the famous reform? The doctrine of the lyric theater defined as its supreme aim the expression of "dramatic truth." In order to achieve this it was necessary to alter not only the structure of the opera seria—secco recitative and da capo aria were banished—but the very hierarchy of the arts: music was to be subordinated to the drama. "I have striven to be more painter and poet than musician," declared Gluck. These ideas were engraved on every memorial tablet and quoted by every writer in every textbook. But who followed the lead of the reformer? There was a small school in Paris—Salieri, Sacchini, Méhul, Cherubini, and some lesser second growth—but they wilted soon and have largely disappeared. Those who survived, like Cherubini, retained certain of Gluck's principles and attitudes but really traveled new and different paths, the main influence being—Haydn! The other confessed disciples, Berlioz and Wagner, are too far removed from the scene to be considered direct descendants. One must come to the conclusion that Gluck made no particular impression on the future of opera, all the endorsements of Berlioz and Wagner and all the textbooks notwithstanding. Mozart was impressed—for a while—but then turned altogether toward the Italians. The latter, bored by the serene nobility of the reform operas, politely suggested that Gluck take up church music. The reform went completely unnoticed in Italy and even in Gluck's own Vienna. As late as 1845, on the occasion of his visit to the Austrian capital, Berlioz complained about "the incredible ignorance prevailing with respect to Gluck's works." Mozart and everyone else continued to use the "chattering recitative" felicitously, and far from eschewing "frivolous subjects," the opera buffa flourished and produced its most delightfully frivolous masterpieces. Leopold Mozart, speaking in a letter about his son's opera *La Finta semplice*, which Wolfgang composed in 1768 for Vienna, says the following: "It is not an opera seria, however, for no operas of that kind are being given now, and moreover people do not like them. So it is an opera buffa." This was said after Gluck's *Orfeo* and *Alceste* had been composed and produced. But, above all, in every successful opera music remained clearly the senior partner in the combination of drama and music.

Gluck himself frequently ignored his own reform. *Alceste* has da capo arias (and they are fine indeed), and the drama was readily sacrificed to the interests of the conventions. In the opening scene of the second act, for instance, when the curtain rises, the real and stark drama of the first act is abandoned because custom demanded a big ballet in the second act. We are witnessing a grand banquet to celebrate the recovery of Admetus. This ballet offers some charming music, but it completely disrupts the drama. The original score says: "A large salon in Admetus's palace"; indeed, "salon" is the word that correctly measures the distance of this scene from classical tragedy.

Next we must examine the reformer's claim that dramatic truth can be attained only through music begotten by the words. Gluck, like all eighteenth-century musicians of the older persuasion, was an inveterate arranger. There is nothing wrong with that; Bach and Handel, together with all other Baroque composers, indulged in copious pasticcio work. *Alceste*, which is rich in such pasticcios, is not merely a slight refurbishing of an older opera, like *Orfeo-Orphée*, but a new creation that, while retaining a good deal of the original, also offers new material and many numbers shifted from older operas. While Gluck borrowed freely from himself, especially in the late reform operas, he often reworked his material in the best Baroque tradition. He was too good a musician simply to clip off the da capo from an old aria and add a makeshift ending; the binary piece he fashioned from it could usually stand on its own. But he could be as sloppy as Handel could when he was in a hurry, and on occasion, when the pre-existing music, composed on Italian words, remained unchanged, the French librettist was compelled to arrange the text to fit the old music. One is constrained to ask what happens to the uniqueness of utterance if substitutions can so readily be made. Furthermore, *Alceste* also has an enforced *lieto fine*, a happy ending. In general there is a certain monotony in this opera, caused by the use of dark-hued tonalities, by a very slow-moving harmonic scheme, and by a somewhat rigidly enforced nobility. The first audiences likened the opera to a "funeral Mass," Mozart *père* referred to its unabated sadness, and one of the contemporary critics asked indignantly, "What pleasure can one have in Jeremiads?" Nevertheless, at its best *Alceste* is truly classical. The fine orchestral commentary, the haunting use of the chorus, the excellent vocal diction, all contribute to an impressive work. *Alceste* is also superior to *Orfeo* in the extent and intensity of the individual scenes, as well as in the characterization.

It is clear, then, that the celebrated reform, ascribed to Gluck alone, is badly in need of thoroughgoing review and study. The source of the reform is palpably literary-philosophical, almost entirely French (even Algarotti's sources were French, with a leavening of Addison) and, as we have seen, valid in France only. To mention one example, surely the flat contradiction between Gluck's maxim that the composer's duty is to second the poet, and Mozart's total refutation of this basic postulate ("in an opera the poet is the obedient servant of the composer") does not indicate acceptance of the reform. The paradox of opera was bound to intrigue the Encyclopedists, and many of the dramaturgical aspects of the Gluckian reform were due to their writings, for the entire range of problems was discussed by the *philosophes* before the musicians took notice of them. Whether Gluck read the Encyclopedists cannot be ascertained, but his reform librettists most certainly did. Calzabigi lived for years in Paris and, as is plain from his own writings on operatic esthetics, was intimately acquainted with the writings of the *philosophes,* notably with Diderot's ideas on dramaturgy. Having been expelled from Paris because of some shady lottery affair, he settled in Vienna, where through the intermediary of Count Durazzo he came to know and work with Gluck. It is here that the reform begins, because before *Orfeo ed Euridice* Gluck did not give any indication of not being satisfied with the type of Italian opera then in vogue. On the contrary, it is quite obvious that Gluck followed the Metastasian operatic code not only because it was the universally accepted one but because he found it congenial and comfortable, as he did the pasticcio technique.

We have heard a great deal about the frosty Classicism of Metastasio, his unreal, distant, and unconvincing drama, but if anyone should be singled out as the overwhelming force in the opera seria next to Alessandro Scarlatti, it is this poet, a thoroughly musical poet. Whether Leo, Hasse, Jommelli, the young Gluck, or the young Mozart, they were all under the spell of this "Italian Sophocles." We tend to ignore the fact that Metastasio was admired even by the arch-enemy of the serious opera, Rousseau, while Voltaire compared him with Racine. No amount of patriotic fervor outside of Italy was able to displace the Italian king of librettists, though some of the ablest literary men, not excluding Goethe, tried it. They did not realize that the secret of Metastasio's success was that he always started from the composer's corner; every syllable he wrote was singable and every lyric invited music. The story has it that before delivering a new libretto to the prospective composer, he secretly set it to music himself to test its suitability. Whether or not this story is true, Metastasio, a trained musician, was perfectly capable of doing so. On the other hand, it must be conceded that Metastasio reduced tremendous historical events to amorous episodes, and his tyrants and regicides always ended up rehabilitated as good citizens. This was, however, the fashion of the times, and he, no less than the musicians, was bound by it. In his earlier years Gluck was considered such a consummate representative of the Metastasian seria that when in 1745 the competing opera company in London wanted an Italian composer of stature to oppose Handel, they invited Gluck, who was billed by the London papers as Signor Gluck. The two Germans were not at all hostile toward each other, and Gluck always remained an ardent admirer of Handel. As a matter of fact, certain of the reform ideas originated during Gluck's London days, though the incentive did not come from Handel's Italian operas—which he himself had abandoned by that time—but from the English oratorios.

The reform declared the secco recitative to be one of the chief obstacles in the path of dramatic truth. In early opera, recitative and aria were sharply opposed—the recitative explained, the aria expressed—and this contrast ruled the opera seria. By the middle of the eighteenth century the composers were endeavoring to make the texture more fluent by the use of transitional types of music between arias, and the orchestrally accompanied recitative, known since Cavalli and Cesti, now came to the fore. But the secco did not disappear, and, as we have remarked, no one used it more happily than Mozart. Actually, it was not until Rossini's *Elisabetta, Regina d'Inghilterra* (1815) that an Italian opera was orchestrated from beginning to end. In this connection we should bear in mind that the French *tragédie lyrique*, which furnished important ingredients for Gluck's reform opera, was orchestrated in its entirety, something new to those used to Italian opera. But upon closer examination we shall find that Gluck did not really "discard the *recitativo secco*"—he discarded only the harpsichord. Many of the recitatives are not true developed accompagnatos; they consist of simple chords struck by the strings—clearly the orchestra merely substitutes for the harpsichord. That a number of the accompanied recitatives are sung over long-held string chords only makes them a trifle monotonous. Actually, Gluck here made general use of a special device drawn from the old Venetian opera, where it was traditionally heard whenever a departed spirit was conjured up. Bach always uses this device in his Passions to accompany Christ's recitatives, but these are brief scenes, and their marked difference from the other recitatives makes them highly dramatic. The growth of the accompanied recitative, the chief carrier of agitated dramatic action in late- and post-Baroque opera, was clear to Gluck. He did not fail to recognize that it changed the schematic recitative-aria contrast, forcing changes in the aria itself. The accompanied recitative was no longer a device without melodic values, but a musically meaningful link in the evolving drama, often turning into arioso, even surpassing the aria in musical significance. It was for this reason that contemporary writers, among them Metastasio, warned against too frequent use of this powerful dramatic agent lest it make the aria anticlimactic. Gluck had magnificent examples of accompanied recitative before him in the works of Handel, Jommelli, and others. At first he did not attempt the thematically developed accompagnato, but later he made the most of this flexible medium. The same is true of the da capo aria, the bête noire of modern opera critics. Since the da capo aria was not acceptable to the French, Gluck had to rework it into a binary form. How strongly he was still influenced by tradition is seen in *Orfeo*, where instead of da capo arias Gluck writes da capo structures consisting of separate pieces: chorus-recitative–chorus, or chorus–aria–chorus, and so forth. Of the proscribed operatic accoutrements, even the castrato returns in *Paride ed Elena*, the third reform opera. A particular difficulty was created in the first reform operas by the restriction of the protagonists to two persons, probably a deliberate return on Calzabigi's part to the pattern of the earlier Attic tragedy. So planned, the third figure, Amor in *Orfeo* and Pallas in *Paride ed Elena*, must appear as an altogether external phenomenon not part of the dramatic fabric.

Now let us examine Gluck's French reform operas, the two *Iphigénies*, considered the summit of Gluck's art and the most classical of his creations. It is interesting to observe that Racine's *Iphigénie* was the subject Diderot suggested and analyzed as the most suitable book for a "perfect" opera, and it was this very subject that Gluck used for his debut in Paris.

The librettist of *Iphigénie en Aulide* was Leblanc Du Roullet, a confirmed admirer of the *philosophes* who was then attached to the French legation in Vienna. Given the guidance received from his French or French-oriented librettists, it was natural for a composer as dependent on the text as Gluck to shed the Italian allegiance and enter the French orbit. The change from Italian to French phonetics was of capital importance with a composer highly sensitive to word values. Gluck's French was excellent, and he was sincerely complimented by eminent men of letters upon his ability to set French words to music faithfully and in the spirit of the language. Still, while ready to be guided, Gluck also explored on his own, and just as he had discovered and absorbed the advantage of the French comic opera for lightness of texture and means of characterization, now he welcomed and tellingly utilized the glory of the French *tragédie lyrique*, the chorus. This was not accidental; Gluck assiduously studied Lully's and Rameau's scores. As early as *Orfeo*, the chorus was given an un-Metastasian importance, and this importance grew steadily in the subsequent reform operas. After *Paride ed Elena* the decision was made to abandon Italian opera forever, and it seems that Gluck even contemplated settling in France.

Iphigénie en Aulide has five protagonists, and this fact alone removed to a certain extent that static quality of the earlier operas. At times the composer's intention to be monumental is a little *voulu*, and at the end, the drama is once more doctored, but the psychological penetration is marked, and there is life in the characters. Of the two *Iphigénie*s, the second, *Iphigénie en Tauride*, is the more highly admired. In fact, it was so admired in the nineteenth century that it offered serious competition to Goethe's famous play by the same title. And its popularity led Richard Strauss, in the amiable way composers trifle with the works of their long-departed colleagues, to patch up this masterpiece, which needs no aid beyond an intelligent group of performers and directors. (Wagner performed the same collegial service for *Iphigénie en Aulide*.) *Iphigénie en Tauride* has a good libretto, perhaps the best Gluck ever set. The young poet, François Guilliard, took

it from a successful tragedy by Guimond de la Touche; nevertheless, it is quite obvious that Gluck's old mentor Du Roullet
still had an important hand in this sombre and difficult work.
The opera contains all the wisdom and creative power of this
worshipper of Classicism, for *Iphigénie en Tauride* does conjure up the spirit of ancient Greece with a success that few
composers afterwards could match. The earnest composer's
endeavor to evoke the grandeur of antiquity makes his
characters at times less real as human beings, but here again,
our own age is responsible for the marmoreal quality by permitting the charming innocence of this music to degenerate
into pompous sentimentality. Though unquestionably a masterpiece, there are curious lapses in this work, mainly owing to
Gluck's preoccupation with ethical and dramatic theories to
the detriment of the musical element. He could give Iphigenia
songs of radiant beauty, but only by falling back upon what
he once so sternly repudiated: the sheer sensuous attraction
and power of Italian melody for melody's sake. He also turned
to the modern musico-dramatic procedure of characterization
in music, and his characters are well formed and steady.
There are instances of the most compelling dramatic power.
Almost the entire second act is strong music, and the clash
between Greeks and Scythians in the first act is quite real.
But there are also unaccountably leaden passages.

There is an element at work here, an esthetic and dramatic
creed, that was unacceptable to the composers in the main
stream of opera. Gluck in his late period was no longer interested in musical invention itself but rather in its dramatic
application. He reached back into his vast reservoir of a
hundred stage works, seizing anything that suited the situation
and thereby violating his own precepts of "dramatic truth."
We know that Gluck's talent was reserved and a little austere,
his ideas hard won, and his penchant for pasticcio marked.
This latter tendency must not be compared to Handel's well-
known instinct for scavenging, for that lordly embezzler always makes one feel that the borrowed stuff really belongs to
the particular spot where it was inserted, whereas with Gluck
it denotes a certain difficulty in keeping the creative flame

going. *Iphigénie en Tauride* has many borrowings, and they do not always fit. There are spacious, almost Handelian arias, delightful Italianate pieces, vaudevilles, stiff French "tragic material," and some silly "Turkish" music with snare drum and cymbals. The harmonic idiom is simple, the harmonic rhythm slow, and the bass line often turgid. As a result, there are serious discrepancies between the "modern" music that characterizes and gets behind the meaning of the words and the old that is merely pretty. The ending, as in most of his serious operas, sags; the masterly treatment and the grandeur are relinquished; the holy conviction is surrendered to the conventions of the contemporary theater. As we stand upon the high point, at the end of Act II, looking over the magnificent music drama, everything appears as true tragedy worthy of the greatest of Greek dramatists, but the end contradicts everything; the tragedy becomes a mere story. The best the tired composer could do was to borrow the final chorus from *Paride ed Elena*.

Gluck was a literary, intellectual musician whose mind, commanded by an iron discipline and great integrity, was seldom permitted to soar uninhibited. Reading his interesting letters one often comes across elaborate descriptions of his intentions, but some of them strike one as pure "paper" speculation, cerebral blueprints difficult to reconcile with lyric composition. In particular, when he instructed a young or minor literary man, like Guilliard, the instructions can be so involved that the poor man must have been hard put to follow them. In Gluck's own words: "The poet-librettist makes the design, the musician only fills in the colors." As we have indicated, this concept is antithetical to true opera. Fortunately, Gluck often strains within his theoretical armor, and in such moments his music convinces. Although he did not attain to the fullness of genius that marks the great Baroque masters or his younger Viennese colleague, when he did not carry his artistic doctrines too far he was unmistakably their kin.

Gluck should not be judged as the representative of an age, a nation, and a reform, but, like all great composers, as an individual creative artist. It was his puritan and uncompromising spirit, proud and single-minded, which was the key to his character, and which gave the composer a deep and inspiring belief in his destiny. The majority of his hundred-odd stage works have aged, much of them beyond the possibility of rejuvenation, but some of them will live forever—because of their music.

Two

OPERA BUFFA

"I T IS AN odd calling," said Molière, "to make decent people laugh"; but a later commentator on laughter, Bergson, ascribed to the comic the high significance and ideals that others applied to the tragedy. Among the many esoteric theories explaining the springs of comedy, two should perhaps be singled out. One is the longing for the innocent world of the nursery tale, a longing which explains why in the comic theater nothing has serious consequences and no grave error costs anyone's head. The other is the comedy's limitless possibilities to illuminate man's character and, indirectly, his views of life. Comedy is the poetry of the other side of the coin, but the insight gained is painless, for it also reminds us of the shiny side, our superior selves, who are not guilty of the shortcomings of the play's characters. In the drama the actor lives before our eyes, engaging in his struggle with such immediacy that the passive viewer in the audience is virtually compelled to identify himself with the incarnation on the stage. It was said that when in Racine's play the Emperor Titus renounced his love for Berenice to satisfy the Senate, "every man in the audience was ready to marry her." In a comedy, such identification and empathy are much more difficult to achieve. More precisely, here the member of the audience is prevented from identifying himself with the comic hero by his love for his own security and self-image. But that

52

a certain empathy does take place here, too, is shown by our anxiety about the outcome of the plot. And in the so-called serious comedy we do feel compassion for the ridiculous hero. Laughter really warns the unsuspecting viewer not to get too close to the isolated, the eccentric, the *inadapté;* it is a defense against undesirable identification. The slashes of irony are enjoyed by the public—up to the first blood drawn; afterwards most people prefer to withdraw so that they may continue in their own way with everything unchanged. We may be unwilling or unable to imagine ourselves in the place of the characters of the comedy, but we feel their attraction, for they are ages old, with millennial experiences, full of movement and life, with sparkles issuing from their fingertips.

Humor often begins where artists, with their own particular vision, see as laughable certain things that others take seriously; often it is nothing but a different viewpoint. So it was with the opera buffa, which arose in the midst of the august and stilted opera seria. It bravely attempted to understand and express the still reticent and unconscious spirit of the wide public as opposed to the tone-setting aristocratic public of the seria. This new theater was no exotic bloom; it was not only the delight of the neglected common audience but a path-breaking departure in musical history that was to have incalculable consequences. Initially composed with simple, even primitive, means, the buffa became the chief agent in the transition from the Baroque to the Classic era, furnishing the latter with the main ingredients of its style. Many musicians and the vast majority of the public were tired of the seria's extreme stylization and lack of action; they found the elaborate decorations and stage machinery ridiculous, as they did the bravura arias and especially their deliverer, the castrato. (The buffa deliberately made the chief protagonist a bass, in order to spoof the castrato.) They also found the eternal gods and heroes of antiquity dull, and disliked the strong contrasts between life and death, Elysium and Hades; the Italian's sunny nature demanded real entertainment and relief from the seria's solemnity. They found much more to their liking the fast-moving buffa—it seemed to have wider dimensions in which men's souls and bodies could find more room—and they enjoyed the pandemonium. The buffa composers' manners are often rude, their mirth unseemly by our standards, but their work is endlessly fascinating. They plumb the depths of naive simplicity, and while their music and satire owe much to the situations, a good deal rests on the amusing and original method of approach, for burlesque and farce are criticism at its most irresponsible and therefore least liable to reprisals. The buffa composers and their librettists knew everyday life and everyday people, their foibles, their language, and they were keen observers of the scene; with them everything happens as it would have happened yesterday and would happen tomorrow, yet theirs is not an uncritical copy of life. The buffa composers were also spurred by a growing appreciation of the nature of the modern theater; the presence of the highly developed Spanish theater in Naples played a role in this. Their operas are usually composed at two levels. They give the ordinary listener plenty of entertainment to carry him along, but to those who are looking for something more, they give carefully drawn characters in an equally solicitously worked score.

How indestructible is the spirit of this comedy: the theme of Puccini's *Gianni Schicchi* comes from the thirtieth canto of the *Divine Comedy*! But it is of course much older than that. Popular comedy always existed and flourished, if perhaps somewhat camouflaged from the historian's eyes because the plays were not written down and were considered worthy of chronicling neither by the clerical nor by the humanist writers. And this spirit of the comic theater always demanded admission to music. Aristotle decreed that the tragedy should evoke pity, horror, and admiration altogether free of the comical, yet such esthetic laws should never be taken so literally as the humanists took them; the statute books of the arts are full of inconsistencies and unenforceable laws. The tragedy as a catharsis to cleanse and bleach the soul did not greatly appeal to the Italians, who in their serious operas eliminated the tragic ending of the classical models and were wont to splice comical elements onto the most hallowed dramas—as well as into sacred music, even the liturgy. Still, it is clear that the comic theater could not have come from any adaptation of the Attic tragedy. In deference to the classical mantle that for so long has been draped over opera, perhaps we should go back to Aristophanes and the Greek comic theater. However, Aristophanes, this "naughty favorite of the Graces," as Goethe called him, this "Heine of antiquity," does not seem to fit the case either. Though his plays are filled with laughter and ribald—even orgiastic—mockery, when we finish reading one of them, especially the passages of choral lyricism delivered by birds, frogs, and wasps, we have the feeling that we have read a great philosophical poem that probes into our most profound moral views. So we must conclude that, unlike the opera seria, the buffa could not claim Greece as its progenitor; its real ancestor was the Roman popular theater.

Though, like the rest of Latin literature, the Roman comedy descended from Greek originals freely rearranged, patched, and sliced, it was Latin not only in language but also in spirit. While Terence was carefully following the Greek models, Plautus, the more influential of the two, was mostly interested in situation comedy, jokes, misunderstandings, and fast, witty give-and-take. We know that there were vocal numbers in his plays—they must have been a sort of ancient operetta. There were many other comic authors and various comic genres. The Atellana delighted in making fun of the figures of small-town life; its humor was drastic and raw, but the plays became very popular. Then there was the Mimus, which was also earthy, and even admitted actresses. The subject of all these comedies was the everyday world, mostly the topsy-turvy aspects of life; and here we already have all the themes of the buffa, though the crude obscenities of the Roman popular comedy were not taken over. Both varieties used the people's language and had interpolated ditties, and, as was the case with the buffa (or with the English ballad opera) they were liked just as much by the intellectual elite as by the lower classes.

While of course there is a long development from here to the seventeenth-century theater—an intricate course of evolu-

tion we cannot follow here—the connection with the *commedia dell' arte*, the improvised comedy in the vernacular interspersed with songs, is obvious and direct. Throughout the
Renaissance the popular comedy flourished parallel with the
literary, and it did so without borrowing from the more
elevated species. This comic theater was realistic and preferred
types that became universally known and loved. There was a
vague traditional plot, but the dialogue was improvised. The
commedia dell' arte, increasingly musical in nature, lived far into the eighteenth century. Then Goldoni, a brilliant playwright, carried the popular figures of the improvised comedy
into the modern theater as contemporary petit bourgeois; now
their dialogues were fully written out. Goldoni, Metastasio's
counterpart in the comic opera, whose innumerable librettos
were as popular as the seria books of his much-admired colleague, did not go back to antiquity for his subjects; he dealt
with the present and with mores valid in his time. His most
famous and successful work, *La buona figliuola*, set by Piccinni in 1760, was adapted from Richardson's *Pamela*.

All this we may regard as the general line of historical development of the opera buffa, but comic elements were never
missing in Italian music, and one encounters them in the most
unlikely places and situations. When opera reached Rome in
the 1630s, in consideration of the exalted status of the capital
of Catholicism it had to add to its classical subjects Christian
allegory. But soon a third element demanded admission to
this curious symbiosis: comedy. The comic element was
slipped into the drama in the form of *parti buffe* or *scene
buffe*. The Roman "sacred opera" was liberally laced with
them and—horrible to contemplate—so was the sacred oratorio. (Carissimi in particular was fond of *parti buffe* in his Biblical oratorios.) The Italian is a classicist and considers Roman
antiquity his own history, but he is also a realist with a strong
histrionic streak. While men of letters and aristocrats were
glorying in Caesar, Mucius Scaevola, Scipio, and Titus, the
man in the street much preferred Colombina, Arlecchino, the
Doctor, the Notary, the Captain, the Music Master, and above
all the wily and resourceful Valet, whom we know as Figaro

but whose ancestry goes back to the ancient Roman comedy. The *parti buffe* often overshadowed the seria in which they were inserted, so they were eliminated by the leading theatrical critics and authors, Apostolo Zeno and Metastasio. It is interesting to observe that Handel, composing Italian operas in England, fully subscribed to the exclusion of comic elements from the serious opera, though he composed some delightful and sophisticated comic operas. The Arcadians' dramaturgical reform was observed far more abroad than in Italy. The humanists severely proscribed "irrelevant comic elements" from the opera seria long before Gluck, but the public enforced its desires. We must realize that the *commedia dell' arte*—like its counterpart, the *théâtre de la foire*—was not only a form of entertainment but a safety valve for the social and psychological needs of the populace. No matter how much they were frowned upon, the comic scenes could not be suppressed, and when they were excluded from the seria proper, the composers found another way to present the people's favorite characters. What could not be included in the body of the opera was offered between the acts, hence the name *intermezzo*. The intermezzo, the tiny interpolated comic play with music, was the direct ancestor of the opera buffa. We know very little about its early stages (as we know little about early opera in general), but by 1720 it was no longer improvised comedy slapped together like the *commedia dell' arte;* it had become a definite genre: miniature opera within the opera. The next step was as obvious as it was inevitable; the intermezzo was detached from the seria and, enlarged, developed into an independent, self-sufficient, and full-fledged opera.

At this juncture we must lay to rest an old and still-flourishing historical fallacy. Pergolesi's *La Serva padrona* (1733) is indeed a milestone in the history of opera in general and comic opera in particular, and it is an unquestioned gem. But far from representing a beginning, it is the crowning of an entire epoch. Leonardo Leo's intermezzos had already created a furor in the early 1720s, and it is quite clear that by the time Pergolesi arrived on the scene the new comic opera was in full flower, ready to claim more than an incidental role in the opera house. Leo's and Leonardo Vinci's intermezzos show good construction, and their "melodic gesture," prattle songs, lightning-fast secco recitatives, arias of action, and vivacious ensembles include all the basic ingredients of the developed buffa.

The subsequent development was rapid, and by the second half of the century a host of able composers produced a legion of successful operas that were played all over Europe. In a brief chapter we cannot follow this historical development in detail—it requires a whole book, which has not yet been written—but we must sketch the most important stylistic changes.

With Leo, Vinci, Feo, and Pergolesi the large musical gestures of the Baroque give way to a small-jointed, symmetrical, and homophonic texture. The stubbornly repeated and thematically woven small motifs and phrases, the fast parlando, and the capriciously leaping intervals in the melody became important stylistic features not only in the buffa but also in the rising symphony. Since the buffa composers responded to instant impressions, there are unexpected rhythmic and melodic turns in their music. They abandoned the da capo aria in favor of a binary construction with a *stretta*. The *stretta*, also known as *cabaletta*, was the accelerated ending of an aria, and was also appreciated in the finales, usually calling for presto or prestissimo. Subsequently, like most other features of the opera buffa, it was taken over by instrumental music, a good example being the finale of Beethoven's Fifth Symphony. It was the close relationship between music and action, and a more developed sense for the living theater, that naturally led to the finale. The serious opera seldom had true ensembles beyond duets, and even the duets usually elaborated the same music for both singers by using contrapuntal imitation or running in parallel thirds and sixths. The opera seria, being a court opera, followed social etiquette: in polite society, especially in the presence of royalty, conversation is not interrupted. The iconoclastic buffa ripped into this convention; nothing was more congenial to the composer and his delighted public than a fast-moving ensemble in which each singer in-

terrupts the other. The innovation had far-reaching consequences, for it was soon discovered that the dramatic force of
the ensemble rests on the tension resulting when characters
express their individual feelings simultaneously. Thus the ensemble became the principal dramatic means of bringing a
sense of action to the static majesty of the seria. By the latter
part of the eighteenth century, it was no longer the aria but
the ensemble, especially its most elaborate variety, the compound finale, that was considered the touchstone of the opera
composer's art. In Cimarosa's *Il Matrimonio segreto* (1779),
the finale, starting with a trio and ending with a septet, extends
to 800 measures. Similarly well constructed scenes abound in
the works of Piccinni, Galuppi, Paisiello, and others, from
whom Mozart learned this particular art. Now we see an interesting reversal of history: the opera buffa begins to have
parti serie. These are no longer spliced in without motivation,
as comic scenes were into the seria, but represent momentary
sadness or foreboding in the evolving plot. Mozart's wondrous
ensembles are discussed in the following chapter, but how
many realize that this art reached its peak in Rossini? The first
finale in *The Barber of Seville* takes seventy-six pages in the
piano score! It is not merely a matter of the composer's fluency running away with itself; he has to plan with skill and
faithful regard for dramatic, tonal, and formal concordances.

This chapter was written in order to bridge the large gap
between Gluck and Mozart; the latter's role in the history of
opera cannot otherwise be understood. Unfortunately, to most
of us this animated period from *La Serva padrona* to *Le Nozze
di Figaro* is largely unknown; none of the operas from the in-
tervening period is ever heard in a professional performance.
But I did hear a performance of Paisiello's *The Barber of Seville*, a student production in a university, done with gusto and
with fresh voices; I must single out this work as a direct connecting link with Mozart.

Like so many neglected masters, Giovanni Paisiello is a
monument, a document, a reference; yet curiously, Verdi, not
given to historical reminiscing, greatly admired him. Even the

casual reader of Paisiello's scores will be astonished when he comes across numerous bits of music that he instantly recognizes—from *Figaro*. Obviously, this Italian composer, sixteen years Mozart's senior and famous when Mozart was ten, had more than passing interest for the Austrian, who of course heard his works sung everywhere.

Paisiello's *Barber* (1782) is the incarnation of the inimitable Italian opera buffa. Mozart's buffa, as exemplified in *Figaro*, though built altogether on Italian precepts, is nevertheless something different. The Italians were conscious of this, and Mozart never became really popular in their country. The difference rests not merely on Mozart's unique musical and dramatic genius, which allows neither competition nor even comparison, nor on his technical and stylistic means, for he used Paisiello and the other Italian buffa composers copiously, but also on the limited degree to which he was willing to go along with the Italian buffoonery—he was not a real Italian. After hearing Paisiello's rollicking comedy, in which the broadest naturalistic tomfoolery freely alternates with delicately expressive moments, one realizes that Paisiello's closest relative is really not Mozart but Rossini. Though on the whole the musical idiom in the first *Barber of Seville* is gracious and refined, some age-old elements that Mozart did not care to use are present. The *commedia dell' arte* and a bit of the vulgarity of the old intermezzo unmistakably poke through this alert, vivacious, melodious, and communicative music. There are also delightful folk materials from the Neapolitan countryside and parody of the serious opera, but there is subtle comedy as well.

Paisiello had a wonderful feeling for both theatrical realism and musical characterization, and used the orchestra with dramatic inventiveness. Those breathless babblings and the fast leaps in octaves and sevenths found their way into Mozart, and while Mozart does not always escape the theatrically irresistible but rather facile prattle, he of course often manages to give it a twist that was beyond Paisiello's powers. But no matter how wild, even crazy, the buffoonery, Paisiello is never rattled; his scoring remains elegant. The motivic-thematic work in the orchestral accompaniment is delicate and imaginative, the woodwinds are used with a fine feeling for their descriptive qualities, and the orchestra is never noisy or coarse, as it became in the opera of the next generation. Every measure of the score is worked out neatly; there are no perfunctory spots. The arias are delectable, even tinged with a little melancholy—Paisiello's Rosina is closer to Mozart's Countess than to Rossini's coquette ingénue. The seccos are carefully planned for realistic effects, but Paisiello is chary of the dramatic accompanied recitative, a fact once more characteristic of the difference between Italian and Mozartean buffa. This is sheer and almost unadulterated farce, without the undertones of human conflict that are never missing in Mozart. But the most remarkable portions of the opera are the ensembles, and here Paisiello is not easily surpassed. One must listen to these ensembles—as Mozart did—with both ears open, because this inventive composer achieved some extraordinary combinations. Especially brilliant is Paisiello's manner of blending parody of the serious opera melody with outright buffa frivolity. The ensemble in which Bartolo's servants, drugged by Figaro, stagger, yawn, and sneeze, illustrates this virtuosity, which represents the height of realistic opera buffa.

This is a viable and highly entertaining work; no wonder Rossini was considered an impertinent upstart when he dared to set the same libretto that Paisiello had made famous. Yet this line of the opera buffa, which continued in Italy all the way to *Gianni Schicchi*, differs from the Italian buffa composed in Vienna. To be sure, Mozart took over the whole apparatus, but the same traditional melodic and rhythmic patterns, the same ensemble technique, became something different when Mozart used them. Mozart, who loved buffoonery, indulged in practical jokes, and was not above frivolity, also knew that humor contains a modicum of sorrow, passion, understanding, and forgiveness; that humor could be the painful smile of maturity that endured much and regrets little. He developed and broadened the amalgam he created from the seria and the buffa, with a wisdom and a happy knowledge of men and their ways, raising the new opera to heights where it became washed by the rays of great art. For a long time it was thought that Mozart's smile reflects joyful but merely innocent merriment, whereas it was really a stubborn peace-offering to life. And there are not a few defeated dreams and aspirations behind the smile that offers peace.

Three

MOZART

FOR GENERATIONS Mozart has been celebrated as one of the most extraordinary phenomena in musical history. His contemporaries considered him a bold "romantic," but the real Romantics who came on the scene a few decades later saw in him the purest representative of classic, formal beauty. By the last third of the nineteenth century the picture has changed to that of a pale Rococo figure, passionless, merely playing with charming and weightless garlands of music. The turning away from Romanticism at the beginning of our century once more changed the Mozart cult. Modern musicological research brought to light many unknown facts and in some admirable essays once more rearranged the picture. Perhaps the most important result of these labors was the discovery of the depth of Mozart's personality, of the recesses of his soul.

Perhaps in our time we should be able to draw a picture of the little Austrian that will do justice to his gigantic stature. However, if we want to penetrate to the core of a genius and search for the genesis of artistic creation, we must realize that creative force can be approached neither by irrational notions nor by rational explanations. Mozart's life work shows conclusively that artistic conception, the origin of musical ideas, is not a process that is necessarily under the influence of the outside world, but is an internal experience. With Mozart the process of creation was like the beating of the heart, a primary function of life; according to much reliable testimony, he could and did compose during conversation, meals, or any ordinary everyday activity, and even while he was listening to someone else's music. With Bach the composition of music was the continuation of creation, with Beethoven it was the redemption of life, but with Mozart it was life itself. Many of the great masters have admitted in concrete words their belief that they are the mouthpiece of some higher force, that their creative powers transcend their human being. Mozart nowhere made such a statement; to him all this was natural and unquestionable. The act of creation often took place entirely in Mozart's mind, before any recourse to written notes. The sketches that were preserved demonstrate that his most dazzling inventions appear not as tentative flashes to be coerced into shape, but as themes and motifs that at their first appearance are already shaped by artistic laws.

The Romantic era was grievously mistaken when it ascribed Mozart's inexhaustible invention to divinely innocent facility. What is most startling in Mozart's music (and there are innumerable examples to prove it) is that imagination and invention are usually companioned by the supervision of an alert critical mind. Mozart himself declared the quartets dedicated to Haydn the result of a great deal of painstaking work. Nevertheless, when he reached the stage at which a composition was committed to paper, the first draft was usually the final one. If he found that the work did not proceed as envisaged, he did not engage in patching operations but simply abandoned the whole thing and started anew. His posthumous papers show such fragments, but few heavily corrected copies.

Pedagogy, and with it public opinion, declared Mozart to be the composer of youth. Indeed, young musicians can do nothing better and more profitable than to listen to Mozart, but they should not believe that they can entirely possess him, for whoever has really arrived at an understanding of Mozart has already left behind the rebellions of youth. Only a nature tried and tempered by experience can win admission to the lively processes of a mind that is no less creative and inquiring for having both the materials and the capacity for judging and weighing.

We usually look upon the second half of the eighteenth century as the age of sonata, quartet, and symphony. Yet, the incredible productivity in the field of instrumental music notwithstanding, the center from which everything radiated was still opera and concerted church music, the latter also a dramatic genre and related to opera. Mozart wrote seventeen complete operas and two or three unfinished ones, a large number of single arias or scenas, eighteen Masses, dozens of smaller church music pieces like Litanies and Offertories, as well as several cantatas and oratorios. That he did not write more operas is due solely to lack of opportunity, that is, commissions; in those days composers depended altogether on patronage. It is perhaps as an opera composer that Mozart has been most loved—and misunderstood. The rage for real, real life on the stage attacks the essence of his operas, and perhaps of opera in general. Realism in opera is not necessarily "reality"; the imitation of life is not the same thing as truth in the world of values. "Music should serve the drama," said Gluck, but Mozart would ask, "How could what was born to rule serve?" The absolute supremacy of music over the sister arts was the key to his whole art. While Gluck created a noble new "serious" opera in which a stylized life was projected onto one plane, Mozart, coming from the domain of the Italian opera buffa, offered life in its entirety, with all its contrasts and conflicts. At times this is done in the glow of innocent play (*The Abduction from the Seraglio*), at others in the wild rhythm of passion and even terror (*Don Giovanni*), at still others with the smile of irony (*Così fan tutte*), but every one of his operas is different, a masterpiece *sui generis*. He draws the broad human scene, the whole of life, with a full-blooded enjoyment that can swing from high tragedy to rollicking farce and can touch both, in the moment of awe or laughter, with a sober and thoughtful tenderness. Such a spectrum of sentiment and of human existence can be realized only by an artist who sees his fellows both from nearby and from far away, with realistic eyes and without illusion, yet at the same time transfigured, and in the rich, beautiful, and cruel current of fate. Shakespeare was one like that, and Mozart. They were the boldest mixers of the tragic with the comic, for more than others they felt the essential unity of life.

The music of the eighteenth century, with its pure, absolute forms, emphasized on the stage all that is permanent and durable. This very fact, the presence of these "closed" forms that add up to the so-called number opera, is what made it so difficult for those living in the next period to understand the eighteenth-century musical stage. They appreciated the wondrous melodies, but every plot and every situation seemed childish to them, a notion that has not yet altogether vanished. Mozart shaped men in their conflicts in such a manner that everything, whether transitory and capricious or eternal and profound, was apprehended in pure musical forms, to appear as the final word. Drama and melody, human characterization and musical convention evolve on Mozart's stage simultaneously. Realistic picture and idealistic rainbow, reality and dream, character drawing and abstract pattern, Italianism and Germanism, all are interwoven. So sure was he of what kind of music a certain spot or situation required that on few occasions he went ahead with the composition on the basis of the general outline of an opera's plot, before he had the actual text. To our elders, who were accustomed to operatic music chained to the libretto, it appeared incredible that Mozart's "absolute" music could have wrestled victoriously with the drama and the stage, yet it is precisely here that Mozart's mastery was never problematical or questionable. Those who are looking for the esthetic values of the stage in opera do not realize that in the world of opera, which is a particular domain distinct from the related spoken drama, the absolute forms of music, while discharging their dramatic mission, also—and nowhere more proudly and with more conviction than in Mozart —adhere to the independent laws and esthetics of their own musical world. It is not a frame in which substance is arranged in certain proportions and thus filled out, but a living organism which in its totality determines the functioning of its parts. These parts are not put together; they issue from the ideal of form as if from a kernel. The connection of the parts is indissoluble. It is this perfection of "form" that furnishes the great work of art with the armor on which the power of time's passing is blunted.

There were uncounted fine operas composed before Mozart, and it seems that we are about to muster the good sense and ability to resuscitate some of them. As we have seen, the oldest of these still to have currency are two of Gluck's operas, but the very fact that Gluck, a particular and unique case in operatic history, stands for "old opera" prevents an orderly and unbiased approach to the immense riches of Baroque opera. Gluck's operas are more a memory than a reality. They are still beautiful but for the most part they attract respectful pilgrims, not a real public, and, with the exception of a handful, they are as dead as the fine works of his great rival, Piccinni. When the curtain falls on *Orfeo* or *Armide* one ceases to be concerned about the characters of the drama. They have been in good hands and everything relevant has been done for them; they engross but they do not impregnate the imagination. But Mozart, at the end of an opera, leaves his figures on our conscience; his operas have an afterlife. What is viable in Gluck represents the denial of many of his favorite theories and aspirations, for Gluck did not want to compose music, only drama. He was a revolutionary and an innovator, a belated Monteverdi, or a Wagner arrived on the scene too early, who fought opera and the fashions of the day and was seemingly victorious. And what remains of the victory? Only some beautiful music, the very thing he scorned.

Mozart proceeded the opposite way. He wanted music, he emphasized music, claiming primacy, nay, absolute dominion, for music on the stage. It is for this reason that his opera is true *music* drama. Every promise and every enchantment of this paradoxical genre of art became reality in him, for Mozart was the great musical mime who could place himself within every character and situation. This he did not because of his lyric wealth—there were others who had that—but because of a dramatic incisiveness and economy which few have ever learned, and none to that degree. The viability and significance of the sung drama, while paradoxical, cannot be questioned, even though in recent history its realization has followed different and even contradictory trends. The great and passionate battle between Gluckists and Piccinnists did not really end with Gluck's victory, as musical historians almost universally proclaim; true to the paradoxical nature of opera, the battle ended with victory for both. The aspirations of Italian opera—drama through song, through beautiful, moving, and bewitching song—found its embodiment in Verdi; here Piccinni was the victor. In contrast, Gluck's efforts to create dramatic truth by the subordination of music to the drama was achieved, though only in a certain limited sense, by Wagner; therefore Gluck, too, was a victor. Verdi's immense theatrical genius utilized every dramatic possibility of singing, while Wagner, departing from the symphony, exhausted the possibilities of the dramatic "gesture music" of the orchestra, upon which he superimposed the voices. Mozart recreated opera neither on the Italian nor on the German model, neither from song nor from symphony (though both figure prominently in his style), but from absolute music itself. The story is really very simple: Mozart discovered the dramatic language of absolute music, compared to which even the very excellent librettos he set merely stammer. The Mozartean cantilena is a perfect and well-defined language which expresses every state of mind with a smoothness and adaptability of which the cantilena was never again capable. Richard Strauss called Mozart's melody "a revelation of the human soul, a total symbol of almost undefinable emotional content." Then he adds that this melody "cannot be grasped . . . it can only be sensed by feeling." Perhaps the beauty of this melody as music comes from the wonderment over beauty itself. Never did music speak in such human tones, never was it so chameleon-like, seducing with Don Giovanni, raging with the Queen of the Night, suffering with the Countess Almaviva, and clowning with Leporello. And yet this music, while universal, is not tragic. All of Mozart's tragic "serious" operas have disappeared from the stage like the older opera seria, even though like the latter they contain much magnificent music. On the other hand, the operas he created after turning away from Gluck and reaffirming the spirit and technique of the Italian opera buffa are all incomparably alive, for Mozart filled the buffa with tragic elements and the singspiels with a profound view of life. This is the meaning of *Don Giovanni* and of *The Magic Flute*, neither of them a tragedy and neither a comedy. These operas are complete and intense, all their exuberance and variety of detail held in check by a unity of characters and style. Mozart's style is perfectly natural yet of an admirable point and concentrated precision. It is as if diamonds were growing like flowers.

The Mozartean melody has no kinship with the robust, twining melody of the Baroque; it is slender, symmetrical, and precise. This gift for melody was of course innate; yet, as is not always realized, it showed an astounding development and —more astounding—became even more radiant and perfect toward the end of Mozart's life, when he was plagued with troubles and death stared him in the face. And Mozart makes the very material sing according to its most natural inclinations. From an oboe he elicits the typical oboe tone, and from the voice the dormant will of the human vocal cords. It is for this reason that, as the keys he selected for his compositions were the final and only possible choice, so is the choice of instruments. This music that conforms so closely to the requirements of materiality is flexible and free precisely because it does not have to counter the resistance of matter. It conquered matter not by subduing and coercing it, as Bach or Beethoven did, but by liberating it.

More than one-third of the 626 items listed in Köchel's catalogue of Mozart's works deal with "entertainment" music. This is a tribute to the period's insatiable desire for refined musical entertainment, which Mozart gladly and most naturally provided. It is true, of course, that, especially while employed in Salzburg, he was compelled to compose such music, but it was not an onerous compulsion. Mozart loved to "play," loved the light, bantering tone, and this playful element is seldom missing in his most exalted compositions; for playfulness does not mean a lack of seriousness of purpose, rather it is the sign of instinctive security. But there is another important fact here. In Mozart's time the sharp distinction we make between "entertainment" music and "serious" music was not yet known—all music had to please, and commercial music had not yet been invented. Mozart was not a rebel and critic of society like Beethoven, nor was he a recluse. On the contrary, gregarious, fun-loving, always ready to joke (just think on those naughty canons), he liked good—even fast—company and hated to be alone. The great overture to *Don Giovanni* was composed in Prague the night before the dress rehearsal, while the room was filled with an animated crowd. Mozart was the type of the urban cosmopolite and had absolutely no eyes for nature; only people interested him. His letters show not only the sensibility of a great artist but, besides the much over-stressed indelicacies typical of the era, a personality of warmth and charm, and though delightfully malicious toward professional colleagues, good-natured in everyday intercourse.

The psychological roots of Mozart's entertainment music are at least as important as the sociological. It gave him pleasure to contribute with his music to that congeniality which he valued so highly, and for this reason he took entertainment music very seriously. Nowhere does he slacken his craftsmanship, and his invention just pours out in abundance in these works that form an important and integral part of his oeuvre. More than that, without this playful streak in his artistic makeup we should not have the composer of the great operas, for the spirit and tone of his serenade music, the divertimento, are present in his weightiest dramatic compositions. Perhaps the most touching and revealing example of this is to be found in Mozart's church music; the earlier Masses are liturgic serenades composed for divine service. To speak of Mozart's entertainment music as if it were lacking in "profundity" is to miss the point altogether; Ernest Newman was guilty of this Victorian view. The word "entertainment" is used not to belittle this music, but to suggest its air of friendliness and relaxation, its just proportion to our everyday mood, not to necessarily rare moments of communion with eternity. Whatever was touched by this delightful serenade music reflected Mozart's love and understanding of that deep-rooted symbolism which colors and beautifies the most trivial and common things in life.

The other side of Mozart, his clear-eyed, pragmatic professionalism, bothered his Romantic apologists, who tried to minimize it. Mozart paid the necessary obeisance to custom and conventions, while going his own way without clattering iconoclasm. In addition to the eighteenth-century composer's dependence on patronage, Mozart, like all his confreres, depended on the forces available for any contemplated production; the vocal parts had to be tailored to the capabilities of particular singers. This, however, did not in the least inhibit Mozart, who never fought limitations as did Gluck or Wagner, but took them in his stride and overcame them. Once he obtained a commission and a libretto he liked, he adjusted himself to the situation with phenomenal ease, mastering any challenge offered by the often very tenuous conditions created by the commission or the available personnel. Following the custom of the times, he would occasionally insert additional arias in a finished work, either on second thought or to placate a singer or patron. While originally extraneous, many of these became integral parts of the operas to which they were appended. Nor was Mozart unmindful of the public's reactions. He wrote to his father that ". . . a great deal of noise is always appropriate at the end of an act," adding that "the more noise the better, so that the audience may not have time to slacken their applause." Here speaks the born man of the theater, who knows that the proper application of the traditional conventions of the stage vitally concerns not only the success but also the nature and construction of an opera. But while observing the conventions, it was impossible for him to keep out, even from the stock figures and thrice-familiar scenes, the savoring salt of his own personality. The planning of an opera was always done in collaboration with the librettist, and as can be seen from his letters Mozart often dictated the procedure. "I have explained to Stephanie [librettist of *The Abduction from the Seraglio*] the words I require for this aria." He was very demanding, and the requests addressed to his librettists show the most imaginative dramatic insight. Nevertheless, it took experiments, and the major effort of a great and somber opera, before Mozart found his own congenial tone and dramaturgy.

The child, guided by his father, began to compose operas at an age when others begin to learn the names of the notes. At eleven he composed the music to a Latin school play; at twelve a full three-act opera buffa, *La Finta semplice*, and a German musical play, *Bastien und Bastienne;* at fourteen a big seria, *Mitridate, rè di Ponto;* and at sixteen the *dramma per musica*, *Lucio Silla*, as well as several others before his first great dramatic work, *Idomeneo*. Thus at an early age he was well acquainted with Italian opera, and his melodic style was formed by what he learned from Di Majo, Jommelli, Piccinni, Paisiello, and Galuppi, not to forget Hasse and Christian Bach, who were more Italian than the Italians themselves. It is interesting to observe that in his early singspiels Mozart's Italianate vocal writing does not always suit the German text. Not that the musical prosody is incorrect, but the Italian melodic clichés often do not fit the German phonetics, and the elisions, natural in Italian, seem contrived in German. The progress Mozart made in this regard in *Die Entführung* is remarkable. But while the Italian influence and orientation were paramount, there are also traces of Gluck and Grétry. The young Mozart knew the entire code of Italian dramatic composition, the aria types, the standard formulas for affective expression, the melodic turns, and so forth, and with his extraordinary musicality and faculty for assimilation he was able to turn out performable operas even at such a tender age. One would not, of course, expect a youth of fourteen or fifteen to deal with heroism or passionate love; like most of his mature colleagues he simply tried to compose attractive music. Nor was he unmindful of the pragmatic wisdom dispensed by his father. "I advise you when composing to consider not only the musical, but also the unmusical public. You must remember that for every ten real connoisseurs there are a hundred ignoramuses. So do not neglect the so-called popular style." This admonition represents the generally accepted attitude of the eighteenth-century composer, who did not find it incompatible with the loftiest artistic aspirations. Among other things Mozart had to learn were the uses of coloratura as dramatic agent and the special operatic relationship between orchestra and voices. But by the time he wrote *Lucio Silla* (1772) the youngster, still short of seventeen, could divine the character of a woman deeply in love. While in technique and vocal writing he could not yet match the great Italians, in dramatic sense and power he had already approached them, because his feeling for the lyric theater was "like the intuition a sailor has of sea and sky." Even in the early operas there are some astonishing numbers that could be placed in his mature works, and the ensembles, the glory of the Mozartean opera, are outstanding; it is here that he first departed from the old opera scheme, going his own way.

As the nineteenth century began, the most popular of Mozart's operas was his last, *La Clemenza di Tito.* At its original performance in 1791 it failed to please, but soon afterwards it conquered all of central Europe; in 1815 alone eight different piano-vocal scores were printed. Although the other operas soon surpassed it in favor, *Tito* remained popular until the middle of the century, after which it faded rapidly, becoming by our time a mere library item with occasional abbreviated concert performances. In contrast, the first of Mozart's full-fledged mature operas, *Idomeneo, rè di Creta,* produced in Munich ten years before *Tito,* was initially well received, but did not become popular. While our books praise some of its qualities, the work, like *Tito,* is declared no longer viable beyond its magnificent overture. The two works are usually bracketed together, and rightfully so, because both belong to the genus opera seria, the old Baroque form of the lyric theater, which by Mozart's time had ceased its natural evolution, its essential character becoming stationary and relying on mere variants of a formula on which a design became more and more obviously imposed. *La Clemenza di Tito* largely succumbed to the formula, for by that time Mozart had moved so far beyond the seria that he could not retrace his steps, but *Idomeneo* is a masterpiece that will again come into its own. It is also a prime example of the profound problem of opera, which, more than any other genre of music, must be brought periodically into a certain conformity with the prevailing attitudes if it is to be kept alive. There is a great difference between absolute fidelity to the *Urtext* of an instrumental work and to that of an opera; the living theater has rights and prerogatives that the purists sometimes do not understand. The tendency is to resign ourselves to the idea that our distance from the world which such a work represents makes the gulf unbridgeable. *Idomeneo*, unlike Mozart's later operas, sees the world through the mask of certain socio-artistic conventions. It was not addressed to the same audience that loved the realism of the opera buffa, it is a pure stylized opera seria. Yet, with careful restoration, much of the ancient glory of such old operas can be recaptured. We must remember also that even though the theater was Mozart's real home, his most cherished musical arena, all of his great dramatic works were commissioned as *pièces d'occasion,* and in the case of *Idomeneo* the commission was hedged in by textual and formal prescriptions which by that time were almost completely anachronistic. The court even chose the libretto's theme by suggesting an old French opera set many years before by Campra. Mozart asked the Salzburg court chaplain, Abbé Varesco, to convert the French text into the required Italian libretto.

The voluminous correspondence between Mozart and his father about *Idomeneo* is most interesting. Besides showing his thorough knowledge of operatic dramaturgy, the correspondence reveals Mozart's attitude to be that of the pragmatic eighteenth-century creative artist: he accepted the conventions and techniques without seeking their moral or intellectual justification, but he was going to deal with this on his own terms. Both father and son disclose a remarkable knowledge of Metastasio, to the point of discussing the master librettist's use of particular words.

We tend to regard the Mozart who composed *Figaro* and the other great operas as the mature artist, and to ascribe all earlier operas to the incredible *Wunderkind* who was the manifestation of God-given talent, a phenomenon of nature. But by the age of twenty-two, three years before *Idomeneo*, Mozart declared to a friend that there was not one famous master whose works he had not studied. Indeed, at that age he was an incomparably trained and superbly equipped composer of mature judgment, infallible taste, and redoubtable craftsmanship. We fail to notice the thoughtful disciplined artist who, on his many trips abroad and under his father's expert tutelage, methodically studied and absorbed all styles and all techniques. All this wisdom and experience went into the composition of *Idomeneo*.

Baroque opera sought its ideal in planned stylization. What Mozart did with the old form was revolutionary: *Idomeneo*, rather than Gluck's *Orfeo*, was perhaps the first great reform opera, though in point of fact neither of them had an appreciable effect on posterity. While the old frame was retained, the new is present everywhere, in harmony, rhythm, instrumentation, tone color, and dynamics; only the tempos recall the old seria. *Idomeneo* has more slow arias and ariosos than the later operas, so there is in this work a measure of Gluck's static quality, but the continuity is excellent, both musically and dramatically. More than in his later operas, Mozart connects recitative, arias, and choruses; instead of reaching full closes with the customary double bar, he proceeds either directly or by providing transition passages.

Then there are the ensembles. No one up to the time of *Idomeneo* had composed anything like the quartet in the third act. It is in these dramatic situations, where several independent characters sing simultaneously without losing their identity, that Mozart leaves the old opera completely behind. There is no longer any compromise with singers, no yielding to librettist or court chamberlain; Mozart himself declared that in the ensembles the "free will" of the composer is given full play. Since the original libretto was a French *tragédie lyrique*, provision was made for a number of choral scenes which Varesco had preserved in the Italian version. The dramatic force of these choruses is unequalled—only in Verdi's *Otello* do we encounter such stormy eloquence. Nowhere in his following operas did Mozart surpass the elaborate orchestral writing of

Idomeneo, and the orchestra he employs is large: it uses a third flute, a second brace of horns, and, in one of the scenes, three trombones. He was of course writing for the most admired and accomplished orchestra of the age, the Mannheim ensemble, transferred to Munich when the Elector Palatine inherited the duchy of Bavaria. But Mozart had some novelties even for this famous body: muted brasses and covered timpani. The characterization is not so psychologically penetrating as in *Figaro* or *Don Giovanni*, but that is owing to the opera seria frame, which demands an unabated heroic tone. The figures are, shall we say, two-and-a-half-dimensional, but even so, in the great recitatives and in the ensembles they rise to genuine poignancy, and the melodic substance is rich and sustained.

It was not easy for Mozart to deal with mythological figures, nor with the Baroque *deus ex machina;* he always wanted believable human beings. The old seria did not appeal to him, and he was prevented from translating into pure drama even those situations that interested him—the conflict between father and son, for instance—because between the human protagonists there was the enraged god Neptune. More to his liking was the relationship of the two women, Priam's gentle daughter Ilia and the passionate Mycenaean Electra, feuding over Idamante. The Euripidean spirit of the third act almost overwhelmed him. In a letter to his father, Mozart says: "My head and my hands are so full of Act III that it would be no wonder if I were turned into a third act myself."

Arrived at this point, the reader may reasonably ask why, if *Idomeneo* is such a masterpiece, it is so neglected, and why Mozart abandoned this genre. The answer is simply that the opera seria could not be carried on to new paths, and Mozart's subsequent blending of all operatic strains into a supreme synthesis has made it difficult for us to give a fair hearing to his work in the older genre. But Mozart himself loved *Idomeneo* and considered it one of his finest operas.

Idomeneo could and should be reinstated in the repertory of all great opera houses along with the Mozart operas we love so well. The work is filled with great music, yet something seems to prevent it from holding the stage. The few performances one sees all suffer from the ills that usually creep into the production of old operas. Admittedly, the libretto is static, but surely an intelligent stage director could minimize this weakness, neither allowing the principals to stand around aimlessly nor resorting to artificial and distracting busyness. What seems to be more damaging is the absence of low voices, a typical Baroque characteristic. What a relief when the first low voice is heard for a few fleeting moments, as Poseidon, sung by a bass, announces his commands. There can be no question that Mozart was inconvenienced by the castrato part; indeed, for a projected Viennese production he rewrote Idamante's part for a tenor. Careful and knowledgeable editing could make this great opera come to life and into public favor. The traditionalists will protest, but actually the "damage" caused by changing the castrato register to a tenor's is less than minimal when compared to the gain in dramatic-theatrical values.

Although all his creative ardor went into the composition of *Idomeneo*, Mozart realized that the seria did not suit him—it was no longer living theater. Then and there he decided to forsake Gluck and the past for the Italians and the present— and that meant the opera buffa. But though Mozart loved the romping buffa, he found that this carefree merriment no longer suited him either, for he had learned that life is not eternal laughter. He was now finding his bearings; all he needed was a good librettist who shared his ideas about life and the theater. This he found in Lorenzo da Ponte.

Le Nozze di Figaro holds preeminent rank among operas, as *Hamlet* does among plays. *Figaro* is not demonic like *Don Giovanni*, ultrasophisticated like *Così fan tutte*, fantastic and dreamy like *Die Zauberflöte*, but a comedy of love and of manners that maintains the most delectable equilibrium between mirth and sadness. Indeed, this is not slapstick comedy but a comedy of love, and despite the air of gentleness and piquancy, the amorous activities do reach an almost dangerous intensity. Every law on the Gluckian tablets is violated in this opera: the librettist, who is supposed to be the master, was made the composer's servant; the banished secco recitative is back as a wonderful vehicle for dramatic action; the marble statues that are the gods and goddesses of antiquity are replaced by those despised frivolous, ordinary mortals who love, cheat, scheme, suffer, and enjoy life. The score is a marvel from the first to the last measure; unflagging in invention, sparkling with wit, brilliant in the orchestral commentary, and full of wonderful melodies. The most rewarding feature of the work, however, is character portrayal in music. Unfortunately, this all-important facet of *Figaro* is the one that is most often neglected. Yes, of course, *Figaro* is an opera buffa, the crowning work of the genre, but it is much more than a "comic" opera; it is a sensitive exploration of love as it is experienced in all walks of life. This was Mozart's favorite subject.

Figaro requires an alert audience to seize the refined shades of its wit. Although there is plenty of humor to delight in, the humor is often a veil for the more subtle shafts from Mozart's nimble mind. The opera is light and swift; the listener is enveloped in a delicious atmosphere; and the generous-hearted composer's laughter, sardonic humor, and tender sympathies are contagious. Yet the comedy also conveys a serious warning hidden by an exquisite urbanity: do not play with fire, for love is a serious thing, whether it affects servant or master. Gaiety is there, as well as the gaiety that suddenly removes the mask and shows us the bare reality. And there is, too, the seriousness of the artist facing the facts of his art.

Figaro is the synthesis of the "serious" and the "comic" opera in which Molière's precept, that life consists of both smiles and tears, is carried out in a manner that has never been equalled in the realm of opera. The Italian opera buffa was the result of the opposition to the opera seria, which had become stilted, formal, and far removed from life. After the middle of the eighteenth century, the buffa swept Italy with irresistible force and, aside from dethroning and dooming the seria, elements of its musical idiom invaded every genre, from keyboard music to the Mass. But the first aim of the buffa was to be amusing, to stress the ludicrous rather than the wicked. Many of them, however, were scurrilous, and while to musicians and

audiences beyond the Alps the buffa proved almost as irresistible as to the Italians, the northerners were a bit baffled by the
Italians' uninhibited ways. The synthesis was the great artistic
feat accomplished by da Ponte and Mozart together, embracing
the libretto as well as the musical-technical aspects of seria and
buffa. Both knew that to understand comedy is to take it
seriously. *Figaro* has a well-constructed text by a master librettist who not only knew the requirements of the lyric stage
but had a wonderful knack for singable verse.

The choice of Beaumarchais's play may be surprising. It is
a biting and brilliant socio-political satire that was widely suppressed by the censors, as its accents had a revolutionary ring
despite the highly polished and urbane exterior. Neither da
Ponte nor Mozart, however, was interested in the social satire.
They saw an exceedingly well-written play inhabited by be-
lieveable figures, and by eliminating the socio-political element
and concentrating on the private human affairs of the protagonists, they found a perfect vehicle for an opera buffa. The
figures of the play and many of the situations come from the
public domain of comedy, yet there is not one conventional
character in the opera, even the secondary personages being
individuals in their own right. Da Ponte performed an admirable job of conversion; the episodes have at once charm,
wit, and good dramatic sense, but above all, the figures of the
play are presented in an altogether new light, and Mozart,
following the librettist's hints, changed their characters to
such an extent that when *Figaro* was first performed in Paris
the press indignantly censured Mozart for "distorting" Beaumarchais's dramatic creations. They were right. Mozart's singing protagonists were no longer Beaumarchais's speaking
figures, but then Mozart did not set to music Beaumarchais's
play. Rather, with the aid of da Ponte—but mainly through
his music—he created new characters who carry only the
names given them by the original author of the play.

As I have said, *Figaro* abounds in comic scenes, but they are
only a vehicle. One look at Bartolo, for example, and we
realize that Rossini's doctor is conceived as a much funnier
character. If, however, we examine the amorous complications,

we find characters who are vastly different from either Beaumarchais's or Rossini's protagonists. The Count loves his wife
but has a roving eye, yet in the end he emerges as a man who
can discipline himself. Figaro is the old, old comic servant
known since Plautus, but he is not comical when he learns
that the Count has designs on his fiancée; he is really shaken.
This happens in the very first scene, and all the cunning he
employs afterwards hides a serious concern underneath the
bravado. Cherubino is a unique character portayal. An adolescent of sixteen, his entire being is invaded by disturbing electric
currents that seem to emanate from every well-turned female
in sight. He does not quite know what it is all about and is
bewilderingly enamored of all the women. Beaumarchais's page
is a mere puppet compared to this creation of Mozart's, and the
difference is solely in the musical version. Cherubino is neither
infantile nor ludicrous, and even though no one takes him
quite seriously as a male, the women—all of them—like him
and permit him little liberties, while the men—all of them—are
uneasy about the budding Adonis and want to get rid of him.

In the original play the Countess is not uninterested in
other men; Mozart gave her a radiant subtlety, and she became
the regal heroine of the opera seria, for she is a suffering
woman and remains one even when she consents to the intrigue. She is morally intact in her innocent duplicity, with the
integrity that belongs to women in love who must lie. Susanna
knows the wickedness of men and is constantly on her guard.
She is willing to flirt a little—within reason—but she is genuinely attached to her sweetheart. The two principal women
in the cast are quite different in character, but they are drawn
together by the clear and present danger. And so this sparkling
and fast-paced opera, composed to a libretto derived from a
"political" play, turned under the magic of Mozart's music into
a gently probing comedy of love, which at one point almost
gets out of hand. In the third-act duet with Susanna, the Count,
who heretofore has given the impression of being rather
flighty, suddenly reveals that he is really smitten. When he
sings "Mi sento dal contento," the melody becomes so sensuously beautiful that one cannot doubt that this time he is in

love. And Susanna, whose fidelity is unquestionable, also gets a little overwhelmed by this ardor and momentarily forgets her role in the conspiracy. The atmosphere becomes fraught with potential trouble, somewhat as in the famous duet between Zerlina and Don Giovanni. Another salient example of the serious within the comic occurs when the Count opens the door and Susanna, the maid, steps out instead of the expected "lover," Cherubino. There descends upon the scene a veil of uncertainty; everyone on stage is seriously affected as guile, distrust, hope, relief, and humiliation breathe from every voice while the orchestra plays haltingly, with a disquietingly sub-dued tone.

The musical construction also shows that *Figaro* is no ordinary comic opera. Aside from the great arias, ensembles, and finales, the quality and pathos of the introductions to the arias go far beyond the usual opera buffa ritornels and pre-ambles, as do the orchestrally accompained recitatives. Mozart particularly excels in the ensembles, in which he proves to be an ardent disciple of the Italian opera buffa composers. The vital difference is that while he faithfully follows the nimble Italian ensemble technique, his figures never lose their identity and individuality, not even in the swiftest and most compli-cated quartet or quintet. And there is of course the orchestra. This is an Italian opera even though it was composed by an Austrian; the voices therefore rule, but the orchestra does not only accompany, it is an indispensable partner. In particular, the four pairs of woodwinds and the horns are played by so-loists every bit as necessary as the singers. They are constantly in demand, and their parts are so transparent, so exposed, and so consistently carriers of important musical substance that one insecure entry or overblown tone may jeopardize an aria. In Cherubino's delightful song "Voi che sapete," Mozart an-swers with the sensitivity and gentleness of his entire being the question "What is love?" His music radiates the poetic first stirrings of a youthful heart, and the song has the fragrance of lilies of the valley in springtime. Yet there are also tenderly sensuous accents discreetly expressed, not by the singer but by the sighs of the woodwinds. These ten musicians should be as pampered as the prima donnas; they should get a day off before playing Mozart.

The finales are tremendous compound structures in which the orchestra is charged with the symphonic elaboration of motifs. In the scene where the gardener hands over the letter he has picked up, one motif is sustained for almost a hundred measures; it wanders all over the orchestra, creating a chill on the stage by its inexorable repetitions in ever-new configurations. This kind of music requires the exacting ensemble playing of chamber music. Indeed, when *Figaro* (or any other Mozart opera) is being performed, the chips are down, because every singer must be an accomplished musician and actor, and everyone in the orchestra a maestro. Every single note upon the stage and down in the pit must be accounted for; neither torrents of sound nor thickness of texture are present to offer refuge to the wayward. Further, *Figaro* calls not only for good voices but voices that will blend in the ensembles. Above all, thoughtful artists, conductors, and directors must avoid behaving like buffoons and turning *Figaro* into low comedy, something that, regrettably, happens too often. This is a delightful comedy which is at the same time the most delicate perception of beauty.

The eighteenth-century stage was full of reciting or singing Don Juans. The subject was popular, and there were a number of plays and operas devoted to "the rake punished." Don Juan, to quote Kierkegaard, is a genuinely musical theme, for the music illustrates not so much Don Juan's adventures as his character and essence. To the very end, when death knocks the cup of life from his hand, he does not repent and does not retract anything, but remains the incarnation of the very love of life which is not overshadowed by reflection and conflict. It was for this reason that *Don Giovanni* was found shockingly amoral, not only by mere theatergoers but even by Beethoven. Da Ponte, who knew both his public and the clergy, was induced to add an epilogue to the finished opera; it did not escape him that the edifying ending was already present in some of the earliest plays. This epilogue falsifies the essence of the opera

by attempting to rationalize, in the oblique form of acknowledged retribution, a character whose heroic hedonism cannot
be rationalized. All the musicians who set the legend before
Mozart were simply afraid—or unable—to tackle its real meaning, a fact well demonstrated by the nature of these operas;
they are all of the pure buffa variety. (All the earlier settings
of the Don Juan legend are now forgotten, but Gluck's ballet-
pantomime and Purcell's setting of Shadwell's lyrics deserve to
be salvaged.) It is unfortunate that to this day many stage
directors think that Mozart's *Don Giovanni* is also a comic
opera pure and simple. But da Ponte understood both Don
Juan and Mozart, the demonic figure of the Latin Faust and
the little Austrian musician in whose soul flamed more than
human powers. Beethoven, who played in the orchestra when
Don Giovanni was performed in Bonn, admired the opera so
much that he copied certain parts of the score and kept them
constantly before his eyes. More than that, he borrowed some
ideas from it, the most notable instance being in the first movement of the C-sharp minor piano sonata. But, as I have said,
he was dismayed by the opera's "immoral" subject, an opinion
that has been shared by many a musician and critic practically
to our own day. Why, then, one might ask, was Mozart attracted to the Don Juan story?

Don Juan is, next to Faust, the most characteristic and human hero type in world literature, a southern Spanish legendary celebrity (though it is not impossible that he was a
historical figure, Don Juan Tenorio) whose valorous deeds,
but even more whose amorous escapades, have excited admiration ever since the fifteenth century. It was in that century
that the godless, philandering nobleman first appeared on the
stage in a play entitled *The Atheist Struck by Lightning*. By
the early seventeenth century, when he began the literary conquest of the world in a serious play, *El Burlador de Sevilla*,
attributed to the great playwright Tirso do Molina, the Don
Juan legend had gradually absorbed other motifs, though the
contours it acquired in the *Burlador* remained fairly constant.
He is a man who enjoys life to the hilt, who is sensitive about
his knightly honor but cynical in love and unprincipled in

everything else. In an everyday sense these traits exhaust Don Juanism, but men of letters have seen in the Don Juan legend a much more profound human and psychological meaning, a meaning entirely at odds with Beethoven's bourgeois interpretation. To them, the Don is the incarnation of the male: imperious, proud, brave, strong. He is not a despicable traitor nor a rapist, but a lover who conquers feminine hearts passionately and hence legitimately; when he is about a conquest his ardor is genuine—though he refuses to bind himself beyond the moment. This passionate ardor with which he woos a woman is the dominant trait in Don Juan, and it is failure to appreciate it that causes him to be seen as a professional seducer to whom variety is an end by itself. His second attribute, cynicism, was carried beyond his love affairs to become a denial of every moral law except the code of chivalry. Thus Don Juan very early acquired the stamp of an atheist, a profane iconoclast, an image which remained with him in legend and literature. Veritable religious mystery dramas, exemplified by the addition of the powerfully attractive motif of the stone guest, were built around the idea of retribution visited upon him. The graveyard statue of the slain father of a recent victim is blasphemously invited by Don Juan to dinner; the statue accepts the invitation, interrupts the Don's festive meal, and tosses the libertine into hell.

The charge of immorality was brought against Tirso de Molina's play (though he was a priest) rather early; the Jesuits thundered against him in Spain, but Don Juan had convinced supporters, not the least among them King Philip IV. Later, the nineteenth century was very critical, and even in the early twentieth one can find derogatory statements by reputable authors. But Tirso de Molina's plays are neither less nor more immoral than those by other playwrights of his time. They contain no language as crude as some of Shakespeare's. The unscrupulousness shown by a lover like Don Juan has no more to do with edification than the actions of a Clytemnestra or a Lady Macbeth. The history of the legend is rich in fine plays, novels, and poems. After a number of predecessors, Molière created a masterpiece in *The Stone Guest*, followed in England by Shadwell's *The Libertine*. The legend made its entrance in German literature with E. T. A. Hoffmann, but this Romantic poet-musician actually started from Mozart's opera. Don Juan's popularity continued unabated: Goethe, Byron, Baudelaire, Rostand, Shaw may be mentioned among the prominent literary figures who found him attractive.

At about the time Byron wrote his poem, Pushkin also entered the competition with a Don Juan drama, but the *bon vivant* of his *Eugene Onegin* comes from Don Juan Tenorio. Onegin is a romantic, half-sorrowful, half-resigned, a decadent man of the world. This unheroic Don Juan, who is even seen weeping, was further watered down by Tchaikovsky's pretty music and became a parlor dandy. Mozart's Don Juan is made of different stuff. Unlike his Russian cousin, he is never in doubt, never vacillates, never repents, and goes to his doom with unbowed head. The composer penetrated into the characters of the legend with a dramatic insight that remains unparalleled. He saw Don Juan as personifying male love par excellence, man as absolute lord over woman, who in her love sacrifices everything, for against her better judgment she believes in her hero. This Don Juanesque love, in which the tragic motif is supplied by the women delivered to the male's insatiable passion, was accorded its most magnificent version in Mozart's opera; it was really he, not the poets and playwrights, who made the Don, Leporello, Donna Anna, and Donna Elvira immortal.

But of course *Don Giovanni* is neither a play nor a poem, and since it is an opera it obeys entirely different dramatic concepts. Da Ponte's libretto has been sometimes called mediocre by critics who judge it as a play—an inadmissible point of view. Da Ponte may have been something of a *dissoluto* himself, and he was certainly an adventurer, but he was a good scholar and knew the lyric stage as had few in the history of opera. As a vehicle for Mozart's dramatic imagination, and particularly as a *dramma giocoso*—that is, the difficult blend of seria and buffa—da Ponte's libretto is in no small measure responsible for the greatness of the work. Da Ponte seems to have been familiar with most of the principal theatrical and

operatic versions of the legend, from the Spanish plays to
Goldoni, and he also knew the tributary motifs that came from
French sources, notably from Molière, but in creating the
libretto he proceeded quite independently and with great skill.
The immediate model for both librettist and composer, however, was a recent opera by Giovanni Bertati with music by
Giuseppe Gazzaniga—*The Stone Guest*. Da Ponte's exacting
task was to reconcile all these sources with the prevailing taste
for opera, and he had to keep a weather eye on the moral
censors. It should be remembered that the original title of the
opera was *Il Dissoluto punito, ossia Il Don Giovanni;* the
idea of retribution was thus prominently displayed. But perhaps the librettist's greatest accomplishment was his divination
of Mozart's powers; he knew what could happen to seemingly
innocuous passages once they were clothed with Mozart's
music, and therefore could attain his aims even if the libretto
without the music were more or less tailored to satisfy the
requirements of the times. (Still, he was careful enough not to
submit the complete text to the censors.) He knew that Mozart
would not be satisfied with a surface setting of any situation in
which his hero found himself but would intensify and enhance
each nuance. Don Giovanni's sense of the intoxicating pleasures
of life, his ardor and the psychic resonance it compels, is purely
in the music, not in the words; it cannot be censored or changed,
for truth in art is truth of imagination.

A good librettist will not only condense an original play,
provide opportunities for set numbers, and adjust the pace to
the altogether different pace music demands but will change
the characters, even the motivations, to suit musical elaboration.
In the various Don Juan plays, Donna Anna and Donna
Elvira assume different dramatic importance, the former especially often being treated as a minor figure. Da Ponte enlarged Donna Anna's role and polarized the characters of the
two women. He cleverly retained Tirso de Molina's way of
bringing out the sheer terror of the denouement by comic
touches that afford relief while sharpening the impact of the
violent end. This suited Mozart, who used humor to serve the
purposes of the drama. But *Don Giovanni*, though containing

moments of genuine comedy, is not a comic opera in the accepted sense of the term, and the Don himself is not a comic or thoughtless character. He is licentious and unscrupulous in attaining his ends, the type of selfishness born to the purple, but he is brave, handsome, and spirited, a courteous nobleman; he is never sentimental, and he has charm, an undefinable attraction that conquers. His courage is so genuine that his composure during the encounter with the ghost convinces us of the horror and reality of the scene. Actually, all the women in the cast are in love with him, and it is this that calls for great skill on the part of singers and stage directors.

Donna Anna is haughty, determined, yet—in spite of her obsession with vengeance—confused. This ambivalence in her character is splendidly realized in her long recitative and aria, where the mood constantly changes from narration and pleading to savage outbursts on the inexorably repeated word *vendetta*. Donna Elvira is much less complicated. She is in love and ever ready to forgive, a sad woman in whom there is always a spark of hope left. Zerlina is often played as an ingénue, which she is not. Indeed, she knows exactly what the Don wants, and she is tempted, but she is aware that there is no future in this kind of liaison and that in the long run a safe marriage with a well-to-do country bumpkin is to be preferred. But perhaps a little indiscretion would not hurt—the dashing cavalier is so much more attractive than Masetto! Was there ever set to music a more delightful, a more tender, a more ravishing and enticing acquiescence to a tryst than "La cì darem la mano"? Don Ottavio is a puppet, a correct gentleman who is a stranger among men of strong character. Mozart lavished on him the most heavenly music, the purest bel canto, but it is music undisturbed by passion. This was the master stroke of the master dramatist. The two buffo parts are quite different. Leporello is, of course, the descendant of the old comic servant, a fixture in comedy ever since Plautus and Terence, and particularly popular in the opera buffa. But Leporello is not like Sganarelle, his counterpart in Molière's play, for while he too is pusillanimous, this fellow is not a mere buffoon; when he acts on behalf of his master he stands al-

most in the Don's place, deriving vicarious pleasure from reflected glory. He is a coward, and he deplores the deeds of
his master, but he too feels the Don's attraction. Masetto, also
a basso buffo, is an innocent who seems to get the short end
in every situation. But again, he is by no means a simpleton;
he has a peasant cunning and is not quite fooled by Don
Giovanni and his valet.

The conductor faces a staggering task in coping with the
fantastic scenes in which lust, bloodshed, comedy, love, and
heroism alternate, all expressed in music of unflagging intensity. After an exceptionally weighty overture, he is almost immediately confronted with one of the greatest scenes in the
operatic literature: the ensemble that follows the stabbing of
the Commendatore, Donna Anna's father. He then has to
sustain two long acts of ever-increasing dramatic pace and
gathering tension, culminating in a finale that is unique in its
power and complexities. And after "the most terrible trombone
chords in all music" have entered with their fearful proclama-
tion of doom, there is no respite until in the last measures the
somber D minor turns into major. The stage director cannot
go wrong if he follows one overriding principle: this is not a
farce, but a drama that begins with murder and ends with the
death of an authentic hero. If the comic interludes, of which
there are many, are permitted to turn into clowning the drama
is completely distorted, for even underneath the lightness of
the comic scenes there is an unseen density.

Stage directors have all manner of devices to preserve the
flow of Mozart's music through two long acts and frequent
scene changes which at times hurt the work's unity. They
want to facilitate instant audience comprehension of each situation and corresponding readjustment to the changing motivation of the musical numbers. What this opera needs, however,
is a complete re-study; it is overgrown with vines that should
be cleared away. A good deal of research is called for, but the
original materials are available, including authentic manuscript
scores that contain many instructions now neglected. It will be
seen that this opera is fundamentally a four-acter, like *Figaro,*

and it was only the growing demand for two-acters that caused Mozart to alter the plan. With some careful editing the four-act structure might perhaps be restored; at any rate it is worth trying. Such an arrangement would not interrupt the music at crucial points and would give breathing spells to both singers and the public. For the Vienna production of *Don Giovanni* (the premiere took place in Prague) Mozart added several new numbers to the opera. Such a procedure is always hazardous, especially in a work like this one in which the balance and relationship of the tonalities employed have an important form-building function. Most of these pieces were added to the second act: the great tenor aria "Dalla sua pace," Elvira's fine recitative and aria, and a fine duet for Zerlina and Leporello. Sometimes these numbers are either omitted or shifted around indiscriminately, but they are valuable extensions of plot and music. The four-act plan would accommodate the additional numbers much more naturally.

Then there is that curious bit of play towards the end of the second act. By a century-old custom, at the dinner scene Don Giovanni is given the company of several ladies who have no singing parts but take turns sitting on his lap. There is no trace of this promiscuity either in Don Giovanni's character or in the original scenario. Anything beyond one female dinner companion at a time is contrary to the spirit of the opera. Finally, one of the most important changes that ought to be made concerns the epilogue. Sung after the opera has really ended with Don Giovanni's death, this sextet comes as an anticlimax on the heels of a relentlessly driven tragic finale. The music of this postscript is equal to the best of the ensembles in the body of the opera, but its text and purpose are weak. After the catastrophic end of the Don, it matters little that Donna Elivira will take the veil, that Don Ottavio still thinks of marriage, that Donna Anna bids him cool his well-mannered ardor for another year, and that Masetto and Zerlina will have dinner. The sanctimonious tone and obviously forced moral are natural neither to da Ponte nor to Mozart: "This is the end of the wrongdoer; his death is as ugly as was his life." With the death of the Don the moral order of the world has been re-established; any further discussion of his demise, no matter how beautiful the music, can only weaken the drama.

Così fan tutte is no ordinary opera buffa but the most sophisticated stylized parody of opera, bearing as much resemblance to the usual fare heard in the theater as needlepoint to a hooked rug. It has the maturity and devotion, the truth of experience, and the transfiguring imagination which all together make what is lasting in works of art. In many ways this is the most "classic" opera of them all, because in it music proclaims its sovereignty and its own authentic laws. *Così fan tutte* is no longer the customary opera buffa; it is a profound caricature of life completely freed of the real and projected into the ideal world. The imaginative truth of the slight story is such that it would be folly to try to dissociate it from the form of stylized comedy which it took and which is so often misunderstood. The opera's warm humanity can be conveyed only by its penetrating humor, avoiding anything analytical or psychological in the method of presentation. Its charm works only if we do not overstep the bounds of operatic story-telling.

This can be very difficult for the real world to understand, and the nineteenth century was completely baffled by the work, regarding it as merely some charming though superficial music on a silly libretto. An ever-recurring theme in the virtuous nineteenth century was the opera's lack of moral elevation, "far removed from the Mozart who in *The Abduction from the Seraglio* and *The Magic Flute* glorified ideal love." Wagner, who in his operas rather liked to create relationships that are on the statute books, declared himself happy that it was impossible for Mozart to invent music for *Così fan tutte* such as he did for *The Magic Flute:* "it would have disgraced music." Strait-laced Beethoven, too, was put off by the libretto, though he greatly admired the music and drew inspiration from it. What an astounding panorama: all three of Mozart's greatest Italian operas were considered "immoral"! Perhaps

this ultra-Victorianism explains how Busoni came to the conclusion that an opera should have no love music at all.

Be that as it may, in order to salvage something from this
terrible debauchery, various improvements were attempted.
Some tried to doctor the original libretto by changing plot and
action; other, more fantastic changes transformed Don Alfonso into Prospero and Despina into Ariel; while in Paris
Shakespeare's *Love's Labour's Lost* was carved up to fit the
music—and vice versa.

Now what was so shocking about this wondrous work that
today vastly entertains us? Actually, da Ponte's libretto is
excellent both in composition and in language. There can be
no doubt that everything in it was planned in close collaboration with the composer, and the outcome was a libretto of
the most sophisticated nature that exactly fitted Mozart's desires and capabilities. In *Così* there is a concentration of expression, a melodic design that is almost severe, and a stylistic
unity in which poetic thought is completely converted into
musical form. Yet dramatic plausibilty is not only present but
is very refined and deftly pointed. The protagonists, three men
and three women, are divided into three groups, each group
being characterized by different music. As the opera unfolds,
there are various permutations in this grouping, leading to the
most sensitively acute conflicts.

Fiordiligi is a woman who stands on her dignity and moral
concepts. She is haughty and imperious, and her suitor has difficulty in making headway with her. Dorabella's concept of
the constancy proper for well-born ladies is much less positive
than her sister's. She is a creature of instinct who likes to love
and readily accepts the flighty chambermaid's advice that one
man is as good as any other—provided he is available. The two
sisters are affianced to men of kindred character, Guglielmo
being the realist, Ferrando the dreamer. When, in the test arranged by Don Alfonso, each pairs off with the other's bride,
the character complex is quadrupled, presenting the composer
with a task only a Mozart could carry out. Don Alfonso is
the real *régisseur* in this opera. This pivotal character is an

elderly bon vivant, an engagingly cynical philosopher determined to prove that *la donna è mobile*—that eternal love is a
serious matter but seldom confined to one. Da Ponte once
more created wonderful foils when he chose as the instrument
of the worldly bachelor's machinations the quintessentially
feminine Despina, the chambermaid.

This situation brought with it reliance on an unusually large
number of ensembles, which Mozart handles with the most
extraordinary skill. The very first scene demands three trios
for men alone, and he was able to avoid the slightest monotony. In the duet "Fra gli amplessi," there is a richness of feeling and expression that is rare even in Mozart. Maidenly fear,
womanly yielding, gentle swooning, and sensuous desire
besiege the double wall of constancy. But there are also many
arias, and they are as varied as they are beautiful. Fiordiligi's
great aria "Come scoglio" is a full-fledged opera seria piece,
the kind assigned in the old opera to goddesses. But when she
avers that her eternal love will withstand every temptation,
all the while singing those frightfully difficult wide intervals,
it becomes clear that this is a parody, even a parody of parody.
On the other hand, Ferrando's "Un aura amorosa" is one of
Mozart's most sincerely felt love songs.

The buffo element is there, of course, and such scenes as
the one where Despina, disguised as the doctor, revives the
"suicides" with a magnet are in the best tradition of the opera
buffa (besides being a parody of the then fashionable Dr.
Mesmer, the hypnotist). But again, at the end, just before the
unmasking of the travesty, Mozart sings the happiness of the
lovers in a canonic ensemble. This is one of his most beautiful
melodies, and the little world on the stage does not realize that
the whole invisible world is making music around them. For
when these marionettes join to celebrate their sham wedding
with a song, the wheels of time pause for a minute while we
hear a hymn of youth and life and love that even Mozart
never surpassed in gentleness and beauty.

Così fan tutte represents the ultimate in classical stylization,
yet Mozart's characters are individuals, not complex, but obstinate in their courses. They are vital, alert creatures who be-

come familiar to us through that mingling of imaginative sympathy with practical craft which alone can create characters in the round. Still, they seem most themselves when the impulse that moves them springs from the intricate ensembles, which are the glory of this opera. The composition of *Così* is more hidden than that of the other operas and its musical language less immediately accessible; it can almost be said to be built on mood sketches, for the events represent only an internal articulation. This music is a gift that first must be unwrapped and assayed, because Mozart is at the height of his melodic inventiveness and offers a whole chain of delicate musical ideas elaborated with the care of fine-grained chamber music. If, as is often done, *Così* is compared with Mozart's other operas, it will suffer—but for the wrong reasons. Next to Susanna or Leporello, the men and women in *Così* seem but figures which at the end of the opera are swept back into the chess box. But they are more than puppets; without embodying any compelling dramatic experience they reflect humanity with a chaste felicity. Since *Così fan tutte* is an ensemble opera, a rare case in the history of the genre, it demands the utmost in musicianship, timing, and ability to keep the pace while remaining flexible—and the catch is that these requirements are mandatory not only for the performers but in good measure also for the audience. It is an exceedingly difficult work, requiring a high degree of artistry from high soprano down to second bassoon. Every one of them, whether on the stage or in the pit, is in an illuminated showcase, open at all times to minute inspection, and the slightest blemish will sound like an air raid siren. Yet at the same time singers and orchestra are asked to deport themselves with agility and grace, with consistent forbearance toward one another, and to pay unusual attention to the conductor. A good performance demands lively tempos, well-phrased melodies, aristocratic dynamics, finely balanced ensembles; and the complicated finales must be whipped up without creating noise. The two leading ladies must handle very taxing parts, whether buffo patter or expansive aria in the opera seria style. They should present a pair of demure damsels who

gradually catch fire. When in their own company they engage in the innocent pleasure of juvenile arguments about
their beaux, but when they face the men everything changes.
What da Ponte—but even more Mozart—wanted to convey
is that the most heartfelt protestations of love become a commonplace if there is an audience besides the blindly believing
beloved. The accents are so delicate that they are easily lost
unless all concerned are aware of them, and the delivery can
easily lose its rare perfume and turn into preciosity by making
false elisions or bending a little cadenza the wrong way.

As for the two swains, when disguised they must try to
bridge the difference in their temperament; Guglielmo is
agreeably gauche and blustery, Ferrando dreamy and suave.
Despina's role calls for a light voice—"light" not in volume
but in freshness that enables it to shine through the ensembles
where her part has the musical lead. All this confronts conductor, stage director, and performers with difficulties they
experience sporadically in other operas, but never throughout
an entire work. Above all, *Così fan tutte* requires the most
sensitive stylization. If performed with refinement and charm,
it will convey to the listener what musical conversation in
the Elysian fields must sound like.

There are many who still think that *The Magic Flute* is an
unfortunate combination of Mozart's "charming" music with
a harebrained libretto; indeed, the latter has been called by a
reputable critic "a hodge-podge of sophomoric symbolism
and bawdy low comedy." It is said that when the plot was
changed in midstream, the librettist failed to adjust the already
composed portions to accord with the new situation; or that
the whole thing was thrown together by two librettists in a
haphazard way, without a semblance of dramatic construction. On the other hand, there are those, especially in Germany, who are convinced that every note and every gesture
in the opera has occult meaning. It stands to reason that given
such extremes both opinions must be questioned.

Emanuel Schikaneder, the librettist, usually described as an
unlettered, provincial theater man, was an experienced actor,

singer, and manager who made his reputation by producing and playing Lessing, Goethe, Shakespeare, and Beaumarchais. He himself wrote plays, composed music, and played the violin—hardly an unlettered clod. Mozart, on friendly terms with Schikaneder since his Salzburg days, often attended the performances (he had a free pass), and it may well have been *The Barber of Seville*, one of Schikaneder's Salzburg productions, that introduced him to the Beaumarchais plays. It was the Emperor who invited Schikaneder to Vienna, where his first production was *The Abduction from the Seraglio*. So much for the librettist. As for the libretto itself, Goethe was moved by its "sophomoric symbolism," as were Herder and Hegel and many others. But above all, Mozart loved *The Magic Flute;* on his deathbed he followed the performance, watch in hand, estimating that "now comes Papageno's song." As a mature composer he never set to music a text he did not believe in, the only exception being a command performance, *La Clemenza di Tito*—and we know what happened. To be sure, this is a text which, set by a minor composer, would be commonplace, as were the "Zauber" operas that preceded *Die Zauberflöte.* Everyone is agreed that it is a strange medley, but the defect of the libretto in no small part arises from what is in no small part its merit: the way the story is told. The action on the stage is always interesting; at no point does Mozart hesitate or seem embarrassed theatrically or musically, and nowhere does his invention slacken.

The Magic Flute was a variant of a well known singspiel type of entertainment whose stock characters, incidents, and other theatrical ingredients were familiar and popular. The singspiel was a very special kind of opera; consistency of musical style was not expected, as the individual numbers were separated by spoken dialogue rather than by recitative and did not need logical or musical continuity. As professional entertainers, Mozart and Schikaneder were, of course, bound to respect this tradition, and indeed externally they held fast to the standard recipe. In none of his mature operas did Mozart use such a wide variety of styles and genres, from German folksong to the dizzying coloratura of the old seria, from solemn choral anthem to lightning-fast buffa ensemble. But while the mixture is heterogeneous, it corresponds to the spirit of the fantastic fairy tale, and the whole is held together by an admirable musical logic based on tonal concordances.

We called the genre singspiel but should qualify it as Viennese singspiel, for it is different from its German counterpart. The Viennese mixture of German, Italian, and French elements is more operatic in nature and tone and demands fully qualified opera singers rather than actors who can also sing simple songs. In Mozart's case we see a strong desire to reconcile the naive German petit-bourgeois song-play with both varieties of Italian opera. He had tried this before, in *The Abduction,* and though that work is delightfully fresh and viable, this first attempt at synthesis did not succeed. In *The Abduction* he divided his characters into two groups: a "serious" couple and a "buffa" couple of the Viennese variety. Both groups consist of tenor and soprano, but they differ not only in character but also in the quality and style of the music they sing. To the serious couple Mozart entrusted the great operatic scenes, to the other the simple songs. In addition there was a spoken part and a genuine basso buffo in the Italian style. This resulted in exquisite Mozartean music and delightful single numbers, but the frame of the work is uncertain. In *The Magic Flute,* with the immense experience of three great Italian operas behind him, Mozart once more tried such a synthesis, hoping to create a genuine German opera. Once more this was not a haphazard procedure, some pretty music tacked onto a silly libretto, but a well-thought-out plan which succeeded to such an extent that we must consider *The Magic Flute* one of the principal foundations upon which subsequent German opera was built. Moreover, the libretto, in which Mozart had a hand, cannot be considered aside from the music, as is too often done, for where the cold print may seem silly and hazy, the music makes the meaning unequivocally clear and noble. The language of the original book is seldom poetic and at times is vulgar, but we must remember that *The Magic Flute* was written for performance in a lower-middle-class suburban district in Vienna, where it achieved a tremendous success. Schikaneder and Mozart combined the popular and the sophisticated in a way that it was attractive to Viennese of all classes. They offered a vision on a double plane; one for immediate appreciation, the other for reflection. To realize the first aim they were careful to provide good entertainment and popular tunes, which alone would not have drawn the fashionable Viennese beyond the gates. But to the more sophisticated they also offered a degree of subtlety, as in the handling of the much-discussed Masonic symbolism.

Mozart was a Mason and, judging from the music he wrote for Masonic purposes, a genuine believer in the movement, which as it existed in those days counted among its adherents not only merchants, civil servants, and artists (Haydn was also a member) but even the Emperor, Joseph II. The audiences attending performances of *The Magic Flute* were familiar with the symbols and rites appearing in the opera, and the outward Masonic symbols are obvious enough even to us. Not so readily perceptible are the "occult" ones. There is, for instance, the mystic number "three:" there are three Ladies, three Genii, the three doors Tamino tries, the three curious chords in the middle of the overture, even the three flats in the principal key of E-flat major. The dramatic mold of *The Magic Flute* is filled with consummate art, and the spectators' thoughts and feelings are guided with a gentle but sure hand. Admittedly, such a plan must either succeed or fall completely; it is either magnificent or nonsensical. In the view of the majority of students of Mozart it is almost always the first; its depth of feeling saves it from becoming the other. In the end we are aware of the excellence of the design and how skilfully the conflict between moral light and sinister darkness has been woven into a fairy-tale comedy.

There are additional reasons for the great popularity of *The Magic Flute* with the German-speaking middle classes from the beginning of its career. The ideas that prince and commoner are both human beings and can seek love on an equal footing, and that light will triumph over darkness, were typical of the Enlightenment. It was this dignity of the individual, the concept of the rights of man, about which they read in the popular translations of Montesquieu, Rousseau, and Voltaire, as well as their own Lessing and other German writers, and they saw these ideas expressed in the solemn and mysterious Masonic rites. But beyond all the lofty ideals, *The Magic Flute* was a real singspiel in the vernacular, every character of which harks back to everyday life. While these figures did rise above the humdrum, they remained recognizable to the Viennese as well as to Germans at large. Even Sarastro is at first sight a benevolent old uncle rather than a sort of Knight of the Holy Grail. The three Ladies of the Queen of the Night have a chat, a marvelously melodious chat, after saving Tamino, but they talk as any three girls would about a handsome young man. Pamina and Tamino may be of princely blood, but they act like brave young lovers from the shores of the Danube. In the making of Papageno the author's task was to produce not a psychologically explicable being but one who would evoke the affection of the audience and would yet be acceptable as entirely human. He is not Rousseau's child of nature but the local jester, Casperl, the traditional Viennese clown known to every urchin in eighteenth-century Vienna. Librettist and composer also made sure that his name should not be Aloysius or Fürchtegott, or even his rightful Casperl, but an Italian-sounding word that permits the fast Italian patter of the buffa, which cannot be rendered in any other language.

Mozart's musical blueprint was extraordinarily original. Each figure in the play was given music according to his or her rank. The light singspiel tone was assigned to Papageno, the full-fledged opera seria style, the great arias with their elaborate coloratura, to the Queen of the Night; the young couple sings tender love music, "princely" music, and Sarastro and his priests "humanistic" music, dignified, serious, quasi-church-music intended to signify the humanitarian principles of Freemasonry. The earnestness of Mozart's purpose—and this should be weighed carefully—is shown by the astonishing appearance in a popular opera of a grave Lutheran chorale over a severe fugue. We are, indeed, in the vicinity of the Requiem and of the *Masonic Mourning Music*, and there are discernible connections between *The Magic Flute* and the religious works. Yet this is still a "fairy opera," the many episodes and transient figures show it and keep the audience amused. One would think that all this adds up to an unmanageable sequence of tableaux, but Mozart delighted in the problem, summoning all his redoubtable skill to create one of the most durable and beautiful lyric plays of all time. The centrifugal force that keeps everything together is the logic of tonal order. Every one of the human types mentioned above— the priests, the youthful lovers, the forces of darkness, the buffo figures—has its own tonal region, and Mozart keeps the various tonal areas in subtle equilibrium, starting with E-flat and after a long "development" section returning to it. In fact, the second finale magnificently recapitulates the entire tonal order of the opera. Musicians, from Beethoven onward, never ceased to marvel at this, considering the organization of the opera a triumph of sheer musical logic. Every once in a while well-meaning persons who fail to see the structure make changes "for the better spacing of the arias." No one can simply step in here and shove around the arias, any more than one can shift the snake from Laocoon's right hand to his left foot.

The musical marvels of *The Magic Flute* are endless, but the real marvel is that the most finicky musical connoisseur does rejoice in Papageno's ditties, while the untutored freely absorb the highly artistic and subtle elements without being aware of their nature. Surely this is the highest tribute one could pay to Mozart and *The Magic Flute*.

Of Mozart's mature operas the first and the last have fallen on evil times. The reason for this seems to be that both were written on the Baroque opera seria pattern, no longer (and not yet) acceptable to our public, nor, in the case of *La Clamenza di Tito*, the last opera, to Mozart either. The first of these neglected works, *Idomeneo*, is slowly staging a comeback in Europe, which it amply deserves, but *Tito* seems to be doomed. *Idomeneo* was of the morning and the May, *Tito* of the autumn and the evening.

La Clemenza di Tito is generally assumed to have been composed in haste, under circumstances of despair and ill-health. The quality of the workmanship does not bear this out: Mozart was often in dire straits without any indication of his mental and physical condition apparent in his music. What inhibited him here was that the specifications set for this commissioned opera went against the grain of his natural dramatic instinct. Nevertheless, *Tito* still brings us in contact with an opera composer of a vitality so overwhelming that he seems more real than most of the musicians whose operas can be heard every day. The libretto is usually ascribed to the great opera poet of the Baroque, Metastasio, but the fact is that the famous book of 1734, set by most leading composers in the first half of the eighteenth century, was "modernized," that is, butchered, by a hack. Mazzolà, the refurbisher, managed to get some action into the static seria pattern but was unable to remove the official and obsequious quality of homage and fealty, anachronistic in an age dominated by the spirit of the Enlightenment. Commissioned for the coronation festivities in Prague, the opera had to be formal in an archaic way, a lightly veiled eulogy to the dynasty. This tone was familiar to the Italians active at the Viennese court—the Habsburgs had been employing them for generations for this purpose—but it was strange to Mozart, who was temperamentally incapable of revealing the train of thought and the sentiments of characters alien to him. Yet again and again, amid much that is perfunctory and a little heavy with solemnity, Mozart delights us with his old felicity and the assurance of his living faculty to rejoice in the beautiful. And in the fine choruses and magnificent finale of the first act, the reflection of the summit falls on this forgotten opera that we know only from concert performances and recordings.

La Clemenza di Tito is weighted down with discord—human, dramatic, and musical. The discord is not resolved, even though Mozart often achieves a unity which is a tense reconciliation of opposites. His concern for uniting the substance with the shadow is consistently apparent in the technical tightness of the composition—the craftsmanship is of the finest. In one respect, then, the music of this opera is successful, often absolutely so, but the contradictions remain. Mozart's operatic technique was by this time a miraculous amalgam of seria and buffa, the latter clearly dominating the ensembles. Da Ponte, who sized up his composer with remarkable insight, wrote his librettos to suit this particular musical style. The libretto of *Tito,* however, offers nothing but unrelieved nobility and *clemenza;* Mozart is able to cope with this to a certain extent in the arias (after all, the Countess's great aria in *Figaro,* to mention one example, is a pure seria aria), but not in the ensembles. Although the latter are very good, and the first finale a masterpiece, the buffo ensemble technique is somewhat incongruous when applied to such texts.

But perhaps the principal discord was created by the absence of Mozart's favorite subject: flesh-and-blood lovers. There are four male characters in the opera, but two of these roles are sung by trebles: one was originally a castrato part, and the other was composed for a mezzo-soprano. In a true Baroque opera, which has few if any ensembles, the castrato part can be lowered for tenor or baritone and theatrical and dramatic illusion can thus be created, at least for those who love the living theater. But *Tito* is not a true Baroque opera; it has fine animated ensembles in which the "men" carry the upper parts, so that transposition would simply destroy the ensembles. So, all we can do is to enjoy the fine music and grieve about the lack of dramatic life, characterization, and vocal contrast. For, indeed, if posterity has failed to find this opera satisfactory, the fault is not with its matter but with its manner: *Tito* is a drama without the full dignity of passion.

CARL A. RUDISILL LIBRARY
LENOIR RHYNE COLLEGE

Four

BEETHOVEN

T HOUGH by the opening of the nineteenth century the Viennese "fairy opera" and sentimental singspiel had become very popular, there was no national German opera comparable to the Italian and the French. Gluck composed Italian and French operas, and Mozart's fame rested primarily on his Italian operas, though *The Magic Flute* was gaining popularity by leaps and bounds. Beethoven, eager to compose an opera, did not know where to turn. An Italian opera he would not compose, partly because of his German national consciousness, partly because of his middle-class moral scruples—he considered Italian subjects frivolous and was unhappy about Mozart's choices. The German singspiel did not attract him either, for this popular genre dealing with everyday people and their everyday lives seemed unsuited to the broad moral, ethical, and political ideas and ideals that interested him, the kind we would call world problems. Though he admired *The Magic Flute* so much that he accepted a commission from Schikaneder to compose a sort of sequel to it, the fairy-tale tone was alien to his nature, and nothing came of the project. Finally he found a congenial form of the lyric theater in the French revolutionary opera, the so-called "rescue opera." Beethoven particularly esteemed Cherubini's *Les deux journées,* a "humanity" opera with a subject that appealed to him, and he unreservedly admired

Cherubini's cool, precise, and fastidious music. This, he felt, was the area he should explore for a congenial libretto, and his sentimental nature—for this heaven-storming bachelor was a very naive and sentimental man—was gratified by the discovery of an inspiring topic treated in another French rescue opera: the triumph of "conjugal love" over tyranny. This was a fine moral subject, and the libretto combined personal drama with the great public issues of political freedom and the just punishment of oppressors. The original French play had been set before, and one of these operas, *Léonore ou l'amour conjugal*, by Pierre Gaveaux, composed on a libretto by J. N. Bouilly, became Beethoven's immediate model. So Beethoven went to work without realizing the grave dramaturgical conflicts that would result from the blending of German singspiel with French rescue opera, both of which had well-settled prototypes that could not help impinging on each other. To complicate matters, the rescue opera itself was an incongruous mixture of the old opéra comique and the early romantic adventure opera. Not possessing Mozart's wondrous theatrical sense and imagination—nor his able librettists—Beethoven still created in *Fidelio* an altogether unique work. Yet, though dutifully admired, it has never become popular in this country. Even among those who like Beethoven's only opera there are not a few who question its theatrical merits. Yet *Fidelio* is a great work that should not be missing from the repertory of any major opera house. It is undeniable that the libretto is marked by primitive dramaturgy and painfully obvious spoken monologues and dialogues, but the musical realization is magnificent. Although essentially an instrumental composer, Beethoven was a musician of highly dramatic imagination, and on the whole, despite the libretto, *Fidelio* is expertly operatic and rises to true dramatic eloquence. While the opera has its awkward moments, it has many more of supreme greatness next to which the flaws pale into insignificance.

What makes *Fidelio* difficult to appreciate is its curious dualistic nature. Those naive words and situations are set to music that may be called romantic in its passion for life, and classical in its insistence on musical logic. Maturity of style does not always ripen simultaneously with maturity of thought, and while there can be no question that Beethoven's musical thought is on as high a level in the vital sections of this opera as in the many masterpieces that originated from the same period as *Fidelio*, he is guilty of stylistic inconsistencies seldom found in his instrumental music. Nevertheless, it is not true that Beethoven had no gift for vocal writing, nor that he was unfamiliar with the requirements of opera. In his impressionable youth he played viola in the Bonn opera house, where the whole repertory of the era, from Gluck to Paisiello, Mozart, and Cimarosa, was heard. After settling in Vienna, he studied with two experienced opera composers, Salieri and Schenk, and made the acquaintance of the most recent Viennese lyric plays. Have the critics of Beethoven as vocal composer ever looked at his Italian pieces, or at the fine early Mass in C? Do they know his sixty-odd songs? And, indeed, have they really examined *Fidelio?* Practically all detractors base their judgment on the finale of the Ninth Symphony and the great Mass in D, which are, of course, fiendish pieces for singers. But in these works Beethoven was altogether preoccupied with the purely symphonic plan that underlies his lofty humanitarian intentions; to the aging Beethoven human larynxes were expendable— they had to serve his exalted plans or perish.

In *Fidelio*, as I have said, Beethoven's sources were the German singspiel and the French revolutionary opera, both of which were mixed affairs containing elaborate operatic procedures but also melodrama and spoken dialogue. What disturbs us is this uncertainty of genre, for *Fidelio* is still a singspiel, if a supercharged one. Mozart had the same trouble in *The Abduction from the Seraglio*, in which he went far beyond the boundaries of the species by incorporating into the innocent "song-play" highly developed operatic elements. Later, in *The Magic Flute*, the problem was overcome, if not solved, and Weber, too, managed nicely with his *Freischütz*; but Beethoven, composing during the period between these two masterpieces, was unsure. It is significant, though, that when Mozart set a German text to music as lavishly operatic as in *The Magic Flute* he still refrained from using recitatives, relying on spoken dialogues; both he and Weber considered the recitative an exclusively Italian manner of musical expression. Living with Italian opera ever since his youth, Mozart was of course able to return from the singspiel to through-composed opera, but whenever Weber tried the latter he failed. The composers of French opéra comique (which paradoxically was not necessarily comical) also resorted to spoken dialogue, and for the same reason as the Germans: they were baffled by the recitative. Lully's exemplary French recitative had long since been forgotten, Gluck had proscribed the secco, and the powerful accompanied recitative of the Italian seria was too much for the French composer, used to the chansons and romances of the opéra comique. The serious disadvantage of these narrative prose passages in an opera is that they disrupt an essentially operatic procedure. The secco recitative may have slight musical substance, but it is still music, and the chords of the continuo maintain a musical continuity, the final cadence leading naturally to the aria that usually follows. In a singspiel, a fresh start has to be made after every spoken interruption. (It must have been this that prompted ill-advised attempts to connect the musical pieces by editorial recitatives. *Fidelio* was the beneficiary of such *Kapellmeistermusik* at the Metropolitan Opera, until Bruno Walter refused to lend a hand to this artistic fraud.)

This sort of stop-and-go music did not suit Beethoven's sense of continuity, and as a result a large part of the uneven first act of *Fidelio* consists of little individual genre scenes; there is little dramatic stuff in Marcelline, Jacquino, and Rocco. But there is plenty of good music, for this is genuine operatic writing imaginatively worked out. Most of the first act is pure eighteenth-century opera, excellently handled within the confines of the style and the genre; the melodies are fine, the vocal writing idiomatic in the operatic sense, the ensembles constructed with skill, and the orchestral part superb even by the highest Mozartean standards. Contrary to all sorts of learned as well as popular opinions, nowhere does

Beethoven show any sign of intellectual discomfort with an "unfamiliar medium"; the music flows naturally until it is stopped by the spoken dialogues, which break the spell and bring us down to a very ordinary earth. As soon as the music resumes the awkward words are forgotten, because the tunes are good and the thematic elaboration in the orchestra never falters. But emotionally involved the composer was not. Beethoven's sympathy and passion were not evoked by the small affairs of the two young people and the old jailer; not a character painter like Mozart, he was devoted to ideas, and ideas are not operatic material. In his embarrassment he relied for guidance on Gaveaux, whose score he not only studied carefully but followed in the general layout and in the types of songs, even borrowing music from the Frenchman. To mention an example, Rocco's song about the importance of money is a faithful copy in both construction and tone of Gaveaux's earlier setting of the libretto; indeed, Beethoven actually used the beginning of the tune.

Suddenly there is a startling change as Leonore appears; now the composer is involved, now the mental states acquire substance and personality, and from this point on even the little folk are ennobled. The quartet that ensues is a magnificent piece, and the following trio scarcely less so. The supposedly naive opera composer here proves himself a first-class musico-dramatist. We are not yet aware of how the dramatic conflict will take shape, Leonore merely joins the three other persons on the stage, yet the change in tone and mood is momentous. The quartet is in the unusual and undramatic form of a canon, so Leonore does not reveal herself except in the inflections of her melodic line, the notes being perforce the same for all four singers. It is the somber quality of the introduction, creating a sudden hush and instantly wiping out the petit bourgeois banter of the opening scenes, that announces the entrance into the drama of a superior protagonist. After this magnificent intimation of what is to come, Beethoven drops back to the singspiel tone and Rocco dispenses his fatherly advice about the need of newlyweds for financial security. While the song is pleasant and well made, it is this stylistic discrepancy that haunts *Fidelio* in its opening stages and again at the end.

With Leonore's great recitative and aria "Abscheulicher! wo eilst du hin?" we have arrived at real music drama; it is fiercely exuberant and rings with the passion of tragic truth. Now the heroine is before us in her ardent and courageous nature. The prisoners' chorus needs no champion; no one can remain unmoved by it. This, of course, is another one of those moments when an ideal—freedom—is invoked, and Beethoven was fully aroused. This curious and interesting source of inspiration is particularly revealing in Leonore's part. In the tremendous recitative and aria with the obbligato horns, Leonore is more heroic than womanly, but in the great duet of jubilation, where Beethoven demands an almost graphically expressive melodic exclamation, she is entirely feminine. The fiercely difficult piece also contains many tender asides that widen the tonal and dynamic range. After the scene with the prisoners, Beethoven composes a traditional act-ending finale with all hands participating. It is a very good piece that once more shows Beethoven to be thoroughly familiar with operatic conventions and techniques.

As the second act opens, we are suddenly hurled forward by half a century. The change is comparable only to the step Beethoven took from the second to the third of his symphonies. It is here that poor Gaveaux is thrown into the shadows, for while *Léonore* is a very good opera that in many ways was of pathbreaking importance in 1798, his elegiac moods could not stand comparison with the shattering power of Beethoven's dungeon scene. The general layout, however—even the role of the horns—Beethoven did copy from his predecessor's work. The somber introduction—one of his few compositions in F-minor—takes one's breath away, and the muffled diminished fifths ticking forth ominously from the timpani sound like our own anxious heartbeats. One can fairly feel the oppressive air of the dark dungeon. Then Florestan begins his great *scena*. He is like the dumb man who struggles to speak, to whom every word is a battle and sharp pain, yet who does speak, first spasmodically, then steadily,

with self-denying heroism. This whole act, from the introduction up to the finale, which once more reverts to
eighteenth-century patterns, is music-drama of the first water,
violent and dark. But even the finale—or rather its original
version—is a fine piece; unfortunately, in 1814 Beethoven
abridged it.

As is well known, Beethoven twice reworked *Fidelio*. The
first revision consisted mainly of abbreviations and reduction
from three to two acts. The second revision, made nine years
after the original composition, was far more extensive, and
it was inevitable that in this version further stylistic incongruities should intrude; nine years in Beethoven's musical
development amount to a lifetime in anyone else's. The
librettist of the final version, Treitschke, a theater manager,
was more skillful than his amateur predecessors and did improve the general dramatic design. Beethoven liked the new
shape of *Fidelio* and proceeded to revise the work from stem
to stern, regrettably dropping some fine pieces in the process.

Fidelio is a very serious matter for all concerned. It cannot
be prepared like an ordinary repertory opera; the musical
forces must be able to cope with both aspects of the score
on their own terms and minimize the stylistic differences between the light precision of the earlier pieces and the dramatic
violence of the later. It has been rightly said that *Fidelio* needs
a great Leonore, a great Florestan—and a great set of French
horns. The horns virtually risk their lives in Leonore's great
aria, but the whole orchestra must be up to the highest symphonic standards. When well rehearsed, under the direction
of an understanding stage manager and conductor, with the
spoken dialogues a bit refined, this deeply affecting opera
must convert even the doubters.

Attempts have been made to reconcile the opera's three
versions, in order to restore the good pieces dropped in the
1814 revision. So far these attempts have not been successful,
but I believe that such a synthesis is feasible without in the
least violating Beethoven's spirit. The four overtures Beethoven
composed for *Fidelio* have caused no little speculation, usually
resulting in deprecatory statements concerning the fourth,

which is now exclusively used. Forgetting the one now designated as *Leonore No. 1*, we of course agree that both *Leonore No. 2* and *No. 3* are great works, but they are more symphonic poems than overtures. The finality of the triumphant close, especially that of the third overture, simply does not tolerate continuation of any sort, as Beethoven eventually came to realize. Discarding the overtures as not suitable for the theater, he composed a fourth that makes an admirable curtain raiser. Palpably modeled on the overture to Cherubini's *Les deux journées*, this is a fine piece, in harmony with the eighteenth-century character of the beginning of the opera, and any comparison with the towering *Leonore* overtures is pointless. The customary insertion of the stupendous third *Leonore* overture before the second act finale only accentuates the discrepancy of styles. Furthermore, the premature appearance of C major, which Beethoven saved for the finale, as well as the repetition of Florestan's dramatic rescue, retold in the overture, obviously hurts the denouement. Since the public loves the piece and the opera is short, the great overture could perhaps be "salvaged" for the theater by playing it as a recessional, after the final curtain. Then it would serve as a grand postlude, a recapitulation of the drama, and everyone would be leaving the theater with those mighty C-major fanfares ringing in their ears. I say "recessional" because some people will of course walk out in the middle of it, but they will do this no matter what is at the end. For the rest of us, however, this triumphant conclusion would be a great if not undisturbed experience.

Five

ROSSINI

TO PERFORM Rossini properly, a conductor used to the formality of the opera house (not to speak of the concert hall) must forget his impressive manners, morals, and dignity, disown his American forebears, renounce the Constitution and even his domestic felicity. He should recall the licentious engravings of the period, develop a somewhat malicious ingenuity, and emulate George II, who, when Queen Caroline on her deathbed enjoined him to marry again, said, with tears in his eyes: "No, no, I shall have only mistresses." He must also leave behind heavy esthetics and forget about grave, passionate arias with their impressive pauses and crashing climaxes, for he must be sloppy with precision, full of irresponsible fun and irony, and brilliantly flexible in rhythm, dynamics, and tempo. I can assure the reader that conductors of recent performances of *The Barber of Seville* pose no threat to the Constitution, and judging by their demeanor, they will have no mistresses either. Performances nowadays lack elegance and real humor—hammy acting is not humor—the orchestras are sober and unsmiling, and, above all, the usual English versions of the libretto are atrocious.

The *Barber* is not one of the ephemera of its day but the masterpiece of a great composer well entitled to his popularity and not likely to lose it. Aside from its eternal freshness and the directness and economy of means which drive this opera unflaggingly forward, drawing the most skeptical listener along, we are dealing with a work that has a special place in New York's history. *The Barber of Seville* was the first Italian opera heard in New York (as it was the first in Buenos Aires and Havana), and ever since the 1820s it has remained a favorite. The *Barber* is an opera buffa, full of fun and rascally goings-on, that should be presented for what it is: delightful comedy for its own sake without any sort of afterthought. Still, it should not be turned into an out-and-out farce, because this is comedy about people; the focus should be on them and not on unessentials. Though Rossini was a contemporary of Berlioz, in the *Barber* he was a man of the eighteenth century. There is no padding in this score and no make-believe, for it represents the great tradition of the classic opera buffa. This heritage goes back in an unbroken line for a hundred years before Rossini's time, though his immediate ancestors were Piccinni, Paisiello, and Cimarosa. And this great tradition reached in him its summit, for the *Barber* is the classic opera buffa par excellence, its date of composition notwithstanding. Verdi himself considered this opera the highest peak in the history of the pure Italian buffa. Nevertheless, there are some flaws in the *Barber* that contradict the spirit of the eighteenth century and demonstrate that its composer lived in the nineteenth. Rossini, who wrote out every embellishment and coloratura so that the singers could not indulge their own whims, often carried the coloraturas to excess, to the detriment of the melodic design. He could also overdo the so-called Mannheim crescendos. In Paris he was called "Monsieur Crescendo," and those frequent long rollers can become rather vulgar; but an able conductor knows how to deal with them.

A curious statement I came across recently is an example of how even those who have ears for music can remain insensible to the very charms in one composer which they extol in another. The author speaks of the two "Figaro" operas, Mozart's *Le Nozze di Figaro* and Rossini's *Il Barbiere di Siviglia*, finding them not only dissimilar, but Rossini's opera vastly inferior, and maintaining that, in view of the priority of Mozart's work and its incomparable artistic stature, it took nothing less than temerity on Rossini's part to attack the same subject. Rossini has also been taken to task for daring to emulate Paisiello and his *Barber*. That Rossini, as were his two distinguished predecessors, was attracted to the Beaumarchais plays is understandable: *Le Barbier de Séville* is an ideal opera libretto. In fact, the play as originally devised in 1772 was a libretto for an opéra comique, and it was several years later that Beaumarchais made a straight play out of it.

A comparison between *Figaro* and the *Barber* is not unnatural; the characters are identical, and even the music shows decided kinship. As to Rossini's "temerity," it certainly paid handsome returns, the *Barber* becoming one of the most successful operas of all time. The truth seems to be that precisely those materials which have already been used may lead not only to epigonic creations but also to new masterpieces. One might conjecture that an august example fairly compels the poet or composer to exert all his powers to justify his audacity. Two qualities, however, are indispensable in such cases. First of all—admiration aside—the composer must have the clearest understanding of his predecessor's merits; second, he must possess sufficient originality and sophistication not to permit the model to rob him of his own concept. Rossini passes on both grounds. He knew Paisiello and Mozart intimately, and his was a most original talent, deeply rooted in the Italian soil. (Incidentally, it was not only Mozart he admired and studied; he was so fond of Haydn and Bach, and learned so much from them, that his fellow Italians called him *il Tedeschino*, "the little German.") There was no more convinced and understanding admirer of Mozart than this volatile Italian, nor was there any post-Mozartean who could approach Mozart's vocal melody, his simplicity and clarity in operatic writing, and his ensemble technique more closely than could Rossini. Both of them share in the fiery love of animated tempos, which, of course, they inherited from the Italian buffa. As a matter of fact, the "rival" opera was so successful that in the latter half of the nineteenth century some able and knowledgable musicians and critics were undecided as to whom to award the palm. However, any valuation based on general impressions, without experiencing, feeling, and appraising the beauties of the works, number for number, technique for technique, manner for manner, is sheer dilettantism. Two works by different composers will certainly not be esthetically or otherwise congruent.

In Mozart's *Figaro* the art of composition is without question superior to Rossini's. When we take as our criterion the symphonic elaboration of the orchestral accompaniment, the thematic interplay between voices and instruments, the "commentary" of the orchestra, then *Figaro* is without a rival. The aristocratic refinement of the texture often affords the same quiet thrill one experiences when listening to a finely wrought string quartet. But Mozart can also create a whirlwind of animated bedlam, like the unexampled finale of the first act, which nevertheless moves with clockwork precision.

Before I say anything about the *Barber* in comparison to *Figaro*, it must be emphasized that we never hear it as Rossini intended it to be heard. The score is mutilated, maltreated, overlaid with arbitrary alterations; the play is turned into slapstick comedy; and the singers do just about whatever they please. The wonderful clarity and lightness of the score are largely lost in the crude "tradition" which surrounds it. But even so, the *Barber* exhibits the same wonderful euphony, the same exhilarating tempo, vigor, and continuity we admire so much in *Figaro*. The art of thematic manipulation cannot compare with Mozart's; nevertheless, Rossini's orchestra, in the eighteenth-century manner, often carries the musical substance, while the singers on the stage indulge in the fastest parlando the buffa has ever known. The symphonic elaboration of entire scenes, built on a single motif, is a remarkable achievement for a supposedly "natural" and "untutored" composer. On the other hand, Rossini's inexhaustible, pliant, elastic melodic invention is fully the equal of Mozart's—a statement that must now be quickly qualified before the chorus of indignation starts up.

Rossini could not rise to the highest melodic level in

Mozart's opera—no one could—but the *mean* level of his melodic invention is remarkably consistent and equals that in *Figaro*. His power of characterization is more restricted than Mozart's; he could not have composed the Countess's aria because he was content to let life unroll, but in the buffa vein he is Mozart's equal; indeed, he is unsurpassed. The reader must bear in mind, though, that Mozart's *Figaro* is a miraculous synthesis of seria and buffa, an altogether personal achievement, whereas Rossini's *Barber* is a pure opera buffa, unencumbered by any deeper feelings or problems. Those who follow the old northern European and American custom of looking down on this type of Italian opera with patronizing disdain and who consider Rossini's technique little more than serviceable should take a closer look as the A-flat sextet in the finale of the first act of the *Barber*. With all his glittering cavatinas, Rossini was the virtuoso ensemble composer, and such ensemble writing is almost unparalleled in the annals of opera—once more, only Mozart can match it.

Some very dubious things can creep into musical works under the cloak of "interpretation," and the *Barber* is due for a thorough refurbishing. The score is full of excrescences that a century and a half of cavalier treatment by singers and conductors have heaped on it, and the English translations are usually laced with silly, anachronistic jokes. Would it not be a heroic move on the part of an enlightened opera house to take the old score, cleanse it, convince—and control—the singers, and give the great work a new artistic lease on life?

Among the last of those operas in which the bubbling world of the old buffa appears as a natural language is Rossini's *Le Comte Ory*. Composed in 1828, eleven years after the *Barber*, this opera falls in Rossini's Paris period. Given the date and the locale, it goes without saying that the libretto was concocted by Eugène Scribe, the fashionable mass manufacturer of opera texts. This in turn means that the dialogue is clever and the comic situations expertly devised. The story is a trifle, but then Rossini did not need much in order to spin his admirably impudent music. The Count Ory, a medieval playboy, escapes from his tutor and, disguised as the mother superior of a religious order, gains entry into the castle of the "fair but chaste Countess Adèle," who has vowed to shun male companionship until her brother returns from the Crusade. The drollery is capital and the situations so hilarious that the audience is rolling in the aisles.

Though not as consistently brilliant as the *Barber*, this music, or most of it, is excellent, at times irresistible, and all of it is viable. Studded with delightful cavatinas, arias, and elegant coloraturas, the opera has many fine choral scenes and ensembles, and the range from delicate prattle to wild gaiety is remarkable. While this is a French opera (Rossini's French musical diction is excellent), and while the idiom at times advances as far as Verdi's *Rigoletto*, it is once more an essentially eighteenth-century Italian buffa, the only difference being that the seccos are accompanied by the orchestra. There are many memorable scenes in *Le Comte Ory*. The opening of the second act is a wonderful genre picture of the ladies of the court at their sewing, as they sing an extended and finely drawn unaccompanied piece. The storm scene—ubiquitous in French opera—is not missing, but instead of the time-honored clichés Rossini gives us an impressive choral-orchestral ensemble. As the storm subsides, the tension is retained with great skill and by the simplest means. The scene where the "nuns" have their basket lunch (with wine, of course) and get a little unsteady on their feet, is one of the funniest things ever seen on the operatic stage, yet it is so innocent that no one could take offense at it.

While Rossini is usually thought of as a fun-maker, the composer of eternally youthful and effervescent music which is the embodiment of the opera buffa, this secretive musician was not devoid of more earnest sentiments. An example is his *Moses*. If it is a bit startling to see Rossini treating a Biblical subject, it is much more surprising to hear lofty choral numbers and dignified vocal lines for the soloists. And none of it is sham.

Originally written as an oratorio, *Moses in Egypt* was

subsequently reworked for Paris as a grand opera. Now the title of oratorio should not deceive us—Italy is not England or America. During Lent Italians were not supposed to indulge in entertainment so mundane as opera—they produced oratorios, but these oratorios were simply unstaged operas (as were Handel's); only their subjects were "sacred." The French version of the original *Mosè in Egitto* shows considerable change for the better. Nowhere else in his dramatic works did Rossini use such extended choral writing, and the conflicts are real and searching. Not a little of Rossini's "past" is in evidence, for his fun-making spirit was irrepressible; here and there the orchestra chortles discreetly and the melody hops and skips. There are also some stock operatic tricks. But the work is strong, inspired, and often very moving. The orchestra is handled with earnest solicitude; it supports the singers, but it also delineates the drama. The writing is always careful and much more elaborate and varied than in the buffa. Clearly, the gay iconoclast was very serious when he composed *Moses.*

Why did this born master of the operatic stage abandon it when he was at the height of his fame? The popular biographies call this man, who composed several dozen operas, lazy, indolent, cynical, one whose only aim in life was good food and wine. True, Rossini loved the good life, but he knew also life's depths and accepted everything positively, courageously, and joyfully, with the confidence of a man who has escaped from a shipwreck and is convinced that he can escape all shipwrecks. Then there are those who believe that Rossini's creative vein simply dried out. This is not true either; witness the fine Mass he composed at the age of seventy-one. It is true that he was frequently in ill-health, but, once more, this alone cannot explain his long silence. We really do not know Rossini, even though he was gregarious, a good conversationalist, and a copious and interesting letter writer. Given the ingrained northern belief that the opera buffa is low-life opera, an inferior species perhaps good for a laugh but not in the realm of high art, and not requiring the kind of supreme command of the craft of composition associated with the great German masters, Rossini is placed low in the hierarchy of creative musicians. But Rossini was a professional from the cradle, even though he had little formal training. At the age of twenty he already had commissions from La Scala, and at twenty-four he had composed a whole fistful of operas, many of them very successful. These we do not know, and we do not know his serious operas either, but Verdi did—Rossini's *Otello* and *Moses* had a decisive influence on his earlier works.

So what was it that silenced Rossini? "I was born for the opera buffa," wrote Rossini in the moving little apology to his *Petite Messe solennelle,* and perhaps this provides the clue, for by "buffa" he meant the classic variety. As we have seen, he tried his hand, and successfully, at serious opera, but like Mozart he did not abandon the buffa technique; he only adjusted it to the seria. This could be done in Mozart's time but not in the romantic era, and here Rossini must have drawn the line. He still wanted pure singing theater, with the orchestra seconding; when he saw where musical developments were leading, that the trend was toward the spectacular grand opera, he stopped composing. He was too deeply devoted to the classical tradition to accept the Meyerbeerian grand opera, even though his own contribution to the new species was considerable. When someone asked the aged master why he had orchestrated the *Petite Messe solennelle,* originally accompanied by only two pianos and a harmonium to make it suitable for the small private chapel for which it was composed, he answered, "because I don't want Messrs. Sax and Berlioz to cover my poor vocal parts with their saxophones."

Alas, beyond the Alps both the man and the artist have been misjudged. The *oltremontani* thought that the man was the sort who begins to love his remaining days at the beginning of his life, while in the artist they saw only a brilliant *farceur* who can keep one amused for an evening if one's esthetic requirements are modest. Schumann, Berlioz, and others abominated him, but jealousy and national pride had something to do with this attitude. Many of the greatest composers were much attracted to Rossini's music, as can be seen from the influence he exerted not only on Italian composers but on Schubert, Weber, and Marschner, and, in France, on Meyerbeer, Gounod, and Bizet. Whatever else may be said, this irresistible if enigmatic man is certainly one of the great in operatic history.

Six

DONIZETTI
AND BELLINI

ITALIAN opera in the period between Rossini and Verdi
was still plentiful, but its tradition was altered. The rise
and success of French grand opera and the attraction
of Romantic literature from the north changed not only the
subjects and technique of the libretto but also the nature of
the music. In the 1830s Paris was a veritable Italian operatic
colony: Spontini, Rossini, Donizetti, Bellini, to name only
the leaders, were all there, composing both for the Italian
and for the French theater. It stands to reason that the serious
opera should acquire elements stemming from Gluck as well
as from Meyerbeer, but even the buffa absorbed a good deal
from vaudeville and opéra comique. Furthermore, we must
henceforth reckon with a new concept: the sharp division
now drawn between art and craftsmanship, something unknown in any era before this time. Scarlatti, or Paisiello, or
Rossini would never permit sloppiness to mar a score, but the
Romantics could condone anything for the sake of expression. It was not that these composers were inadequately trained
in the craft of composition. Donizetti, who wrote seventy
operas, most of them quickly thrown together, not only re-

ceived a good vocal training but was himself an excellent basso buffo, a good viola player who loved to play chamber music, and an experienced conductor. Like most opera composers from Monteverdi onward, he was well versed in church music, as can be seen from the fine Requiem Mass he composed on the death of Bellini, a work that must be considered the forerunner of Verdi's *Manzoni Requiem.* And there are some other echoes from the past. The sextet in *Lucia* shows that Donizetti knew and understood the polyphony of Lotti and the Venetians. Bellini, too, came from a family of solid church musicians, yet he could be very careless with his score. It is interesting to note that all these musicians, from Rossini to Bellini, made an early and fond acquaintance with the chamber music of Haydn and Mozart, and Donizetti composed a dozen quartets and some symphonies himself. Yet their good schooling and the great music they absorbed did not prevent them from sacrificing sound craftsmanship for the sake of convenience.

Donizetti, like his contemporary and rival Bellini, belonged among those opera composers who permitted themselves to be led by the prima donna and primo uomo. He worked for them and through them, for to him the flesh-and-blood singer represented the earthly fulfillment of that God-given gift, song. Unfortunately, in his song there no longer lived the holy worship of bel canto of the old Neapolitans and of Handel and Hasse; and there is an admixture of superficiality, even sloppiness, and a generous obeisance toward the gallery such as we seldom see in Bellini. Donizetti's was an age in Italian opera when the composer was altogether dependent on the public's mind and temper, forcing him to surrender to the interpreters of his art, the adored star singers. Thus developed a very specific art in which everything is projected out of the stage, straight at the public, the prima donna and the tenor standing under the proscenium solely concerned with the requirements of the moment. Donizetti was a master of this technique and style, a versatile musician able to give contours to this peculiar art made up of recipes, effects, and tricks of the vast Italian operatic arsenal. His hand was light and his sense of the beauty of the human voice nearly infallible; he could satisfy both the public's hunger for catchy melody and the singers' desire for a suitable vehicle for their talents. Donizetti possessed an incredible facility, as well as humor, and literary and linguistic ability. But despite—or perhaps because of—this versatility, and his considerable though undisciplined talent, this composer of scores of operas failed to achieve true greatness in his serious operas.

Lucia di Lammermoor, like all of Donizetti's dramatic operas, is not a well-composed work; there are some wonderfully arresting moments, even entire scenes, and the famous sextet is stunning, but the composer was too facile and superficial to grasp larger units. So while his comic *Don Pasquale* is a worthy romantic sequel to Rossini's classic comic operas, *Lucia* is only a tentative herald of Verdi's earlier serious operas. Almost the whole first act of *Lucia* is a concert, without the slightest dramatic-theatrical force or even implication. The only thing that can save it is great voices for the concertizing. The sheer sensuous beauty of the human voice can make us forget the lack of theater. Then, in the second act, this operatic profligate suddenly gives us real music drama and for a good stretch everything comes to life. But the characters in the opera are not the kind who, given a reasonable chance, might have insisted on living a life of their own. They are treated with a magnificent gravity that makes them all the more improbable. Lucia, mostly pale and characterless, perhaps evokes our pity, but we cannot truly sympathize with her. She is given some fine songs until her big moment arrives. The mad scene is an old operatic device, but in itself it is not dramatic, especially when accompanied by shallow and meaningless roulades. (Whenever I hear it I cannot help recalling Sheridan's line, "O Lord, sir, when a heroine goes mad she always goes into white satin.") Once more, its performance can be made exciting only by the quality of a fine Mediterranean voice. Edgardo is the sort of dull character on whom the composer's dramatic pains are likely to be wasted; the portrait seems to be a faithful one but remains dramatically lusterless. Even with such a subject as Lucrezia Borgia,

Donizetti altogether missed the unholy fascination of the female poisoner.

If Donizetti's tragic operas have become period pieces that only extraordinary singing can make presentable, in the comic vein he was the last of those great buffa composers who created work after work with incredible facility and prodigal invention. Here he was a man of the theater to his fingertips, full of temperament and, though a true romantic, essentially a buffa composer of old. Rossini outlived him, but since the older master ceased to compose at a relatively early age, Donizetti's *L'Elisir d'amore* and *Don Pasquale* are the last genuine works in the spirit of the classic opera buffa which began in the seventeenth century and for well over a hundred years exerted irresistible attraction not only on all opera but on music and musicians of all types. Romantic grand opera killed this engaging genre, and not until the aged Verdi's *Falstaff* were its elusive charms once more recaptured. What distinguishes Donizetti from Rossini is his Romanticism, which made him one of the natural intermediaries between the "Jove of music," as the Italians called Rossini, and Verdi.

L'Elisir d'amore is the work of a musician whose imagination was absolutely vocal, endowing his melodies with that broad, elastic, and freely soaring quality that makes Italian opera what it is—the glorification of the human voice. This melody is in love with the singing voice, and while in a sense it is a prisoner of this love it also has the power to arouse the voice to all the passions of song. Even in the recitatives we feel its dramatic fervor, but supremely in the wonderful ensembles where each voice seems to encourage the other to exert itself to higher flights. Obviously, first-class singing voices are a requirement here as much as in the "concert" operas, but in addition, since we are dealing with an opera buffa, the possessors of these voices must be good actors. *L'Elisir d'amore* is one of those operas that delight everyone not yet fossilized. When it is well produced one can hear laughter—so rare in opera—and see smiling faces. Even the long-suffering husbands who are dragged to the opera can enjoy themselves.

Although composed in 1842, Donizetti's *Don Pasquale* is

still a genuine opera buffa in the great tradition of the eighteenth century. Some of us may be too jaded to appreciate still another story about the fat old guardian or uncle who wants to marry a pretty young thing, and perhaps the notaries, doctors, and cunning servants are a bit too familiar, but to the audiences of former days its formality was a challenge. They knew the layout and they were interested in seeing what the composer could do with the thrice-told story. *Don Pasquale* offers a very good variant of the master copy, and even the libretto is well made. The music is bouncy, witty, and thoroughly enjoyable. It is true that the overture is nothing but a slapdash potpourri and the prelude to the second act a tear-jerker of a trumpet solo, but that should not deceive us. Donizetti was a full-blooded opera composer to whom pure instrumental music was a necessary chore; once the curtain is up he is an undisputed master. Interestingly enough, as soon as the orchestra ceases to exist for its own sake and turns to the business of seconding the voices, Donizetti shows an almost Mozartean finesse in handling it. From the moment the first singer opens his mouth everything is ship-shape; there is no waste motion, the cavatinas are melting, the recitatives are spirited, and the ensembles are as skillfully put together as they are sparkling. Donizetti's serious operas appear more faded as the years go by, but these two buffas are masterpieces that will retain their freshness as long as we shall have singers and conductors who can communicate their spirit.

Bellini's operas present great difficulties to audiences beyond the Alps, let alone beyond the seas. The main difficulty non-Italian audiences experience with this all-embracing melody-opera is that from the point of view of sheer theater, the "action music" to which we are accustomed, and the still influential Wagnerian esthetics, it appears vastly inferior, a sort of drama in merely decorative silhouette. In reality, however, Bellini's particular musico-dramatic conception is valid and viable, but nothing less than superlative singing can do justice to it and bring out its qualities.

If we look at Bellini's dates (1801–1835), we see not only

that he had a tragically short life—like Schubert, four years his senior—but also that he was born into a period of transition when the ablest Italian composers were in Paris, working on the renewal of French rather than Italian opera. The old traditions had loosened, the influence of the great Viennese composers was not directly fruitful, and opera had become the possession of the singing stars. The composers spurned everything that was not suitable material for arias, because the Marchesis, the Rubinis, the Pastas, and the Catalanis demanded arias to sing, not well-constructed operas. Bellini studied at the Naples conservatory, whose maestro, Nicola Zingarelli, a mediocre composer, was carried to world fame by the larynxes of his singers. Born before Mozart and Beethoven and outliving both as well as Bellini, Zingarelli never once mentioned to his students the names of his great contemporaries. Thus Bellini had to find out by himself about the wonders of the "age of form and style and lucent reason," before he entered that strange, disturbed, and brilliant era known as the Romantic. But he must have known the works of Piccinni, Paisiello, and Cimarosa, as well as those of Jommelli and Pergolesi, from whom he should have learned that on the stage lyricism demands variety. However, all these composers were gone, and in the diluted musical atmosphere the only contemporary inspiration he could have received must have come from Rossini's music. In the absence of an understanding teacher, Bellini could not clearly discern the full meaning of Rossini's musical philosophy, for that capital entertainer was also a thinking musician. Rossini had already recognized the danger of this cult of the aria, this carefree Italian singing that violates the spirit of genuine theater. He therefore did not wrap himself altogether in the arias; rather rising above them, he fitted them into place from above, like building blocks, and made them surrender a good deal of their prominence to the ensembles. In a word, he constructed his operas, if in a happy-go-lucky manner, still always with sovereign security and with a truly marvelous economy. But, then, unlike Zingarelli and many others, Rossini knew his Mozart intimately.

This comprehensive view and wonderful theatrical instinct and security Bellini could never have learned; it was uncongenial to his romantic nature. While Rossini too had to make concessions to the tyrannical singers, he did not permit a character to say the psychologically impossible. The attitude of Bellini's dramatic figures is more passive than active; such persons experience life rather than mold it to their own patterns. Bellini supports with mellow sounds the hard staccatos of dramatic events. One has the feeling that his figures are looking back on these events, echoing what has happened to them, which makes their tragedy take on the mood of a requiem. Bellini was an emissary of Sicily, like Alessandro Scarlatti a century and a half before, with the mission of bringing new forces into Italian music from the peculiar moods of southern melody. His soul was so completely immersed in the happy melodic world of this Italian song, with its joyous abandon, that all his desires, memories, and passions fainted into a cheerful intoxication. With such a disposition, Bellini was scarcely destined to contribute to the displacement of the aria; on the contrary, he was to give it a natural, expressive quality greatly admired by Chopin, and one that made his arias worthy to occupy a central position in opera. In order to achieve this, Bellini was not compelled to engage in revolutionary moves; the world that reigns in his melodies does not mirror such an anvil-wrought personality as that of his ancestor Scarlatti. Bellini leans toward melancholy; he is tenderly elegiac, and compared with the serene and arching melody of the older Neapolitan arias, his intoxication seems caused by a lighter wine. In consequence, his formal frames are not so steely and solid as those of the old opera from the golden age of Naples, and he could let himself be carried by the looser and more frivolous forms of his day. All he had to do was to pour his dark and deep melancholy upon the colorful romantic horror drama that was rising with the new grand opera; the garish colors became instantly ennobled, the sensation-seeking noise toned down, and everything that heretofore had been mere theatrical decor now became the symbol of a poetic imagination.

The core of Bellini's operatic thought is the closed arioso; thus he arrived at his concept through the medium and the desires of the reigning singers. When planning his debut in Milan with *Il Pirata*, he retired with Rubini to the country so as to be able to tailor every line to the famous tenor's measurements. Ever since, the success of every Bellini opera has been connected with the names of celebrated singers—Pasta, Grisi, Tosi, Malibran, Patti, and all the others. But while the procedure may have been opportunistic, his melody transforms the star singer into a human being. For this reason there are few schematic types on Bellini's stage; they may not be well-drawn characters, but they are live men and women who converse with one another through the language of melody. The most beautiful examples of this are to be found in the duets, where melody speaks to melody directly. As Bellini matured, this power of the arioso gradually affected all other ingredients of his opera. The recitative became melodious, leading to the aria almost without a break, the chorus contributes only deeper shadows, while the orchestra confines itself to basic colors—nothing must be permitted to intrude on the melodies. Bellini was not universal, like Verdi, nor did he dominate all Italian music with the robust power of his great successor, but whatever musico-dramatic configuration he touched, gently and almost as if by chance, received a higher meaning through the accolade.

Bellini's Italian period culminated in *Norma*, a great opera for great singers but most perilous for lesser artists. There is nothing but singing in it, no idle declamation, no mere effects, only melody that pours from every throat and every instrument; and this melody while of course in the tradition of Italian dramatic song, is Bellini's own. It is impossible to characterize it, for it is at once infinitely complicated and incredibly simple, as simple as a dipper of fresh water, a calm, reticent, and elegant musical poetry, utterly sincere and serious. This expressive melody penetrates even the recitatives, which acquire a solidity and substance rare in opera at any time. The trouble is that Bellini's melodies do not always rise from the songlike to the dramatic and are often extended beyond their tensile strength, so that what should have been a profoundly serious situation easily becomes mere diluted ornamentation that belies the sentiments expressed. Even the famous "Casta diva" aria ends in a sort of conventional march that breaks its spell. This Bellinian melody must exert its full charm if the shortcomings of his operas are not to become too noticeable, but since most if not all roles were custom-composed for singers whose art must be recaptured, this is not easily achieved these days. *Norma* is perhaps the most difficult of these operas to present to modern audiences, for apart from the excessively ornate vocal parts, the staging is a director's nightmare. The scenes are stock operatic scenes that cannot be varied or improved upon, and their pace is awkward, the choral numbers being particularly unwieldy. The chorus streams into the sacred grove of the Druids, sings, and is dismissed. Then, when it must return for a brief appearance, the singers all come back on the double because the score barely given them time to get into position. The true opera composer's inspiration also depends to a considerable extent on visual impressions; the genre demands a scenic imagination, which Bellini possessed to a rather limited degree, thus often failing to make the human message of his operas visible.

At this point in his career, circumstances forced a change in Bellini's concept of opera. In 1833 he went to Paris, where he found an altogether different climate, created by the rising French grand opera. This rich and pathetic new form of the lyric stage—as well as the personal advice of Rossini, who knew the local scene and befriended his compatriot—tempted Bellini to strive for sharper dramatic accents and richer orchestral commentary, thus granting more independent life to all the components of his opera hitherto imprisoned by the sorcery of the aria. In *I Puritani* there appears the measured, tragical, funereal pomp and pathos of the military Romanticism of French grand opera, together with its neat but artificial ensembles. The new orientation had serious drawbacks. The pretty triteness that was an occasional defect in Bellini's astonishing lyrical fluency now becomes more evident amidst the stronger accents, and his original style, which may be called "purple" without irony, loses some of the naturalness of this dangerous color.

I Puritani has a story of the kind to which opera fans of Sir Walter Scott's era were gratifyingly susceptible, with tears always trembling not far away. It is a tragedy with a happy ending that baffles our understanding. But, then, family prayers and family reading by the fireplace have vanished—who can read *Ivanhoe* by the radiator? Perhaps this is the reason Scott and his confreres are no longer popular. At any rate, the score of this strange dramatic concoction is fluently and fervently composed, and a good deal of it is very beautiful, but it possesses little insight into the nature of music drama. Creative artist though he was, Bellini was not the creative psychologist that a dramatist must be, but rather a highly refined musical poet who lost his way in Utopia. Here he shows a curious disregard for characterization, but he was handicapped by the fact that his librettist's theme is pathological rather than spiritual. The quality of this opera is quite variable. The songs often have little substance and more charmed and charming affection than revealing passion. But not infrequently this music has a fragile and lovely melodic beauty that is altogether Bellini's own. The same is true of *La Sonnambula*. Although only the most unresisting listener will fall under the spell of this story's illusion, and although the opera's tenser episodes—the sleepwalking scene in particular—may cause a smile rather than a shudder, it too has many fine scenes.

I must return again and again to the warning that this music is falsified by merely adequate singing. Moreover, it requires singers with that undefinable animalism that will carry them through the emotional situations, which cannot be resolved intellectually because this music is addressed not to our intelligence but to our sensibilities. The singers must be adept at those little inflections and accents that musical notation cannot indicate, and they must be able to scale the heights unflinchingly, effortlessly, and with secure footing. Bellini's early death shattered all possibility of his reconciling the new stylistic elements with his own heritage, and we shall never know whether he might have done so, and whether another true giant would have arrived on the musical earth. One has the feeling that at the end of his short life Bellini was still groping for a solution to the problems of Romantic opera. He broke with the Neapolitans, loosened traditional aria construction, and tried to come to terms with the new French ideal of opera. Yet, like Donizetti in his serious operas, he was structurally unable to build an arch or span a roof. He did not know how to wed restraint to richness; his defect was in being too mellifluous. Nevertheless, Bellini's influence was considerable. I do not have to point out Verdi's indebtedness to his predecessor, nor even the palpably Bellinian turns in Chopin's nocturnes; but even Wagner, who in a curious way admired Bellini, shows the effects of this admiration from *Rienzi* to *Lohengrin*. And no one who composed prayers in the nineteenth century could escape the dark sweetness of Bellini's *preghiere*.

This young composer, whose life ended at thirty-four, was a genius in transforming dramatic conflict into pure expressive melody, but real music drama he did not give us because he never learned to create characters in the round. It is this extraordinary musician's tombstone that should carry the epitaph mistakenly placed on Schubert's: "Music has here entombed a rich treasure but much fairer hopes."

Seven

FLOTOW

AND NICOLAI

O F GERMAN opera following *Fidelio* nothing is to be heard in New York until we reach *The Flying Dutchman*. Weber's *Der Freischütz* should not be missing from the repertory of a major opera house, but then it is quite clear that even *Fidelio* holds a rather tenuous lease on life in New York. Could it be true that there exists no obviously eminent German opera in the first half of the nineteenth century beyond these three works that are still alive in the repertory? Judging by one of the revivals I heard, *Martha*, the outlook seems indeed bleak.

Its creator, Friedrich von Flotow, was a composing baron, the issue of an old noble family. This alone should not disqualify him, for there were some princely—even crowned— personages who proved to be fine musicians. Regrettably, on the occasion neither of Flotow's birth nor of his subsequent activities did the world tremble. He was born one year before Wagner and died one year after him, yet a greater contrast between contemporaries could not be imagined. Flotow's musical education, taste, and technique were French; he studied in Paris, spent a great deal of time there, wrote French operas, and was a member of the Adam, Auber, Meyerbeer, Rossini,

Gounod circle. He probably would have settled in France permanently except that he was too much of a nobleman to stomach the revolutions.

Flotow's music, elegant if dated French Biedermeier, the kind the French call *musiquette*, is nicely worked but short-winded. Some of the tunes are pretty; the harmonies are conventional; the rhythm is tame, always following set patterns. On the other hand, the orchestration and the vocal writings are quite good—in a cautious way. Though French in tone and reflecting the *vaudeville* with its succession of completely un-operatic tableaux, this music does not hide its German sentimentalism, which accounts for Flotow's borrowing of a soulful Irish melody, "The Last Rose of Summer," which he used as a sort of theme song. The libretto, juvenile and hapless, has repeatedly been subjected to a change of venue. In the present undistinguished English version it finds a resting place in "an imaginary England of c. 1830."

The opera is little more than competent in its own way, but its rootless eclecticism of sentiment denies the work any real solidity. *Martha* has a built-in vivacity that is not convincing. From its casual, comfortable atmosphere of easy emotion and unworrying indebtedness to the period's bourgeoisie, its pat structure and pleasant if conventional tunes, there rises a rather stale warmth. Not one person in the opera is other than pasteboard, and there is scarcely an emotion registered that is other than pasteboard emotion. Every character sings in the same style, and the style is not that of a living person. It is almost pathetic to watch Lady Harriet as she tries, somewhat vainly, to make us believe that her stocking is no longer blue, that she also is a woman. This sameness of tone deprives the work of expressive high points and makes it seem very long indeed.

The other mid-century German opera, *The Merry Wives of Windsor*, is made of different timber. Those who still think that opera is always a lugubrious or sentimental affair should hear it. They will be treated to a surprise because this comic opera is a barrel of fun, a rollicking lyric play that must be placed among the best in that genre.

Otto Nicolai, the composer of *The Merry Wives*, reminds us of those grand old musicians who were just as much at home in church music as in opera, who could play, conduct, and even talk intelligently about music—for he did all this. The founder of the Philharmonic Orchestra in Vienna, he also organized the Berlin cathedral choir and had a hand in all sorts of other musical organizations. Nicolai studied old music, wrote about it perceptively, and then performed it. His conducting was admired even by Berlioz. While *The Merry Wives* is as little Shakespearean as Gound's *Faust* is Goethean, it is a masterpiece in which the mirth of the Italian buffa is blended with German harmony and orchestration, producing a singularly happy, elegant, and well-tempered music. Although Weber and Mozart rub elbows with Rossini and Bellini, one is always conscious of a definite and very engaging personality. The arias are beautifully singable, the ensembles piquant, the recitatives perhaps a little perfunctory but always well turned, and the orchestral accompaniment full of life and wit. Nicolai's felicitously successful attempt to combine Italian with German opera was as consciously planned as Mozart's. From the Weberian horn calls and racing strings to the Rossinian ensembles everything is naturally compatible. Nicolai is one of the few Germans after Mozart who could really manipulate an ensemble, and the dramatic pictorialism of his orchestra is remarkable. The frequent comparison of *The Merry Wives of Windsor* with Verdi's *Falstaff* is mistaken and irrelevant. Half a century separates the two works, and the two composers had totally different aims. Verdi created a magnificently sophisticated aristocratic opera, Nicolai a popular opera in the sense that *The Magic Flute* is a popular opera. This able and sympathetic musician, who died at the age of thirty-nine, also wrote an Enoch Arden opera called *Il Proscritto*. In this fine Bellinian work he is fully the equal of the young Verdi, whose early operas are now being revived. Perhaps one of our more literate conductors might look into this; he would not regret it.

Eight

VERDI

THE AMERICAN operagoer takes it for granted that *Rigoletto* and *Aïda* always have been and always will be, nor would it occur to him to question the genius of their great composer. But recognition was not always universal. While the "people" were almost immediately captivated by Verdi, and in Italy he was beatified in his lifetime, the intelligentsia of the Transalpine world was, until relatively recent times, puzzled, cautious, and in many cases hostile. To assess Verdi's ultimate victory we must survey his rise not from a "neutral" country such as ours, where opera is an imported commodity produced largely for a select audience, but from one such as Germany, where the massive figure of Richard Wagner must either be met head-on or bypassed by the intruder. The Germans were wary of this Italian, for he challenged their great reformer of opera who had done away with "Italian tinsel" on the lyric stage, who indeed had done away with opera altogether by establishing what was considered a higher category known as "music drama." Yet by the 1920s Verdi had clearly overtaken their idol in his own world. Though justly proud of their symphonic heritage and conscious of the alien tongue and of the technique so different from, and so independent of, Wagner's, they found the communicative power of Verdi's music irresistible. Is this popularity due to the attraction of the "different" or to the craving of the unenlightened for easy melodies that by the standards of German critics (e.g., Moser) are only "half-legitimate"?

The critics who raised objections were more puzzled than hostile, even granting Verdi a certain power to enthrall the listener, but they pitied those arias, those marches and duets, which they considered the dead bones of the musical past in contrast to the innovations and profundity Wagner brought to the species. For this creator of half-legitimate melodies clung to the tradition that melody is an essential means of dramatic expression in opera, that the projection of the dramatic in the lyric theater is principally a matter for the singers, not for the orchestra. Except for the Italianized among them, German composers were more interested in the richness and variety of abstract musical substance than in the subtleties of the theatrical representation of sentiments. It was the Germans who brought fugue, sonata, and symphony to their culmination, but opera took root in their music only slowly. The Italian's wealth of expression is immediately carried over to anything he does, yet it is not so much its wealth as its vividness that is characteristic. The Italian does not lean to contourless brooding; the objective realism of his view seeks men in action—the theater.

A true Italian composer and a man of ardent nature, Verdi was also a clear-eyed realist and a conscientious craftsman whose demands the librettists learned to respect. Unlike the romantics, especially the Germans, he did not seek refuge in metaphysics and symbolism, and avoided the supernatural. His aim was the transfiguration of the sensuous, and he was never oblivious of the requirements of métier and matter. He did not particularly care whether the story he set to music was rounded and well motivated; he demanded from his librettists "bold subjects and unique characters" because he wanted to do a much greater thing than tell a story—create authentic human beings in song. His heroes may indulge in bombastic pathos, but their personality does not have to be explained in commentaries; it reaches the listener with gripping immediacy. It is because Verdi was interested mainly in characters rather than events that he emerges victorious from most difficulties created by his librettists. Yes, the operas of the early and middle periods of his career have quite a few of the "easy" melodies, but almost every one of them gradually and almost imperceptibly darkens and deepens into powerfully expressive characterization and mood.

Verdi wanted to represent in his music not things seen but things divined; as in a portrait, not the faithful copy but the truth perceived is the real art. Historical and philological accuracy, so dear to Wagner, meant nothing to Verdi, nor even the sets and costumes (though he was extremely solicitous about good theater); he wanted his figures to sing so that the listener forgot about everything else and saw human experiences. Because he could not throw overboard what had come to be regarded as the necessary commonplaces of Italian opera, he retained and ennobled them. To rise above tradition without destroying it is the rule of taste, the natural instinct of the great artist, and this is what endeared him to his compatriots and even to the puzzled foreigners. And yet he was never really satisfied with the subjects his librettists provided. How long and with what fervor did he seek the literary man who could mediate between him and his adored Shakespeare, but none suited him. Then, in his old age, he found Arrigo Boito, a kindred soul, with whose help the septuagenarian rose to the pinnacle of drama in music. *Otello,* the terrible tragedy of jealousy, seemed to be the ultimate, consuming achievement of a great creative life; but at almost eighty, like Monteverdi and Schütz, his creative power intact, Verdi was able to ascend into still higher regions. For then, at the end of a marvelous career, with the wisdom and experience of great age, he turned, with *Falstaff,* to comedy. Thus ended sixty years of artistic growth that was steady and always rising to higher spheres.

Verdi was a simple man with an incorruptible moral and social sense; his considerable wealth was left to the charities he had supported during his life. He was sincere as a man and ruthless as an artist, with the sincerity and ruthlessness of a healthy personality. "Healthy" is indeed the proper term to characterize him and his art. Unlike his great contemporary Wagner, who was constantly pursued by the past and craved the future, Verdi was in everything the man of the present; a peasant who read Manzoni, Schiller, and Shakespeare; democratic, close to the soil and to his people; straightforward, proud of his art and always willing to fight for it. In this remarkable man there was not a trace of personal ambition for fame, riches, or political power, though all three were within his reach. The money— and he made millions—he ploughed back into the soil to make his country estate a model farm, and he endowed hospitals and a home for aged musicians. Political power was there for the asking, because Verdi took an active part in the *Risorgimento,* and several of his early operas had strong political connotations, setting off patriotic demonstrations. The whole nation looked up with admiration at the *Maestro della rivoluzione*—"Viva Verdi! was the equivalent of the forbidden "Viva Vittorio Emanuele Rè d'Italia!" As to fame, his only ambition was to write better operas, but characteristically he told his countrymen to refrain from building theaters and save all their resources for the cause of unification. Like every healthy, uncomplicated personality, he did not look inward, painfully examining himself, but outward, into the world. And through this sound and simple soul we see, as through a window, the world in its natural colors, rushing by and at the same time immobile, like a great waterfall. He felt free to give the world the whole of himself, and the whole of Verdi is something like the whole of humanity.

Nabucco, the earliest of Verdi's operas performed in this country, was Verdi's third, which in terms of the usual productive Italian composer would place it at the age when the formula is supplemented with some solid food. Verdi himself stated that his artistic career began in earnest with *Nabucco.* The opera is somewhat static and uneven, the libretto atrocious, but *Nabucco* has fine moments and good melodies. Amazingly enough, the young composer's ensemble technique is remarkably developed; the quartet in the second act is a grand piece. However, while Verdi displays many signs of his future power, his musical ideas have a short breath, reaching a cadence after a few measures, even though some of the tunes have great possibilities. The arias and recitatives are sometimes a little jerky, because they are frequently interrupted by little meaningless coloratura cadenzas that are evidently not part of the melodic design, as they are in Verdi's later operas. There are innumerable holds that slow down everything, the tessitura for the vocal parts is uncomfortably high, and the succession of high notes is often abruptly followed by unmotivated low ones. The characterization is rudimentary—Verdi did not yet know how to create a woman in music—although there are moments when Nabucco himself really comes to life. Nevertheless, *Nabucco* is a significant work, for while Verdi closely observed the operatic conventions of the time, everything, including the Rossinian and Bellinian touches, is imbued with a personal and masculine quality.

The titles of the operas preceding the famous trio *Rigoletto*, *Il Trovatore*, and *La Traviata* indicate Verdi's strong patriotic fervor, which was avidly accepted and admired by his compatriots. He had a certain flair for keeping his head in dealing with inflammatory material, and his judgment as to its effectiveness rarely erred. But this very quality makes these works difficult for us to appreciate. Boito, in a letter written fifty years after the 1842 premiere of *Nabucco*, said that no foreigner could possibly sense the feeling which "Va pensiero," the famous unison chorus, evoked in his compatriots. Perhaps this statement sums up the situation for Americans in the latter part of the twentieth century. "Va pensiero," deprived of its nostalgic, patriotic, and historical significance, is to us just another good tune. It is nice to hear *Nabucco* once or twice— it contains clear indications of genius—but I am afraid Boito was right: this opera is not for "foreigners," at least not as a repertory piece.

Ernani was Verdi's first opera to acquire international renown. While an early work—composed in 1844 by the thirty-one-year-old maestro—it presents something of Verdi as we know him, if rather sketchily and with a strength that is more potential than actual. The building of motivic unity which characterizes the mature works is still undeveloped, only one of the figures of the drama, the King, being fully delineated, and not consistently so; and in contrast to *Rigoletto*, or other later works, the characterization is perhaps interesting but seldom moving. The introductions to the arias merely give the pitch to the singer; they represent a perfunctory vestige of the old "motto aria" beginning, of which Verdi made excellent use in his later operas. Still noticeable is the plain orchestral commentary, serviceable but often awkward, and the crude use of the brasses and percussion can be disconcerting. A knowledgeable conductor can, of course, minimize all this by keeping the meaningless fillers played by the brasses inconspicuous and muzzling the percussion—in this particular opera the snare drum needs constant restraint. This most dangerous of instruments can be unleashed in Siegfried's funeral music, where its contribution to the din is magnificent, but in *Ernani* only a *soupçon* is permissible, to avoid accentuating an already harshly accented texture.

After enumerating all the shortcomings of *Ernani*, we still have a work of considerable persuasiveness, and this in spite of the silly libretto. We must beware of approaching and judging this Italian opera from the point of view of German or French opera. Even at this stage, Verdi was already the lawful heir and successor to Rossini and Bellini. Those who call this "barrel-organ music" do not realize that these melodies come straight from the heart of the Italian people; they are the issue of Italian folk music, hence their simplicity, strength, and humanity. These early operas represent probings, with varying success as to details. One element was, however, new, or rather significantly expanded: the chorus. Verdi made the chorus one of the protagonists rather than an occasional agent of relief or emphasis. His reason was patently less dramatic than patriotic. The great Italian expatriates—Rossini, Bellini, Donizetti—could never achieve, or even fully understand, Verdi's profound identification with the nation's aspirations. The young musician is very much the national composer, the musical Garibaldi who in his melodies, especially some of the choruses, unites Italy. We have already mentioned the great popularity of "Va pensiero," but "O signore, dal tetto natio" (*I Lombardi*), or "Si ridesti il Leon di Castiglia"

(*Ernani*) are also folk hymns that became veritable national anthems.

Everyone speaks of Gluck's great reform operas, but even two or three generations later no one in Italy had heard about them. When Verdi's *Macbeth* was composed in 1846, the Italian lyric stage was still dominated by singers who merely wanted to show off their voices. The grand old opera seria was long since dead and the brilliant, witty, and delightfully frivolous opera buffa had become watery. Then came *Macbeth*, the first of the transition works leading up to Verdi's mature period; and suddenly the Florence opera house, where it was produced, was confronted with demands—musical, dramatic, and technical—that were unknown to the age. For this is real music drama; one admires the assured competence with which the young composer, whose operas immediately preceding this Shakespearean essay were quite conventional, is able to fill his hearers' minds with an eerie, strongly charged atmosphere of psychologically penetrating drama. And there are elements in *Macbeth* that become of decisive influence for the future.

As we look at Verdi's librettos we notice that though beholden to the inescapable Italian *scrittura* industry, his dramatic instinct drove him to Schiller and Shakespeare. The romantic element in Schiller made him more accessible to Verdi's librettists, and the composer stayed with the German poet until *Don Carlo*. For many years he tried mightily to establish artistic contact with Shakespeare, searching for decades for a suitable version of *King Lear*, but he could not find an understanding librettist until the autumn of his life. For *Macbeth*, he took matters into his own hand. The prose version as well as the scenario he planned himself; Piave, the librettist, was largely restricted to the versification. Though *Macbeth* is not one of Verdi's popular operas, it does not fail to impress by the tremendous force of the dialogue, by the vehemence of the dramatic musical idiom. This must be ascribed to sheer genius, because nothing of the sort was then known in Italian opera. We must also remember that *Macbeth* antedates *Rigo-*

letto; it is a work of transition from the Bellini-type "music opera" to the "music drama." Whenever a modern audience listens to *Macbeth*, there must be quite a few people in the audience who feel somewhat embarrassed by what some critics call "the stereotyped Italian opera applied to Shakespeare." Yet despite a certain feeling of guilt at listening to a "hurdy-gurdy tune" when Macbeth is in the throes of passion, they cannot help being seized by the opera's mixture of doom, pity, horror, and stark drama. For Verdi was a natural composer of tragedy, divining the true dramatic accents even when his librettists supplied him with only the bare operatic essentials of the plot. This must have been the reason for his apparent belief that there was no need for a new musical procedure even when Shakespeare was the source of the libretto; his predecessors had already handed down the Ten Commandments of opera. He saw from such depth the problem of tragedy, and felt so keenly the tragic nature of events, that in his experience basic pattern and individual event became one.

The opera *Macbeth* is quite different from the original play. The difference that seems to me the most subtle, and at the same time the one upon which hinges the dramatic unity of this somewhat uneven masterpiece, is Macbeth's changed character. When conflict resolves into suffering, dramatic action slackens, confronting the dramatist with his most difficult task, for drama then tends to dissolve in lyricism. But music is eminently capable of turning suffering into inner, lyric action, eliciting forces powerful enough to become, paradoxically, dramatic in spite of its lyric nature. Verdi was already a master of this unique dramatic lyricism. Yet, despite its virtues, *Macbeth* is not a good opera, and its weaknesses are rather conspicuously in evidence. The short scenes and frequent curtains dissipate the momentum, break up the dramatic continuity, and of course make for a proliferation of curtain calls, which destroy the mood for both audience and performers. There are too many instrumental preludes and interludes of a rather perfunctory quality that nowhere match the violent intensity of the drama. The secondary characters, particularly the tenor parts, are treated as an afterthought; on the other hand, Verdi's plan to give the principal parts to bass and baritone admirably suits the dark subject of the drama. Shakespeare's three witches have been expanded into three choral groups which, following operatic custom, even dance. These scenes claim too large a share for the good of the drama. The opera is also marred by the erratic procession of episodes of violent action and somewhat precious reflections put into the mouth of the chorus. But if the pattern is disorderly, its lack of unity comes not from poverty of thought but from wealth of interest. If *Macbeth* were less tumultuous it would not be so richly vivid. It can be presented so that its harsh realism does not altogether cover the elusive strangeness of human dreamings and the stirring mystery of human relations. *Measure for Measure* is flawed as a play no matter what apologies are offered on its behalf, and so is *Macbeth* as an opera, but talent is less likely to make such mistakes than genius. *Macbeth* has enough great moments to remain not only viable but absorbing and enjoyable.

The success of the Risorgimento relieved Verdi of his patriotic duties, and beginning with 1849 there was a change in his dramatic aims. Now purely human problems came to the fore, the impersonal élan was replaced by very personal human characters. Clearly, the "middle period" represented a new stage in Verdi's development, and the three operas forming its core have become universally loved and constantly performed wherever there is an opera house. The public's attitude toward these great favorites is unique, almost proprietary. "Caro nome" is about to be sung and the big auditorium is hushed. The patrons know what is coming, high notes, long-held ones, trills, and coloratura; this is the real stuff, and they do not want to miss a single note. The soprano sings Gilda for the first time. She will be measured, note for note, against the other heroines of *Rigoletto,* past and present; her fate is inescapable, because everyone knows every turn in "Caro nome" and the firing squad awaits the transgressor.

Il Trovatore has a libretto that is almost impossible to accept; it is a concoction in which from first to last the most doubtful expedients are offered in the guise of plot and action. Then the curtain goes up and a miracle takes place; what seems silly or preposterous when read becomes warm human passion when sung. This libretto, fashioned from a dime novel, carries all the trappings of romantic grand opera: duel, suicide, Gypsy vengeance, a nun about to be professed carried away by her lover, a besieged fortress, and other assorted and gory pictures in profusion. There is a great deal of swordplay, while the "crowd" behaves like the crowd at the other end of the house: they are standees. Yet all this is immaterial, because the music makes everything believable. More than anyone else, Verdi knew the power of music to convert dismal melodrama into noble human sentiment, and he knew his own powers too. Though *Il Trovatore* is lacking in logical dramatic action, the music, while uneven in style and development, is remarkable in characterization. Verdi had found the great motifs of hate and love that henceforth dominated his musical tragedies.

 Unlike *Il Trovatore*, *Rigoletto* and *La Traviata* have good dramatic plans, but they too often move in scenes or episodes which, while magnificent, are more or less isolated. Such works, especially *Il Trovatore*, should be approached not as a coherent whole but as a series of individual scenes that are self-contained dramatic entities. In *Il Trovatore*, Verdi even gave titles to the acts. This is the technique of the great moments, a technique that rules the operas of Verdi's middle period. Each figure comes fully alive only at certain points in the drama, at which time he ceases to be the pictorial background for the fate of the others. These are the moments when his fate and character fall in line with the progress of the drama. The force accumulated in the great intensity of these moments conjures up real character as it throws illuminating light on the past and into the future. On these occasions the dramatic figure is developed in the smallest nuances. If we insist we may call this naturalistic detail work, but in reality Verdi concentrates on the essentials of characterization which, while simplified, can nevertheless represent complicated mental states, like the mock laughter violently imprinted on Rigoletto's face, which conceals his sorrow. The extremely popular arias, especially in *Rigoletto*, are not "hits" for easy enjoyment; they are the prime vehicles of what I called the technique of the great moments. They are consciously planned surfaces under which the drama brews until it breaks through. A magnificent example of Verdi's newly won dramatic expressivity is the ragged dialogue between Rigoletto and the bandit Sparafucile, sung over a dusky march tune. In the arias we often find dance and march tunes, easy on the ear but saturated with passion.

In *Rigoletto* the art of characterization in music is fully achieved; every protagonist is an individual, not an abstraction; and the entire opera is rich in sharply drawn dramatic scenes of great variety and contrast. Such dramatic characterization had been unknown in nineteenth-century Romantic opera, and *Rigoletto* represents an unproclaimed operatic reform within the traditional principles. With this opera Verdi left the world of Donizetti—even of Bellini—far behind. The dramatic situations are not lightly passed over, as in Donizetti, but are realistically and psychologically deepened. The public was a little taken aback seeing a hunchback on stage as hero instead of a king or high priest, but Verdi expressly stated that he found it glorious that this person of passion and dignity should be a "ridiculous misfit." It is nothing less than a stroke of dramatic genius that the composer gave Rigoletto few real cantilenas; his stammering recitatives are of a poignancy unknown in the earlier Italian opera.

The first performance of *La Traviata* disappointed the public because the music did not exhibit the muscular arias of the previous works. Nevertheless, the three operas form a unit; all three deal with love and guilt, and the difference between *La Traviata* and the other two rests on the intensity of the passions: *La Traviata* is gentle and subdued. Nevertheless, this opera represents a change in more than one way. For the first time Verdi uses a modern subject and a modern problem; there are few protagonists and practically no choral participation; the tone is intimate, and long stretches are in parlando rather than in the affect-laden arioso. This opera provides a testimonial—if such is needed—to the extraordinary musico-dramatic gifts of the composer of *Il Trovatore* and *Rigoletto*, who could cast aside the familiar mold in favor of a thoroughly bourgeois Romanticism. Verdi was aware of the hostility that would greet a contemporary theme on the Romantic operatic stage and fully expected a debacle, but his producer shrewdly changed the milieu from the mid-nineteenth century to around 1700. This permitted him to use the lavish and colorful costumes of the age of Louis XIV, something that the public expected and relished. Today, of course, we see *La Traviata* staged in the original period.

The play from which the libretto was fashioned was not so much a *comédie larmoyante* as it was a moral dissertation in the form of a play. Dumas *fils* drew his pen in defense of the sanctity and purity of family life. But he was also a romantic, and the fragile courtesan had to be presented in a light that was romantically gentle and bittersweet, even affectionate. The difficulty was created by the thesis: no matter how sympathetic, the fallen must be vanquished by the stern power of bourgeois morals; love comes too late, and must end in renunciation or death. Such a story can, and often does, end up on the operatic stage as a tearjerker or as Puritanical sermonizing; it is entirely up to the director and the singers whether they take the words of the libretto or Verdi's music to guide their realization of the opera.

It is moving to watch as Violetta is invaded by feelings heretofore unknown to her but, seeing herself indelibly marked by her past, she tears herself away from the tender thought. The changed mood is expressed in brilliant coloraturas, crystalline, flexible, and beautifully projected. Through her faithfulness she becomes transfigured in death, like her sister, Manon, because both are like the holy women of the medieval legends who, thirsting for life, fall in order to be redeemed. The elder Germont is in truth a far more poignant figure than his son, who is something of a weakling, and should properly dominate the scene. With his appearance the moral thesis begins to operate, and it takes great artistic strength to balance its weight.

Simone Boccanegra (1857) is one of those operas of Verdi's middle period which were first unsuccessful and which he later extensively reworked. While never so popular as the celebrated trio of operas that preceded it, the refurbished *Boccanegra*, its libretto improved by the able Arrigo Boito, gradually gained ground, though it does not yet occupy the place it deserves. This is a tremendous opera, alive with human passion and seething with drama. Verdi found opportunities for genre painting, for dramatic confrontation, and for characterization of passionate force; the hand of the future composer of *Otello* is upon the pages of *Boccanegra*. The revision came more than twenty years after the original composition, when the aging Verdi had already written *Aïda* and the *Manzoni Requiem;* the immense experience and development of a seasoned and serene master were behind this revision of his old score. *Boccanegra* is an absorbing, intense, and poetic opera, with scenes and finales as powerful as anything in the best Verdi. But this power and dramatic tension are interspersed with refined delicacy and an attractive story-telling quality. One can search high and low before finding such an overwhelming musical portrait as the principal figure in this opera. Boccanegra's is a vibrant, tragic, and mesmerizing portrayal. When he vents his wrath on Paolo one can feel the man crumple under the terrible malediction; it is an unforgettable scene.

Verdi's next opera, *Un Ballo in maschera,* encountered difficulties even before its first performance. Because the censors objected to the assassination of a monarch, the local and protagonists had to be shifted to the faraway American colony of Massachusetts, whose governor could be slain without planting subversive ideas in the minds of royal subjects. To right the historical wrongs we have tried in this country to restore the original version, but the result is the introduction of new artistic errors. Colonial Boston was exchanged for the original late-eighteenth-century Stockholm; the British governor became a Swedish king; the two conspirators, Sam and Tom, were elevated to the peerage; only Ulrica remained a witch, and surely a bit too exotic for either clime. However, historical accuracy matters little. Whether Riccardo be the King of Sweden or Governor of Massachusetts, Verdi makes him a man wrestling with his conscience.

Un Ballo in maschera has a wide range of singing styles. There are the fast, almost buffa-like staccatos in "Ogni cura," then the elegantly lilting melody of the Barcarolle, and there are many expansive ariosos in the grand pathetic style. On the whole, however, Verdi stays within the code established in the great successes, though the musical language is richer, darker, and the dramatic shortcomings more dramatic. *Un Ballo* also shows a great refinement in Verdi's melodic design; much of this music is graceful and light, the muscular élan is toned down as the great "white key" tunes assume coloration. Renato is one of the well-realized characters in the opera. When the trusting friend of Riccardo discovers what appears to be betrayal, he changes from devoted companion to aroused foe. This is not the insane jealousy of Othello; Verdi conveys with subtle variations in vocal timbre fluctuating desires for vengeance but also for pity. As a rule, Verdi lavishes particular care on his heroines, who are often stronger and more complicated characters than his heroes, but here, largely owing to the poorly spaced libretto, Amelia is somewhat pale as a dramatic figure. In the first part of the opera, though much beautiful music is allotted to her, she does not really come to grips with her own tragic situation, and it is difficult for the singer to make a whole woman of her. Nevertheless, if she holds her own until the impassioned duet with Riccardo in the second act, a plausible personage emerges, and in the third act Amelia really comes to life as an operatic creature, as she pleads with her husband for her lover's life. This is Verdi's very own territory, and he does not fail to overwhelm us with compassion. The witch's role is also difficult; it calls for an ample voice and good control of the widely separated vocal regions, and she has an important part in the complicated ensembles. The figure of Oscar, the page (sung by a soprano), is dramatically overdrawn and almost distracting, because he gets a larger share of important music than his role in the drama warrants.

But again, Oscar is invaluable in the ensembles, where "he" is in charge of the topmost line and often carries the burden.

There are many opera librettos that tax not only one's imagination but one's sanity, though few of them can vie with Piave's brew that became *La Forza del destino*. After Meyerbeer, Romantic grand opera always reveled in the grandiloquent gesture, fairly dripping with patriotism, noble resignation, filial love, vengeance, and religious fervor. At the same time it loved swordplay, and corpses carried away by extras were a familiar sight. Piave managed to cram into *La Forza* pretty nearly every one of the great themes, and one would not expect a thoughtful opera composer to touch such a book. As we have seen, Rossini, diffident and haughty, retired from the scene rather than submit to the trend emanating from the Paris Opéra, but Verdi was willing to see what could be made useful for his style. Unhappily, *La Forza* did not turn out well, remaining diffuse and at times bewildering, though it possesses a generous quota of powerful music. The version used nowadays is supposed to tighten the sprawling work, but it achieves the opposite effect. Granted that it looks back upon an honorable bowdlerized past, still it is hard to see why illogical and unmusical traditions should be observed in modern theaters. The shifting of the overture to preface the second scene, as practiced recently at the Metropolitan Opera, is musical larceny, as is the omission of some fine scenes in favor of long stretches of conventional music. The way the opera now starts gives one the feeling of stepping into a hole. But *La Forza* has real Verdi stuff: love and hatred, curse and blessing, personality as fate opposed to pride. Musically, the opera comes from *Il Trovatore*, though it is more refined, while at the same time it prepares for and prefigures the future. Surely, Leonora's last aria foreshadows the last scene in *Aïda*.

Verdi must have realized the necessity of breaking with French-influenced dramaturgy, for he returned to one of his two most admired dramatic poets, Schiller. *Don Carlo* was an attempt to reconcile Italian with French grand opera. As we have said, all of Verdi's operas from the late middle period, notably *Un Ballo in maschera,* owe a great deal to Meyerbeer and French grand opera. Like his immediate predecessors Rossini, Bellini, and Donizetti, he went to Paris, the new Mecca of opera, for he wanted to move with the times; but his heritage made this difficult. That many years later he reworked *Don Carlo* testifies not only to the composer's faith in the work but also to the fact that it contained some un-Verdian things which the aging composer wanted to eliminate. The refurbishing was done with the mature master's sure hand, yet Verdi did not erase the youthful qualities of the opera, nor could he, for that matter, remedy some of the basic dramaturgical flaws that originated with Schiller himself. Yet *Don Carlo*'s lack of popularity is altogether unjustified, for this is a great and fascinating work of immense power, and some of its characters are among the truly great musico-dramatic portraits. We might note that when *Don Carlo* was performed in St. Petersburg, Mussorgsky was working on *Boris Godunov.* There are unmistakable traces of its influence in the Russian's opera, especially perceptible in certain traits the Czar shares with King Philip.

Don Carlo was written for the Paris Opéra, and against his instincts Verdi was compelled to conform to the French grand opera pattern. The themes of the enormously long opera were the then popular subjects: tyranny, liberalism, nobility, the defense of the oppressed, the conflict of church and throne, all of which the librettist found in Schiller's *Don Carlos.* In spite of the inhibiting factors, Verdi's work was a great setting filled with wonderful music, and the master loved it even though in its French form it was not congenial to his compatriots. Almost two decades after its composition, and after the tremendous advance made with *Otello,* Verdi returned to *Don Carlo,* resolved to "Italianize" it. The result was the majestic opera we know. Yet what a difficult libretto this was even after the experienced Ghislanzoni tightened it to a four-acter.

One would expect the drama to present the age-old conflict between father and son, King Philip and Prince Charles,

but the key figure in the libretto is the prince's friend, Marquis
Posa. Schiller's aim was a moral one, and it is Posa's liberal
idealism that motivates everything and without which the
play would fall apart. This idealistic fanatic, concerned with
the fate of downtrodden Flanders, sees human beings and their
relationships as mere tools for the attainment of his purpose.
Since hopeless lovers resigned to separation could not advance
the cause of mercy and liberation, Posa deliberately rekindles
the love his dearest friend, Prince Charles, harbors for the
youthful Queen, his stepmother. Because once this is achieved
the Queen is no longer needed, the principal soprano, though
given some exquisite music to sing, is a pale figure as Verdian
heroines go.

When the opportunity arises for Posa to influence the King
directly, he is immediately tempted to follow this new possibility, in a way betraying Charles though retaining him as a
likely trump card, while the Queen recedes further in dramatic
importance. The complicated intrigue bogs down, but by this
time the original plan, based on Charles's nomination as Vice-
roy to the Low Countries, is no longer feasible; in his last attempt Posa risks his own life, again to no avail. Thus Posa
presents the perplexing picture of the most transcendental
self-sacrifice combined with monstrous egotism; the great
ideal made him cruel toward everyone, including his best
friend and even himself. This is not workable drama for a
composer, for Posa's acts are full of attitudes, of rhetoric, and
of unresolved detail. This figure was created by an esthete,
not by a dramatist who experiences the conflict sensuously.
Accordingly, Posa and the unfortunate Crown Prince, a mere
pawn in his hands, also sing very beautiful music, but they join
the Queen as wasted principals in the drama.

The uniformly beautiful eloquence of Schiller was the perfect means of expression for the eighteenth-century man, always acting out of a firm belief in the rational principles of
the age, but Verdi was no longer an eighteenth-century ra-
tionalist; like Shakespeare, he ignored abstractions, finding
drama in human personalities and not in their ideals. Fortunately, there were some scenes in the drama which went beyond

Schiller's original plans, even disturbed them, but which contained potential expressive power suited for music. Verdi espied them and by placing them in the center of the opera at once changed everything.

Verdi's King Philip is a man, not an idea, a man tortured by doubt, ambition, pride, love, and he is in overriding conflict with the power of the Church. His son, and everyone around him, are weaklings with whom he has no patience, but the Grand Inquisitor is another matter. In Schiller he is only an accessory, but Verdi makes him into a principal, an apparition that casts a spell over everything. The old and infirm Cardinal, ninety and blind, is the wrath of the Church incarnate. The meeting of these two powerful individuals results in a scene virtually unmatched for dramatic impact.

Verdi must have been unhappy with the timid female characters presented to him by the libretto. There was nothing he could do about the Queen, but there was the Princess Eboli, who is in love with Charles. The composer bides his time. In the early parts of the opera he gives Eboli some fine coloratura song, but when jealousy begins to make her desperate, Verdi turns her into a magnificently passionate character. This is the miracle of *Don Carlo*, the ability of music to recast anything and everything in its own way. So much power and eloquence is worked into these three parts that the radiance emanating from them illuminates the whole opera. We still have principals and secondary figures, but a reversal has taken place; the force of the music itself has transformed Schiller's accessory characters into dominating personalities.

Aïda is the most successful nineteenth-century grand opera in the repertory, and while it offers the ultimate in spectacular splendor it also offers unfailingly great music. The public loves it, and all kinds of musicians love it. *Aïda* is also a singers' opera and the singers must have big voices, for their parts are designed to fit the colossal Egyptian architecture. Verdi had no free hand in the subject of the libretto; given the occasion and the locale, the celebration of the opening of the Suez Canal in Cairo in 1870, it had to be a "pharaoh opera." What

Verdi could not achieve in *Don Carlo*, largely because of the libretto, is here accomplished with singular felicity—Ghislanzoni gave him an excellent book. *Aïda* is the combination of the most elaborate grand opera with bel canto and with a modern orchestral technique, but all this on Verdi's terms; thus *Aïda* does constitute a new stage in the composer's development and also a new style. The opera is now a century old, yet it has not lost one whit of its artistic freshness and is one of the most universally admired and popular operas. It is also the first among Verdi's many to abandon the technique of the "great moments" in favor of an integrally composed work. The drama grows and flows inevitably; the spectacular scenes are a logical part of the dramatic composition; and where the earlier Verdi tended to weaken, in the connecting passages between the great scenes, is precisely the place where he now triumphs. The set pieces are still there, but they are always motivated and blended into the evolving action.

Verdi's acquisition of the métier of composition was a slow process, and for some time his workshop wisdom could not even approach Rossini's. Furthermore, he was saddled with the traditions of the *scrittura* practice, which demanded medieval plots with measurelessly passionate heroes. This had become a hard and fast cliché which all romantic composers were expected to follow. Where Verdi departed from Donizetti and Bellini was in his concentration on the depiction of character. The difference was caused by his preoccupation with Shakespeare, a preoccupation that extended to his entire life. Before *Aïda* Verdi's taste could nod; even *Rigoletto* and *La Traviata* have numbers and passages that can hardly be reconciled with the high points in these operas. In fact, all three of the great middle-period operas have a good deal of the faded, stereotyped, *scrittura* opera, awkward and useless cadenzas, and perfunctory sutures between arias; but these are more than offset by the splendid and profoundly felt characterizations and dramatic scenes. And they show remarkable development in every aspect of opera: melody, harmony, orchestration, and formal organization. The great scenes are poignant, even when Verdi uses a simple recitation, but most attractive is the warmth of the steadily flowing lyric invention. Now in *Aïda* there are no commonplace or conventional spots; from the remarkably fine prelude to the soaring duet at the end, the listener is fully engaged. The prelude is no longer the usual romantic Italian potpourri overture; the material quoted from the body of the opera is not used haphazardly but built up dramatically so that it becomes a genuine prologue, an essential part of the opera itself. A particularly praiseworthy feature of *Aïda* is Verdi's way of dealing with local color. Instead of make-believe exoticism and orientalism, he used altogether Western means, harmonic, melodic, and orchestral, to evoke a distant, attractively strange atmosphere, and in the Nile scene he virtually advances into Debussy's domain. Needless to say, this is still drama in song, but now the orchestra is a senior partner, full of color and subtlety, while always in the service of the stage.

crit

Certain operas that form the core of the repertory are repeated so often that at times even the best will and the best voices fail to dispel the ennui that settles on them like smog. But *Aïda* never fails to delight, and therewith Verdi has arrived in Mozart's company.

Otello, composed many years after *Aïda,* surprised even those who had known Verdi well and for a long time. The surprise was not due to some unexpected new direction, to a basic change in style and manner; Verdi remained what he had been. His sudden new flourishing after years of silence was not a baffling "new phase," only a new season, but it was the fulfillment of an ideal for which he had begun to search more than half a century before. What is really surprising is how faithful he remained to himself and yet how new this sudden explosive spring was, how natural and still full of wonders. *Aïda* was the culmination of Italo-French grand opera, yet it was not this, the first of Verdi's "through-composed" operas, that led to the final masterpieces. *Aïda* was homogeneous, of one piece, without stylistic inconsistencies, and one would think that if any further development was possible it would naturally issue from this accomplished work.

But the struggle for the final operatic concept took place in *Simone Boccanegra, La Forza del destino,* and *Don Carlo,* although they are uneven and in a sense incomplete. Significantly, these were the three operas which Verdi later reworked seeking to solve their particular problems—and his own. The reworkings were undertaken after *Aïda,* and while he did not change these operas in their essential features, he must have clarified the problems for himself. And now, at the end of his life, he found the perfectly built and balanced music drama. While one can still discern the outlines of aria and recitative —Verdi was an Italian composer who never forgot the national tradition—the aged master integrates them into a seamless musico-dramatic fabric that is as inexorably woven as the unfolding drama itself. The orchestra is very large and very articulate; it comments on everything and has a thousand hues, but those who speak of Wagnerian influences simply fail to see that the drama is still on the stage and not in the pit.

As early as *Macbeth,* Verdi endeavored to combine set numbers with a freely flowing "operatic language," thus wrestling with a problem no Italian composer of the century had yet faced: the reconciliation of musical form with dramatic content. One realizes with astonishment that, different as they were in everything, the two dramatic giants of the century, Wagner and Verdi, were basically seeking the same ends. At the time of *Macbeth,* the Italian composer was not yet able to abolish conventions and the conventional, and they are present for some time to come in the best of his works, but there can be no question that the problem was clear to him at this early date. And now we witness a most interesting phenomenon: the two grand old men of Italian opera, Verdi and Monteverdi, meet across the centuries to affirm the ideals of this most Italian of all musical inventions. One look at the vocal line in Monteverdi's *L'Incoronazione di Poppea* will show the kinship of his recitative-arioso with that of Verdi in *Otello.* This is an infinitely varied and expressive musical narrative that can follow every inflection of the words, every accent, and every gesture.

Otello belongs at the summit of drama in music. It opens

with a tumultuous scene surging with sound, but following this there begins the relentless psychological process of the disintegration of a mind maddened by jealousy. Every scene and every episode propels the action to its tragic culmination. When Emilia's "Buona notte" is answered by the agonized cry of Desdemona, the premonition that has ominously hung over the scene from the beginning of the act erupts with an intensity that leaves everyone with a tightened throat. The "Willow Song" is simplicity itself, but the asides between the verses tremble with terror, and the "Ave Maria," utterly moving with its halting beginning, is the last prayer of a woman overcoming her terror at facing death.

Of the participants, Iago, the originator of the action, is in the foreground—Verdi's first intention was to name the opera after him. He is the very epitome of wickedness, who commits foul acts almost unselfishly, for wickedness' sake, rejoicing diabolically in the misery he causes. In the play he wheedles money and jewelry from Roderigo, but in the opera this is left out; here his sole motive is malevolence. None of Shakespeare's villains, not even Richard III or Edmund, can touch him in sheer inhumanity. Otello is the victim of this wretched schemer, and once again, no one matches his simple nobility; it is this nobility that causes his downfall. Verdi not only understood Shakespeare's concept and motives but developed and enhanced them. There is no force in Iago; he is odiously shrewd and has the ability to hide his own evil nature while deriving a devilish pleasure from the ease with which he manipulates people, the way he plays with them; and indeed Roderigo, Cassio, Otello, and Desdemona act and move at his bidding. Otello is not one of those we often meet in plays and operas to whom jealousy is a congenital illness, a mania with which they were born. Such men are either pitiable or, as Molière so superbly showed, comical; Otello is of a different breed. He is simple, heroic, trustful, a soldier who does not know much about the world, and since he takes it for granted that most people are equally decent, he does not distrust others and believes what he is told. Iago exploits this openness and trust to the hilt, and torments the Moor until he becomes a maddened beast bent on destruction. It is here that Shakespeare and Verdi rise to the summit of dramatic art: they did not want the tragedy to culminate in the ravages of a blind passion. As Otello prepares to kill Desdemona he seems to have awakened from his stupefaction, becoming a human being who tries to think objectively. Desdemona must perish, not as the victim of sheer revenge, but because honor demands it; she must be judged. The great soliloquy in the play, "It is the cause," is omitted in the opera—music needs only hints— but the idea is there, as Otello tells Desdemona to "think of thy sins . . . take heed of perjury." Otello sees himself as the executor of a higher justice. When he learns that he has been betrayed, the victim of a terrible misdeed, he deals with himself just as resolutely. Desdemona, the immortal perfection of womanly goodness, is gentle, faithful, and forgiving. Verdi loved her and we love her, and we cannot forgive Otello for doubting the innocence of such a woman.

In its ever-mounting tension, in its marvelous character portrayal, and in the infinite suppleness with which the music follows the masterful libretto, *Otello* demonstrates that it was indeed "from Harmony, from heavenly Harmony, this universal frame began"; and further, that this Harmony is the ultimate region of expression where mere words no longer suffice and must yield to song. The intensely concentrated force of expression of the septuagenarian composer awed but also somewhat baffled audiences. The last two operas were not commissioned; Verdi wrote them "for himself," and he no longer made concessions to the public's tastes and wishes. Nevertheless, *Otello* was successful from the very beginning, and if not so popular at *Rigoletto*, it had an overwhelming power that was irresistible. But the public was not at all prepared for what was to come.

There are instances where a composer courts disfavor with open eyes. In Verdi's life work there was a critical moment after which he stubbornly forged ahead though even his tremendous popularity could not protect him from adverse reactions. He felt that if he wanted to realize his artistic ambitions he must take a new road, though knowing that on this road many of his admirers would not follow him. These admirers felt themselves cheated; the master had forsaken such much-applauded Italian operatic dramatists as Ghislanzoni, and he had "lost his gift of melody." *Falstaff*, though it represents the aged composer's artistic summit, was accorded respect but no love. Many decades later, the public at large still does not warm to this incomparable masterpiece—Franz Werfel wrote a famous novel about Verdi in which *Falstaff* is not even mentioned. The opera has never been popular because Verdi steadfastly refused to use any of the time-honored and expected operatic forms and effects, creating a score that at first, and even after repeated hearings, only the schooled ear and intellect can fully savor. *Falstaff* is not really an opera buffa though it has many of the age-old buffa elements in greatly refined form. One would call this opera weightless in the sense that state is understood by physicists. Spirited contrapuntal repartees, sparkling motion, clarity and perspicacity that applauds and smiles at the slightest impulse, a gourmet-like savoring of the ensembles that make the contrasting simultaneous, all these, leave the hearer breathless in this capital comedy in which there is no guffaw and no make-believe. The large orchestra is used like a chamber music ensemble; piquant, witty, and delicately colored. In truth, *Falstaff* is a unique work—Boito called it "an absolutely new art form." (Incidentally, so is the *Manzoni Requiem*, often decried because of its "theatrical qualities." But there is nothing like it either in opera or in church music; only unhearing ears can find it "theatrical"—whatever is meant by that.)

Comedy is more individual, national, and contemporary than tragedy, and for these reasons more transitory and perishable. It can be divided into two main types. One is realistic, seeking those regions of the real world where mirth can find a home. Molière was the greatest master of this genre. The other gives more scope to fantasy as the play carries us into a fairy world; this is Shakespeare's comedy. French comedy stays close to the real world; in its caricature it emphasizes the characteristic traits of life. Shakespeare's comedy is poetic, fantastic, lyrical, and humorous. Here it is not the laws of necessity that rule, for everything turns out for the better; even the dead reawaken, or, more propitiously, men do not die at all.

Shakespeare wrote genuinely comic plays in his earlier career; later he tempers his comic vein with a certain melancholy and resignation. In contradistinction, Verdi, after a life spent in creating severely tragic plays, returned, at the twilight of a long life, to comedy. It is interesting to observe that Verdi's first and only opera buffa, *Un Giorno di regno* (1840), is shallow, and follows all the clichés of the genre without any personal involvement; it was a complete failure. But now, many decades later, the meeting of Shakespeare and Verdi in *The Merry Wives of Windsor* was a memorable and subtle occasion. The original Falstaff is not the innocent humorist he is often taken for; we must stalk him carefully if we want to catch him. He is jovial and can amuse himself hugely; the tavern is his home because his type needs company, and he takes charge of this company. He is a coward, but if necessary he may remember that he is a knight, and he lies gloriously to escape from a bad situation. The Falstaff of *The Merry Wives* is different from the splendid rogue in *Henry IV*, though Boito skilfully spliced lines from that play into *The Merry Wives*. A rogue he remained, but he is also an amorous, cooing, adventure-seeking gallant, characteristics that make him more appropriate for operatic treatment than Henry's erstwhile boon companion. Now it is not that he plays with men: the women play with him. Furthermore, in this version the hero is lifted out of the historical context; this also favors the musical concept. This is the only one of Shakespeare's plays that seems to take place in his own time (as well as the only comedy set in England), presenting on the stage the middle-class life of an English town. *The Merry Wives* is really the first bourgeois comedy, a genre which was unable, however, to prevail against the aristocratic tendencies of the theater; the eighteenth century had to start it all over again.

At the end of his life Verdi looked back on many triumphs,

but also on much disappointment and disenchantment. The serene old man appears, like Cicero, to have seen old age as the time when the soul has fulfilled its servitude to the passions and becomes its own master. The old musical poet welcomed the young playwright's vision of frolicking everyday people, creating from Boito's libretto a brilliant musical picture of life. There are the ladies, gay, vital; their voices tingle, their words dart. They are alluring, cleverly sober, a little vulgar; and the way they hold their own is thoroughly middle class. Falstaff has a great deal of trouble with them as he shakes up their commonplace existence, and he gets his punishment for it. But the great liar, the paunchy scoundrel, the swaggering poseur is also a poet who has an eternal love: his own reveries. What would reality be without reveries, what would these gray, ordinary people, who make Falstaff the butt of their derision, be without him? Then, in the midst of the amusing frivolity, dowry hunting, and flirting, there is a tender love story, so fleeting, so delicate that we get just a glimpse of it. There are neither ardent arias nor melting love duets, the innocent lovers meet only for brief moments, but the young heart of the octogenarian composer makes these brief moments unforgettably tender. So in the end this foolish, empty life can be made beautiful, and the song of youthful love sweet by eternal comedy which is the world of dreams and fantasies. "The world is a jest; man was born a jester. . . . All are cheated. . . . Every mortal being laughs at every other. . . ." says Verdi in the great final ensemble, and with it he reveals the role of the dreamer in the prosaic reality of life, at the same time raising the composer and his dreams above it. *Falstaff* is the bitterest self-confession of Verdi's art, but also its most eloquent defense, the crowning of the work of one of the greatest musico-dramatists of all times.

Verdi's relationship to Shakespeare has been the subject of a good deal of speculation. If we acknowledge *Otello* and *Falstaff* as what they are, incomparable masterpieces composed with the aid of excellent librettos, the early Verdi of *Macbeth* cannot, by comparison, be regarded as a true Shakespearean.

But to accuse him, even at this stage, of misunderstanding the great dramatic poet, whom he worshipped, is unjust.

Shakespeare's age did not very much bother with the unity of composition; the tragedy grows from all sorts of accidents, but these accidents are strongly dramatic. Verdi welcomed these dramatic accidents, they fitted his technique of the "great moments," and he even succeeded in improving, we may dare to say, on Shakespeare; the endings of both *Macbeth* and *Otello* are superior to the endings of the plays. As for *Macbeth*, with the ruthlessness of its characters working against the establishment of any real connection between the destroyer and the destroyed, it is difficult enough for modern audiences as a play, let alone as a subject for opera. Nor was it popular in the Romantic era, when Verdi decided upon the composition of his opera. It was the composer who presented Piave, the librettist, with detailed instructions on how to proceed, and this at a time when the theater, both spoken and lyric, was largely under the influence of Scribe's dramaturgy, entirely based on audience psychology. Since the generally admitted aim of the drama was to keep an audience occupied and interested for a few hours, such extremely complicated characters as Macbeth and Hamlet were judged unsuitable for the contemporary theater. The colorfulness of Romanticism was the many-sided glitter of the reflection of things, rather than the things themselves, and hence of life itself, whereas in Shakespeare the concept of the human, and even of stage technique, contained the material of poetry; life in the Shakespearean drama was extensive, varied, and polyphonic. Dumas openly expressed his dislike of *Hamlet* and *King Lear,* and doubted, with many others outside of England, that the "bizarre particulars" of Macbeth's fate were suitable for tragedy.

But Verdi was a much more profound connoisseur of drama than many of his literary confreres, not to mention his fellow musicians, some of whom wrote successful "Shakespearean" operas; but whether Massenet, or Gounod, or Zandonai, they quite misunderstood Shakespeare—as they misunderstood Goethe. Verdi divined what those who objected to the "bizarre particulars" failed to realize: that Shakespeare had close connections with the popular stage, and that his figures are not abstractions or types, but human beings to whom the audience can correlate. Some of us still tend to ridicule Verdi's "barrel-organ tunes," but they achieve the very closeness to the audience which Shakespeare enjoyed. These tunes may be just as accidental as the Shakespearean turn of events—and are just as intensely dramatic if properly presented and understood. But Verdi's vocal flourishes must be taken unblushingly and without apology; only thus can their true dramatic force be realized. Verdi clearly saw that Shakespeare's motivations are much less severe than those of modern drama, they are purely mental-emotional, always resting on individual causes, and therefore are eminently suitable for musical setting. And he realized that in the end the essence of dramatic stylization is to portray a single adventure from a man's experience in such a manner that it will stand for that man's whole life, so that this isolated bit of living becomes an entire life, an entire character.

What made many of his operas before *Otello* so indestructible and dramatically poignant, never threatened by the great Wagnerian wave, and easily surviving the periodic attacks of the highbrows, was Verdi's realization that in the life of every man there comes a moment when the driver of his star yields the reins and he becomes master of his own destiny. It is at these moments that the great, uncomplicated, and devastatingly telling melodies appear and with uncanny certainty take command of the situation. This is the secret of opera, a secret few have known so intimately as this great, patient, and dedicated composer, who never rested until satisfied that he had found the right tone at the right place. *Macbeth* is still uneven, because the young Verdi did not yet see that the Shakespearean drama, with all its similarities, differs considerably from the Romantic. He did not yet succeed in pulling together a number of scenes into one operatic condensation, the thing that makes *Otello* such a gripping music drama. The problem was, of course, to present Shakespeare in terms of Italian opera without losing Shakespeare in the process, but try as he would Verdi could not get his librettists to understand his concept. For many years he was occupied with a libretto based on *King Lear,* longing to set it to music, but since he could not reconcile the emasculated libretto with the drama he envisaged, nothing came of it. When, late in life, he encountered Arrigo Boito, a musician-writer as cultivated as he was understanding, and superbly qualified for the task, he had finally found the man who could condense Shakespeare's drama to the exact proportions and density opera demands without jeopardizing its original qualities; the road to the summit was opened.

Shakespearean adaptations are a perilous undertaking. Boito's skill in drawing on two of the great plays for his librettos is the more remarkable in that though he "arranged" them, hardly anything in the books, including the dialogues, was the product of the arranger's invention. *Otello* and *Falstaff* are in fact very carefully founded on the originals, though they have an air so spontaneous that anyone not acquainted with the details of Shakespeare's own texts would not realize how much skill and literary savoir-faire went into Boito's adaptations. This time Verdi was careful—he knew it was his last chance to realize the lifelong dream that had begun with *Macbeth*—so there were preliminary experiments for the collaboration with Boito. Verdi put him to work on the reshaping of some of his older operas, and soon the young poet-composer earned Verdi's approbation and friendship.

Until recently it has been the fashion to ascribe Verdi's remarkable development from *Aïda* onward to the beneficent influence of Wagner. Various arguments have been advanced in support of this theory, but today we see that none of them holds water. In the first place, it was commonly accepted that Wagner emphasized the drama, Verdi the music. Aside from the fact that, his protestations and writings notwithstanding, Wagner too was a musician first and foremost, this is an absurd statement, resulting from the inability of the Transalpine critics to understand the Italian composer's psyche. Like Mozart, Verdi did not manipulate his human figures from the orchestra pit, he lived among them, up on the stage, in the great melodies, in the arias, cavatinas, cabalettas, ensembles, and finales. It goes without saying that plot and action were important to him, but only to a certain degree. The centuries-old heritage of the Italian composer is the certainty that human life, drama, and melody are inextricably bound. "Cantiamo"—let us sing—says Desdemona facing death, because it is only melody that can dissolve hopeless human fate in beauty, that can transfigure forlorn and perishing life. Italian melody never lost the roundedness it acquired from Alessandro Scarlatti, and it is this that distinguishes it from German dramatic music. And while Verdi gradually departed from the "closed" forms and melodies, he never really abandoned them even in his last, through-composed operas that appear to be seamless. It is here, in the melodies, that Bellini's strong influence makes itself felt; Verdi himself expressed boundless admiration for Bellini's "long, long, long melodies." The Italian idea of opera is purely musical, and so it was with the Italianized Germans—Handel, Hasse, Christian Bach, and Mozart. It is fruitless to compare this southern concept of drama in music with the northern; each is legitimate in its own sphere, but they are not interchangeable, for they fulfill different needs.

Verdi's orchestra was contemptuously called "a monstrous guitar" playing inconsequential accompaniments, but Verdi was just as careful with his orchestra as the Lord of Bayreuth. However, extended symphonic elaboration had no place in his scheme, because the point of gravity was on the stage, in the singing voices. Wagner proceeds from the old accompanied recitative and from the so-called melodrama of the late eighteenth and early nineteenth centuries. The melodrama was a specific kind of stage music where spoken or half-spoken words were accompanied by music. Scenes such as the dungeon scene in *Fidelio* or the Wolf's Glen scene in *Der Freischütz*, exerted strong attraction on Wagner even though later he expressed reservations concerning this species of dramatic music. The human voice in his operas is generally drawn within the orbit of, or superimposed on, the thematic-motivic orchestral melos. Verdi started from the aria, gradually approaching "speech-song" through the arioso. In the end, both great musicians reached a similar goal, the continuous operatic narrative, but the "endless melody" so created remained in the voices with the Italian, while the German made his orchestra the more eloquent of the partners. Verdi, immersed in the Italian tradition, considered the Wagnerian concept unsuitable for Italian opera.

This brings us to the frequently expressed opinion that it was Wagner's leitmotif technique that made possible the unity of the last three of Verdi's operas. Once more we are dealing with faulty analysis and lack of historical insight. As a matter of fact, the first time Verdi heard a Wagnerian opera, *Lohengrin*, was after *Aïda* had been composed, yet he used leitmotifs—more precisely, a variety called recurring motives, or motives of reminiscence—quite early. It must be remembered that Wagner was not the inventor of the leitmotif, which, once the "number opera" was tightened and made more homogeneous, was a natural means of maintaining continuity of the musical narrative. There are traces of leitmotifs in *Macbeth*, then in *Rigoletto* the motivic correlation is integrated with the unfolding drama. These recurring motives are not to be equated with the Wagnerian species; Verdi uses a few *themes* that return at salient points like a leitmotif. There is, for instance, the "murder" theme in *Rigoletto*, or the music associated with the burning stake in *Il Trovatore*, or the "kiss" theme in *Otello*. These recurring themes have an eminently dramatic function, but they are not, as in Wagner, subjects for elaborate symphonic treatment.

Verdi shared with the Scarlattis and Bellinis a profound suspicion of everything musical that came from beyond the Alps. It was essentially northern opera, the "opera of words and of musical instruments," that he mistrusted, even though he had a deep and genuine admiration for Wagner. His sober realism, the honoring of tradition, and stern self-criticism saved him from the many perils of Romanticism, but especially from the theories so dear to the northerners (whom he called the "quartettists"). "Not theory but music," he protested. Yet this man, to whom music was synonymous with the lyric theater, who did not care for anything abstract, who even deplored the tendency in his time to foster in Italy orchestral and chamber music on the German model ("we are descendants of Palestrina"), ended *Falstaff* with a great fugue, the most sparkling and virtuoso piece of ensemble writing in an "abstract" form in the entire century.

Nine

VERISMO

NATURALISM, engendered by French literature, was bound to find its way to the lyric stage, and it burst upon the operatic world with *I Pagliacci* and *Cavalleria rusticana*, later to become known as the celebrated "double bill." Both Leoncavallo and Mascagni were small-time musicians until they took part, around 1890, in a contest; as prize-winners they became world-famous composers overnight. Their popularity is undimmed after more than three-quarters of a century, and there is no repertory opera house in the world that does not have the twins among its sure-fire offerings. Surely this is a phenomenon that bears a little investigation.

What makes the situation puzzling is that while Verdi and Puccini, Massenet and Debussy, even Mahler and Sibelius admired one or the other or both operas, the majority of critics, historians, and, more recently, musicians of all persuasions condemn them out of hand. Yet the vast popularity of these two operas is not restricted, as some would have it, to Italian barbers and uninformed music lovers; the public of both hemispheres rates them among its greatest favorites. True, some of these admirers certainly make strange bedfellows. William II and Queen Victoria, both notoriously unmusical, were altogether taken with Leoncavallo, and the Kaiser commissioned him to compose a German national opera for Berlin. It was duly composed, delivered, and performed, though with deplorable results; the Kaiser, however, still liked it. To complete the story, neither of the two composers was able to repeat his tremendous success, though in Mascagni's case this fate was undeserved. I know only his *Iris;* it is a much finer work than *Cavalleria* and was undoubtedly the model for *Madama Butterfly*. Unfortunately for the composer, it does not offer the crass realistic drama that carried along his prize opera, and the work did not cross the Alps. Although *Cavalleria* and *I Pagliacci* have much in common, they are the products of two differing musical personalities. While the Naturalism in *Cavalleria*'s liberetto is powerful there is still a good deal of the pathos of late Romanticism in Mascagni's music, and he is less harsh than Leoncavallo.

Toward the end of the last century and in the first decade of ours, Naturalism was the battle cry. All the dreams and ideals of Romanticism as well as its idols were lost, its élan and enthusiasm were extinguished, and cold sobriety took their place. The sharp, inexorable light of reality chased away the last rose-colored clouds, romantic values and beliefs were rejected as outmoded, and whoever was conservative enough to believe in something—the soul, God, or the hereafter—beat a blushing retreat. But why Naturalism, and what is it?

One kind of writer or painter looks at life and finds it beautiful. He conceives it the task of all art to approximate this beauty without "interference," that is, without permitting his own personality and imagination to intrude upon the perceived beauty, for if interpreted or stylized this inherent beauty will be diminished. Then there is the other kind of realist, who holds a mirror before the world to terrify it with its own ugliness; it seems that the musicians were particularly attracted to this kind of realism. They had a grateful public, then and now. A corollary to this attitude was that both creative artists and their public could see dramatic problems only as sensual violence.

Romanticism was a literary movement, but one might say without undue exaggeration that it culminated and ended in music. Naturalism also started in literature, but its musical phase was not successful, and it ended by being practically re-absorbed by literature. The one truly great Naturalist opera that succeeded and became an honest *musical* triumph is *Carmen; Cavalleria rusticana, I Pagliacci, Tiefland, Il Tabarro,* and all the others have been—and some still are—very popular, but they are musically insignificant compared to Bizet's sparkling score. The next step was to be Impressionism, which produced only one outstanding specimen, *Pelléas et Mélisande,* but here music is not the senior partner as it should be in an opera; it does what Gluck and Wagner preached but never really practiced: it surrenders to literature. The two prize-winning operas assign a more positive role to music than does Debussy. Nevertheless, it is the play that carries the day; the music only contributes to the successful theater and has small intrinsic value.

As a young man, Leoncavallo met Wagner, who made a deep impression on him and encouraged the fledgling composer to be his own librettist. It should be remembered that Leoncavallo was by trade a writer, the holder of a doctorate in letters, and that *I Pagliacci* was accepted by Sonzogno, the music publisher, on the strength of its libretto rather than of its music. Galsworthy called *I Pagliacci* "a fascinating hybrid, one of those rare operas in which the story takes complete possession of the music and fuses with it perfectly." Mascagni, in his turn, consorted and collaborated with eminent literary men, like D'Annunzio, and had an abiding faith—if poor luck —in the literary guidance the composer should accept and follow. Incidentally, Leoncavallo, an able playwright, had a hand, one way or another, in the librettos of *Manon Lescaut* and *La Bohème;* the latter he also set to music, but the opera failed.

"Truth" was, then, the great slogan—hence *verismo.* As the name implies, veristic drama aimed at true-life realism and tried to capture, especially in its musical version, raw instincts and passions in action, unprocessed and untrammelled, without embellishing and moderating them. Its disciples found it very annoying when human beings were made into symbols, puppets, or for that matter into saints, but they forgot that in art verisimilitude is not necessary to attain truth. Homer's Cyclops, Shakespeare's Ghost, and Mozart's Queen of the Night are just as true as Leoncavallo's Canio, who stabs his wife and her lover before our eyes. Violence and sudden death are promising themes, but to catch the imagination they must not be treated in the bald manner of verismo; the bloody convulsions of the battle of the sexes, which was the preferred subject, can seldom be sustained by appropriate music for any length of time—thus the one-acters. The drama is condensed and the catastrophe is reached without many preliminaries; there is one milieu, one mood, one situation—and one act, so that the spectator has no intermission during which to recover from the suggestive mood. (Though *I Pagliacci* nominally has two acts, the curtain between them signifies no more than the Intermezzo in *Cavalleria*.) This limitation to one act is also clearly connected with the limitations of the composers' talents, because a one-acter can seldom conjure up the completeness and universality of great drama; it merely gives us a piece of life, or life seen from one angle. The men and women in such a drama come from the outside, they walk into the play ready for the conflict, and they have no complicated relationships. Accordingly, both construction and dialogue are designed with the greatest simplicity. Whenever the composers of the uncompromisingly veristic opera attempted to create a full-fledged three-act work, they failed; they were unable to maintain dramatic continuity and reach a plausible climax. Bizet and Puccini succeeded, if at different levels, because Naturalism was only one aspect of their musical makeup; they were basically dramatic lyricists and could unite realism with Romanticism. But when Puccini did compose an altogether veristic opera, *Il Tabarro*, it was a one-acter, and when Leoncavallo tried to return to the eternal spirit of the buffa he produced only miserable operettas.

One would suppose verismo to have originated from popular sources, and it actually did start from such premises, but soon struck out in different directions and became sensationalism. The Calabrian and Sicilian peasant scenes in the "double bill" have nothing in common with the attractive popular realism or the humor and earthiness of the Neapolitan peasant, so engagingly—and lyrically—depicted in the works of Salvatore di Giacomo.

Both Leoncavallo and Mascagni were considerably influenced by Bizet, but were too noisy and overemphatic to grasp the finesse of the Frenchman's verismo. Their lovers have no tender words for each other; they break into frenzy, slashing, biting, killing. Without wishing to argue that the world is all sweetness and light, one wonders why realism should be so peculiarly unpleasant. Teniers, with his brush, made drunken peasants fit to be hung on the walls of aristocratic living rooms, but in these plays no one knows peace or warmth or goodness, and no one ever smiles. The music, though in many ways palpably within the tradition of Italian opera, is similarly unsmiling. Yet neither of these composers was false; the whipped-up passion pours out convincingly in melody, and while much of the composition is trivial, it is not without merit. Although the music faithfully follows the restricted moods, it is well timed, and it has a certain crude verve supported by solid dramatic-theatrical knowledge; in the end the libretto is much more veristic than the music.

What called forth lasting reaction to this sort of Naturalism was that it substituted instinct for the soul, denied the freedom of the will, and proclaimed determinism. Naturalism has a narrow horizon because it concentrates only on such things as can be seen and grasped immediately, and it does not permit music to follow its own bent and its own pace. While it had considerable influence and contributed, with its violence and its favoring of dark subjects, to the enlargement of literary themes and musical vocabulary, it failed as a movement. The aging Mascagni himself admitted this failure, and composers once again learned that art cannot live without discipline.

Ten

PUCCINI

PUCCINI is as universally loved by the public as he is condescended to by the highbrows. Almost all critics and historians of consequence (and this includes even a few Italians) gauge Puccini's artistic stature at a rather low level. His tremendous popular success, attained with unusual rapidity, is of course undeniable; but is it merely the result of a well-calculated appeal to the less refined instincts of the public? Some of the poster-like climactic scenes, with touches like the shrieks of the tortured Cavaradossi in *Tosca*, or the bloody card playing in *La Fanciulla del west*, would support this conclusion, as perhaps would the sentimental passages that make the cinema-like situations even crasser. It must also be admitted that at times Puccini is given to proclaiming his ecstasy too explicitly, instead of distilling it. But blanket condemnation is a little too easy. Curiously enough, no competent author has yet attempted a serious full-length study of this music, which also shows genuinely inward and highly artistic qualities. These qualities are evident through most of *La Bohème* and, to cite a few other examples, in the last part of *Manon Lescaut* and in many moments of *Madama Butterfly*; and, together with the rich, colorful, and attractive musicality of such scenes as that in the coffee house in *La Bohème*, they easily and emphatically tip the scales, fully justifying the composer's enormous success.

It is little known that Puccini, like Bach, was the issue of a musical dynasty, and that his ancestors, like Bach's, were organists and church musicians. Indeed, the composer of *Tosca* was earmarked for the post of cathedral organist in Lucca— practically a hereditary post—before his legs could reach the pedal board. The lineage of the masters to whom earlier Puccinis were apprenticed is also significant: Padre Martini, Paisiello, Donizetti, Mercadante, though their instruction was usually begun by their fathers. Giacomo's father was a musi- cian highly regarded for his knowledge of counterpoint. At the age of fourteen the son was already a practicing organist, so we see that, aside from natural talent, he came by his abilities logically. Puccini combines the plastic melody of Verdi and the theatrical instinct and elegance of Massenet with naturalism and with exoticism, yet his musical idiom is original and ad- venturous. The doubters should examine the composition date of the introduction to the second act of *La Bohème*, 1895 —to mention a good example—and then look around to see what was being done in those days in opera scores. Actually, while retaining many—and some of the worst—features of verismo, Puccini turned the movement in a neo-romantic direction.

Indeed, his detractors should not overlook the very real connection with Verdi. From *Il Trovatore* threads lead to *Tosca*, from the fragile courtesan of *La Traviata* to Mimi in *La Bohème*, from the oriental pomp of *Aïda* to the exoticism of *Madama Butterfly* and *Turandot*, while the exacting buffo manner of *Falstaff* surely inspired the virtuoso parlando of *Gianni Schicchi*. It is true that in every instance the format was reduced, but it was also brought closer to its time. It is also true that what in Verdi is overflowing passion, in Puccini can border on excitability. Still, it is easy to see why, beginning with *La Bohème*, he left far behind those who considered themselves Verdi's heirs: Mascagni, Leoncavallo, Ponchielli, Giordano, and all the others. He was an artist of what may have been a declining period, but an artist he was to his finger- tips. The workmanship of his scores is excellent, ranging from leitmotif to tightly thematic orchestral commentary. His harmony is always interesting and shows a steady development. He learned a great deal from verismo, but he also learned from Bizet's dramatic economy and from his classically closed forms, as well as from Massenet's elegant sentimental lyricism. Puccini was remarkably alert to the developing musical scene; he studied Debussy, but *Pierrot Lunaire* and even the young Stravinsky also left their mark on his music. His talents were strong enough to enable him to absorb all this and to mold his multitudinous sources into a pronouncedly personal style— Puccini never imitates. It is interesting to note that while the critics and historians belabor him, many composers, among them Debussy and Webern, praised him. Try as one may to dismiss him, it is impossible to do so because many a notable score, from *Salome* to *Lulu*, shows his unmistakable influence —and the influence of his most garish work, *Tosca*, at that.

La Bohème is Puccini's finest and most convincing work. Its musical invention is not subjected to the glaring constrasts exhibited in *Tosca*, the rapport between composer and librettists is close, and the atmosphere is attractive because it reflects Puccini's own world and cultural milieu, which he could convey with warm and sympathetic authority. And *La Bohème* is well balanced and satisfying because here Puccini stayed wholly within the boundaries of his genuine powers. The lyric-sentimental and bourgeois attitude in this opera is, of course, diametrically opposed to Verdi's heroic vein, and yet one still perceives the ties that bind the younger to the older master. *La Bohème* has an excellent libretto congenially set to music, and besides, Puccini was clearly in love with Mimi.

Tosca is an example of that painfully coarse naturalism with which second-rate French dramatists, like Sardou, momentarily captivated the world. It has been called a mixture of vulgarity, brutality, and cruelty, and it may appear that the inherent garish theatricality of Sardou's play is often heightened by the music's rather distressing shade of purple. Yet a closer look will show that, aside from some raw spots, Puccini's music actually minimizes the worst features of the libretto. The melodic flow is strong and combustible, and there is psychological force in the characters. The opening "Scarpia motif," which as a leitmotif is heard throughout the opera, is a penetratingly sharp musical image of the unsavory secret police baron, and its rapid change from B-flat to E-major captivated many musicians, as the "Tristan chord" fascinated a previous generation.

Madama Butterfly was composed in the days when Asian and other exotic art fascinated Europe. The painters watched Gauguin, and the musicians listened to the Javanese gong orchestras. When Puccini saw Belasco's play he immediately joined the camp of the exotics and fell in love with the little heroine, as he had earlier with Mimi. While the orientalism is mere decor, and the collision of the *Star Spangled Banner* with Japanese tunes a bit obvious, the close of the second act, where the geisha, the child, and the nurse wait with touching faith for the impossible to happen, is as fine as anything in all post-Verdi Italian opera. *Butterfly* is usually given in an "authentic" oriental presentation; not only are the sets and costumes careful replicas of Japanese originals, but the singers are taught gestures and motions genuinely Japanese. One may wonder whether this authentic local color is justified in an opera whose music is absolutely and irrevocably Italian, sophisticatedly Western. Actually, the antipodes get along well precisely because only the subject and the setting are Japanese. Puccini did use a few Japanese tunes, but never for an instant did he relinquish his birthright; whatever sounds Japanese, that is, exotic, is the exoticism a Westerner would create for his own use. Actually, Puccini is less successful when in order to create local color he borrows alien musical material, as in *Butterfly* and *Turandot;* these tunes always remain foreign incrustations. He must have realized, at least instinctively, that such syntheses are dangerous. We may recall that in eighteenth-century Europe it was highly fashionable to collect Chinese art, but its devotees completely missed its nature and point of view. This was once more true during the second wave of oriental influence, when artists like Degas and Whistler, taking their cue from Japanese prints, attempted the impossible task of reconciling a system of design founded on two-dimensional concepts with three-dimensional content.

Many look down upon *Madama Butterfly* as a tearjerker.

They could not be more wrong, for while the tears are plentiful, many of them are warm and honest. Throughout the opera there are many felicitous scenes and passages that display Puccini's mastery in handling delicate themes with a superbly controlled orchestra.

There is good evidence to show that Puccini was by no means a facile exploiter of the public's tastes. He could have gone on forever composing *comédie larmoyante*, making even more money than he did, but *La Fanciulla del west* shows that he had largely lost faith in the expressive and technical means he was using heretofore: the work is poor because there is little conviction behind it. It seems that after what we may call feminine-sentimental operas he now turned toward masculinity, and what would be more masculine than the American Wild West? Externally, the changes are considerable. We see the familiar interior of a bar instead of a salon, six-shooters instead of daggers, kerosene lamps instead of chandeliers, and moonshine whiskey instead of champagne. We also see the most unlikely operatic heroine who ever graced grand opera. Minnie laughs at the fellow who drinks his liquor with a chaser, is quicker on the draw than any pistol-packing prospector in the house, has never been kissed, and in the best sourdough tradition reads the Bible to the rough gentry. Then there is the tough Sheriff who swears in Italian but handles his Colt idiomatically. (There is a posse, too, but the presence of live horses is not Western realism. Though of course fraught with certain hazards, whether in *La Fanciulla* or *Götterdämmerung*, the use of livestock on the opera stage represents a status symbol: no small house can afford them.) Then comes the most American touch. The Sheriff and the Fanciulla engage in combat on the field of honor with Dick's life as the prize, not with pikes or swords, but with that deadly native weapon, poker. Minnie, an old hand at this sort of thing despite her Bible reading, keeps a few extra aces in her stocking, just in case. Well, I suppose this libretto is no sillier than the eternal medieval romances or regicides, and to a Milanese or Venetian audience it should appear as exotic and remote as ancient Egypt or even medieval Florence is to us, though in English and with realistic American touches *La Fanciulla* would be a disaster in an American opera house. What is fatal to *La Fanciulla* is that the music is saddeningly indecisive. The Puccini stamp is there, as is his great theatrical skill, but real and convincing dramatic melody, his real strength, flares up only once or twice. Unfortunately, this time he was not in love with his heroine. Repeatedly Puccini makes one feel that the lush tune is just around the corner, but after a few wing beats the music resumes its earthly course, vacillating between Debussy and Strauss in a way not becoming to this fine and original composer.

A pause followed after *La Fanciulla,* and a search for a new direction; Puccini tried a triptych, three vastly different one-acters for a full evening's fare. *Il Tabarro* is the last of Puccini's naturalistic operas; he must have realized the genre to be a cul-de-sac from which he must back out to save himself. The traditional French love triangle is here a pretty gross variant of the usual brilliant give-and-take, and Puccini did not succeed, as he did in *Tosca,* in attenuating—or enhancing— the garish lines and strong situations with strong music. The principal purpose of this opera, almost a Grand Guignol piece, seems to be to rouse the audience's emotions rather than to give expression to the dramatic characters. In *Suor Angelica* the composer did back out of the cul-de-sac, but a little too far. Here he gives us a nun's tragedy, teetering on the treacly, especially since men's voices are banished from the score. The opera is uncomfortably theatrical, even though blood and guts have been exchanged for tears and sighs. This is no longer the sincere and attractive lyricism of *La Bohème;* full of artifice, it represents an enervating slackening of Puccini's gifts.

The third short opera, *Gianni Schicchi,* however, is an authentic small masterpiece, a comedy that revives the great traditions of the classical opera buffa with astonishing fidelity to tone, manner, and substance. The story is somewhat maca-bre, but its whirling and drastic humor, its scintillating vir-tuousity, and its theatricality (this time in the best sense of the word) make the macabre actually very funny. The marvelously handled orchestra gives us an endless scherzo; bright, brilliant, never halting, and always entertaining.

It is often said that in Rossini's *Barber* the opera buffa reached its crest, and thereafter was no longer in the mainstream of Italian opera. It is true that in the period following this early-nineteenth-century work Romantic grand opera dominated the scene, but the buffa never ceased to attract composers, and several masterpieces grace the literature between Rossini and our era. We no longer have opera buffa specialists as in the eighteenth century, but it is most interesting to note that each of the two great Italian opera composers of the late Romantic period, Verdi and Puccini, after a life spent in setting to music Romantic drama, returned to the buffa to compose their most mature works. In reality the buffa always slumbers in every Italian composer's bosom. The buffa requires an approach and treatment quite different from serious opera. Tone, pace, melody, orchestration, everything is lighter and faster, but above all there are the ensembles, those romping and scintillating pieces which are the acme of operatic virtuosity and enjoyment—that is, if they are properly executed. When Gianni Schicchi explains to the assembled "mourners" his plan to fool the notary and make a spurious last will seemingly legal, there ensues one of these animated ensembles that are a wonder of minutely organized chaos. The Italian is not a Puritan, nor can he long be satisfied with romantic grandiloquence. Among his most engaging traits are his earthiness, his independence of authority, and his scorn of sanctimoniousness. The Anglo-Saxon is a little uncomfortable when the body of the just deceased Buoso Donati is unceremoniously dumped by the mourners as soon as a scheme has been found to prevent his money from going to the Florentine clergy. The Italian calls a spade a spade and more than hints at the real feelings of the heirs waiting for the estate to be disposed of. The solemn gathering of family and retainers for a similar function is common enough in our world, but the true sentiments are always camouflaged; the Italian goes openly to the root of the matter. Puccini caught this rather ghoulish humor with a sure and virtuoso hand. Strauss and the other erstwhile Wagnerians had to fight their way out of the immense gravitational pull of Wagner, but Puccini was not a whit inconvenienced by the towering figure of Verdi. He went straight back to the eighteenth century and to Rossini, as is clearly shown by the spirited ensembles and the remarkable thematic work in the orchestra.

American performances of this little masterpiece often misjudge the tone, so that what should be a saturnine smile often turns into a guffaw. But what hurts the opera most of all is that the American public misses much of the wit and satire because of the strange tongue, and is reduced to the appreciation of such comedy as is conveyed by the situations and acting. While it is true that in general it is essential for vocal works to retain the original language, in the case of a brilliant theatrical piece in which, with the exception of a few arias and duets, the singers are engaged in a rapid conversational tone, the audience's own language should be used. This, however, does not mean the usual "vocal-score English," but a lively, faithful, and thoroughly modern translation. It can be done.

The great artistic ascent of the aging Verdi was not granted to Puccini. To be sure, he advanced steadily in every department of the composer's art, but richer melody, harmony, and orchestration cannot substitute for concrete artistic convictions. While *Gianni Schicchi* was a masterpiece, the opera buffa could not solve Puccini's problem; he still wanted to salvage his original operatic art, but by now he had lost touch with real life. In Puccini, Verdi's healthy Romanticism turned into exoticism, and the melancholy that was part of his nature and never left him now came to the fore. *Turandot* represents both a crisis and a climax, for while Puccini could not find the true new tone he was seeking, he nevertheless liberated his music from the excess of naturalism—and found his last and most attractive love in Liù.

Turandot, though unfinished (Alfano completed the last act), is a remarkable work, distinguished by fine melodies, advanced and always interesting harmonies, superb orchestration, impressive choral scenes, and pleasant Chinese local color.

Moreover, Puccini, who as a rule worked with smaller, nicely constructed mood scenes, here attempts much larger constellations that show him at the height of his powers. Yet he did not quite achieve his ambition. The antithesis between the cold and cruel Princess Turandot and the warmly human slave girl, Liù, perhaps Puccini's noblest operatic figure, is not fully realized in the music, though the attempt results in some telling dramatic contrast and characterization, and in a powerfully atmospheric style attained without the benefit of veristic underlining. Also, some of the incidental elements, like the part of the three court ministers, appear to have been dictated not so much by wisdom as by confidence in virtuosity. All in all, the opera exhibits vigorous invention and brilliant theatrical knowledge, with dream-like rather than real characters. *Turandot* deserves more attention for its own sake than it is accorded merely on account of its being the last opera by the famous composer of great favorites.

Puccini always had many professional and critical enemies —all successful men have them—but this essentially modest and likable man never answered the challenges and innuendoes, and in general shunned publicity. He did not always travel on the true path of the great tradition, but he never remained static and was always receptive to new stimuli. Whatever his limitations, he was the legitimate heir to the past grandeur of Italian opera.

Eleven

FRENCH OPERA

FRENCH opera has fallen on lean years in this country. Little of it is heard, as this is written—not even *Faust*, once so much a pillar of the Metropolitan Opera's repertory that a witty critic called the staid old institution a Faustspielhaus. *Carmen*, of course, still holds the boards, as it will forever, but that the rest are in need of conservation measures is demonstrated by the formation of a society calling itself The Friends of French Opera. Yet if we do not hear much French opera, from a certain point of view French opera still lives on in Italian—even German—disguise: many of the librettos of the standard repertory were derived from French plays of the Romantic era, and grand opera of the nineteenth century itself is a French creation. During my years as a critic, I encountered (in unstaged performances) a pair of works by two of the important ancestors of Romantic grand opera. As was so often the case in French musical history, neither Gasparo Spontini (1774–1851) nor Giacomo Meyerbeer (1791–1864), the two paragons of the new lyric theater, was a native of the country, but they found success and fortune in Paris, and they recall a most colorful and flamboyant phase of operatic history.

Like any other mortal, Richard Wagner had artistic ancestors who deeply influenced his music. Weber and perhaps Marschner, among them, are familiar to most friends of opera, but Spontini, whose imprint on opera was lasting, is unknown to present-day audiences. When we look upon his life and work, we discover that, as with Wagner, his operas reflect the entire social and political climate of his times. This austere, haughty, and choleric artist was the musical spokesman of the Napoleonic spirit of aggressive nationalism.

Spontini was Roman with a vengeance. What he saw in Paris, where he moved as a young man, rekindled memories of the great historical past of the Roman Empire. He enthusiastically threw himself into the grandiloquent atmosphere of the short-lived Napoleonic Empire, forging a French-dominated cosmopolitan musical style of brilliance and power that delighted the Corsican. What David's famous historical paintings could not achieve with their frosty Classicism, Spontini's sonorously radiant operas did, for opera thrives on the grand gesture which is less congenial to painting. The imperial composer had only one rival, Lesueur, Berlioz's teacher and the first of the "monumental" composers using a very large orchestra. Lesueur was fond of the brasses, which he made blow often and loudly, something which then and now is greatly appreciated by the public. But Spontini used more trombones and trumpets and used them better. Wherever one looks in Wagner, not only in the early operas like *Rienzi* or *The Flying Dutchman*, but in *Tristan* or *Meistersinger*, there are many scenes that are pure Spontini.

Nor was Spontini merely a composer of glittering ceremonial music. A real dramatist, he could write with élan and passion, but he was more interested in massive scenes than in the characterization of individuals. People against people: this was his favorite subject (no wonder he loved Handel), and these crowds he manipulated with the tactical skill of a general, watched with awe by every contemporary composer. The trouble with concert performances of operas like Spontini's is that since the visual element, the spectacle, is carefully devised and integrated into the drama, very little of their nature and character is communicated. *La Vestale* (1807), which I heard in such a performance, was the first modern *tragédie lyrique* calling on the participation of a large orchestra. This orchestra, full and brilliant, was handled in a novel way, and it is here that it begins to assume the role in opera that leads to Wagner.

The Roman-French imperialist reached the height of his power and popularity when Napoleon's empire was at its zenith, but with the Restoration Spontini's star began to decline. He tried to convert the imperial manner to the more sedate Bourbon taste, but it was not his real nature. The public was no longer the same either, and since this proud and uncompromising artist, rich in honors and earthly goods, was not an opportunist, he was ready to retire to a musical St. Helena. Then a curious thing happened. Frederick William III, King of Prussia, a bitter enemy of Napoleon and his French, fell in love with the military pomp of Spontini's music and invited the composer to be the music czar of Berlin. The Roman did not understand a word of German, but he understood German music: his favorites were Haydn, Mozart, Beethoven—and Bach! It must be remembered that the time was 1820, and it is very characteristic of the man that he fully recognized Beethoven's greatness at such an early date. While Weber, the German musician, who was Spontini's junior by a dozen years, rejected Beethoven's Seventh Symphony, this peasant-born aristocrat, who knew what power meant, performed it at his own benefit concert in 1824. He was also renowned for his fine performances of *Don Giovanni*, which he was the first to introduce in Paris.

At first the Spontini craze in Germany knew no bounds. After Prussia chased the marshals of France beyond the borders, after Napoleon was exiled, the erstwhile musical field marshal of the Emperor ruled Prussia. For over twenty years he reigned from the Berlin opera house as an absolute dictator, but gradually he alienated too many people with his boundless arrogance, until finally he had to retire. In 1841, during a performance of his beloved *Don Giovanni*, the Berlin public forced him to leave the conductor's stand, never to return. In 1844 he once more appeared as conductor of his famous opera, *La Vestale*, in the fine opera house in Dresden, the memorable performance having been prepared for the distinguished guest by the resident conductor, Richard Wagner. After this, Spontini disappeared from the musical scene, retiring to his birthplace. There he passed his declining years, infirm but always accessible to people in need. The hard-bitten autocrat was at heart a very charitable man who left his considerable fortune to the poor, a rather un-Wagnerian gesture.

Aside from this, the two musicians had many things in common. Like Wagner, Spontini was a thorough student of the historical and national background of the subjects of his operas; like the German, he was a great and demanding conductor; and like the future ruler of German opera he was endlessly involved in debates, issuing manifestoes and pamphlets at the slightest provocation. When the news of his death reached Berlin, where he was so much admired, feared, and hated, the Prussians were in no mood to remember the musical emissary of Napoleon I; another Napoleon was beginning to rise. The great General Music Director's passing went unnoticed. One wonders how Wagner, who always retained a certain admiration for Spontini, felt about it.

There are few great musicians—for a great musician he was —in the history of music so difficult to judge as Meyerbeer. A man highly gifted, superbly trained, with sovereign command of the craft of musical composition, he had a remarkable theatrical sense, fine and delicate lyric invention, a bold and colorful art of orchestration (to which Berlioz was indebted), and he was immensely successful—yet history was cruel to him, and the cruelty started with his contemporaries. Weber, who was one of his fellow students, denounced him, as did Marschner and later Wagner, but perhaps the most unkind words came from gentle Schumann. It is difficult to unravel the reasons behind this hatred. Anti-Semitism was one of them, though originally it was not noticeable; Mendelssohn was a contemporary, and he was universally loved and admired, particularly by Schumann. The anti-Semitic antipathy started later, with Wagner, and then blossomed in recent German musical histories. German national pride was another factor in the hatred of this musician who was German in harmony,

Italian in melody, and French in rhythm. Weber and Schumann, both of whom dreamed of a German national opera, resented Meyerbeer's international leanings. The romantic era was nationalistic; after the Napoleonic wars composers could no longer switch from one national style and language to another without being considered artistic traitors or worse. Weber conveyed this quite frankly and indignantly to Meyerbeer, berating him for thus misusing his great talents, and many other German composers and critics objected to Meyerbeer's various "conversions" from a German composer to an Italian, then to a French, and back again to a German. But the same accusations could be—but never are—levelled against Hasse, or Christian Bach, or Gluck, or Handel, none of whom ever wrote a German opera and all of whom triumphed in Italy, or France, or England.

Then there was the accusation of the love of Mammon, never suggested in the case of Wagner or Strauss but instantly hinted at in Meyerbeer's case, though he was wealthy, in no need of money, and always scrupulously honest in such matters. His detractors mention with horror his "rapacity" for establishing the system of royalty payments to composers, forgetting that it helped every German composer, although he himself did not need the income. Nor could the dislike have been caused by aloofness or professional jealousy; Meyerbeer, by nature a friendly and generous man, went out of his way to help less fortunate musicians, the young Wagner being one of them, something the latter, once his own star rose, conveniently forgot. While General Director of Music in Berlin, occupying the post vacated by Spontini, Meyerbeer did everything in his power to improve the lot of the musicians under his care; the composers were awarded larger commission fees; German composers, including Wagner, were given a good share in the repertory; and the best available German conductors were engaged. The great successes in Paris were real enough, but once more history was unkind and inaccurate about Meyerbeer's doings and dealings and far too kind to the members of the cabal working against the much-abused composer.

Even to a man as famous and successful as Meyerbeer, the

road from the composition to the production of an opera was fraught with the most exasperating skulduggery and wire-pulling. A successful opera in Paris meant a fortune to the theater, the composer, and the publisher, and since the stakes were high the methods were not unlike those employed in expensive Broadway productions: "angels" got into the game intent on making their artistic altruism pay. Meyerbeer was already a celebrated opera composer when the premiere of *Les Huguenots* took place in 1836. One would think that a composer of his reputation would have had easy sailing, yet he had to overcome formidable obstacles before the opera could be produced. The success of the work was unparalleled, and the money poured into the pockets of all concerned. Now we come to some edifying details of operatic life that exceed by far anything a present-day composer may encounter.

This great success was too much for some fellow composers, as it was to publishers and to competitors of all sorts; it had to be whittled down, and they did everything within their power, which was considerable, to do so. Efforts were even made to reach the singers so that they would "throw" the opera. (This sort of thing was not unknown in French operatic history. During the Gluck-Piccinni "war" the prima donna who sang Iphigénie in Piccinni's opera was so inebriated that the wags called the fine but ill-fated opera *Iphigénie en Champagne*.) The influential publishers, the brothers Escudier, having been unable to secure the publishing rights to the opera, left no stone unturned to hurt it, and a good deal of money found its way to the press, not difficult to influence in those days. But the press was nevertheless remarkably unanimous in praising *Les Huguenots*. Even Berlioz was laudatory; Balzac and George Sand wrote veritable hymns of praise; and nothing could thwart the work's overwhelming success. Meyerbeer was exceedingly sensitive about criticism, and it was rumored that he spent large sums to keep the Paris critics in line. Not the slightest evidence could be uncovered by a number of conscientious researchers to substantiate this charge or any other charge of unethical dealings.

Now the poet Heine appears on the scene. Living in circumstances of dire poverty in Paris, he wanted a slice of this operatic prosperity, aiming for a position which today we would call that of Meyerbeer's press agent. Heine, who became next to Goethe the most popular poet with song composers, knew little about music and cared even less, which is assuredly a curious fact since his influence became decisive in the lifework of such major composers as Schumann. There are more than 250 different settings of his *Du bist wie eine Blume* alone, and his *Die Loreley* has become perhaps the most beloved German "folksong." All this by virtue of the exquisitely musical quality of his lyric poetry; yet he did not appreciate music, and the sole reason for his interest in the opera world was hoped-for gains.

So Heine wrote an elaborate review of *Les Huguenots* for an important German paper, enthusiastically describing the premiere; he knew that Meyerbeer, who had always retained a fondness for his German homeland, would be pleased by the appearance of a favorable review there. The poet and the composer became fast friends, but Heine's unsavory money operations—surprisingly similar to Wagner's—eventually led to a complete break between them. The review was fine, indeed, the only hitch being that Heine never saw that premiere. True enough, the piece was so written that it would be difficult to pin him down to any misstatement, but the evidence is incontrovertible: the poet saw the opera for the first time after he wrote the review. Heine had to pay for this partisanship, for when the Schumann circle raked Meyerbeer over the coals in their periodical, Heine was also liberally singed.

The warring publishers, Escudier and Schlesinger, each supported an influential musical journal; the former's *France Musicale* plugging Italian interests, while the latter's *Gazette Musicale* was devoted to German music in general and Meyerbeer in particular. The competition was bitter, and neither fair nor foul means were neglected. Here again Heine's role was less than edifying. Escudier used the poet to try to woo Meyerbeer away from Schlesinger, but when that proved to be impossible, the publisher assigned him the task of promoting the cause of a possible rival. In 1847 Heine was writing for the same German paper he once used to ingratiate himself with Meyerbeer, only this time he sang the praises of the young and still-unknown Verdi. It was a sordid game. None of these people championed Verdi because of remarkable perception into the young Italian's future greatness—it was all a cold business gamble. Throughout these moves and countermoves the only one who showed dignity and integrity was Meyerbeer.

Whatever the facts of Meyerbeer's life and activity, in the end we must judge the creative artist, and here posterity, while perhaps harsh, was not unjustly critical. Meyerbeer's fine native musicality, his fresh invention, and his zest for the theater served him well, but underneath there were always serious doubts. A lack of real artistic integrity and conviction, an uncertainty about the limits of his talents, and other deeper conflicts constantly troubled him. And there was an obsession— the fear that he would not succeed, or not finish his task triumphantly. Meyerbeer desperately wanted to be successful, admired, and loved, and this led him consciously to seek overwhelming effects, to seize every chance for the theatrically sensational that would please his public. Every one of his operas was subjected to years of patching and polishing until every possible theatrical trick was spliced into the proper spot, while in the process the finest lyric inventions were sacrificed. We could apply to him what Balzac said about Stendhal: "I believe he writes his works twice. On the first occasion he writes them sensibly, on the second he decks them with a nice neologue style." Forgetting Wagner's personal malice, it is difficult not to agree with the gravamen of his indictment that Meyerbeer used "effects without cause," that he "emphasized the unimportant" in the drama. Here is one, we might say, who but for the grace of God could have been a great composer but today is held up as one of the great failures in musical history. Perhaps so, but we must also reckon with his pervasive influence, which reached every corner of the musical world, not excluding Wagner and Verdi; and since a century of operatic history was determined by this influence, we had better take a closer look at the events that took place in Paris.

Settled in the French capital, Meyerbeer's first collaboration with librettist Eugène Scribe, *Robert le diable* (1831), resulted in a success that reverberated all over Europe, enthroning for an undisputed reign of a hundred years the species started by Spontini, Auber, and Rossini—the spectacular Romantic grand opera. The auspiciously-begun Meyerbeer-Scribe partnership turned into a veritable institution as the recipe worked unfailingly: *Les Huguenots; Le Prophète; L'Africaine.* The public admired the noble religious themes, the strong contrasts of black and white which conveyed the massiveness of the contending forces, and greatly rejoiced in the spectacular scenes—as it still does in such pieces as the second-act finale in *Aïda,* which is unthinkable without Meyerbeer's precepts and techniques. It was one of those rare times in musical history when opera became a box office attraction and running an opera house a profitable undertaking. At this juncture, however, we must consider the contribution of Meyerbeer's librettist, Scribe, to the establishment and continued success of grand opera (which, I must remind the reader, is not a generic term applicable to all opera but a specific designation referring to the type that had its inception during the aftermath of the Revolution, receiving its constitution and bylaws from the celebrated pair under discussion). And Scribe's influence was just as lasting and important as Meyerbeer's, for not only did the spectacular grand opera of the second half of the century derive its forms and patterns from him, but even Donizetti's buffa, *L'Elisir d'amore,* with a libretto by the able Felice Romani, goes back to a play by Scribe.

The poet and the novelist, when faced with incomprehension or rejection by their contemporaries, can at least hope that posterity will distinguish between artisan and artist. The dramatist is in a different position—better or worse according to our caprice—for he must be an artisan even when he is an artist. His lack of professional theatrical routine is judged by posterity even more harshly than by his own age. On the other hand, a solid scaffolding will support his play long after its soul has departed and its flesh has rotted. If playwriting were not a profession requiring a great deal of technical savoir-faire,

Eugène Scribe could never have made his fabulous career, which also significantly affected the history of opera. He lived from 1791 to 1861 and by his twenty-fourth year was lord and master of the French stage. Hated by poets and critics, as was his musical partner by other composers, his popularity, like Meyerbeer's, was unprecedented; as a librettist he was sought after by every composer. Only Metastasio's popularity in the preceding century is comparable to Scribe's. Today we wonder what made for this boundless esteem and popularity. Character delineation was not his forte; his dramatic figures are capable only of being manipulated like marionettes at the end of a string. This "string," *la ficelle*, has become legendary, because Scribe could pull it with marvelous virtuosity. No matter how impossible the premises from which a scene starts, it ends with a telling point; no matter how tenuous the little, scattered motives, in the end they give the impression of thoughtful preparation for the great scene. And here we are: *préparation* and *scène à faire*, the two cardinal rules of Scribe's theatrical rubric, are also the main pillars of grand opera. Incidentally, since Scribe started out with vaudevilles, it was quite natural for him to proceed to opera. *Vaudeville* is a specifically French term, not to be confused with its modern English usage. It designated light, satirical chansons that were inserted into spoken plays, whence the name became applied to the entire play. The vaudeville was a predecessor of the opéra comique but also existed concurrently with it, and in the nineteenth century Scribe gave it a new, more elaborate form called *comédie à vaudeville*.) When Scribe, who did not have one atom of poetry in him, tries to suggest the infinity of destiny and aspirations, he suggests only the void; nevertheless, he developed a theatrical technique that corresponded admirably to the requirements of the age and suited the taste of the bourgeoisie that made up the theater and opera audiences. What he represented was not so much the bourgeois reaction to the excesses of Romanticism as the horror the petit-bourgeois spirit felt towards anything that violated its code of the sanctity of status, career, money, and family ethics. At most they would allow the successful dramatist such nobility as all of us can muster—as spectators, that is, in a situation where our own pocket is not involved. In France, where literary tradition is more deeply rooted than anywhere else, and where everyone builds on what his predecessor has created, everything turns into tradition and pattern. Since Scribe maintained a drama and libretto factory where a bevy of hired literary hands worked out the plots sketched by the master, not unlike draftsmen in an architect's office, the technique was well known. The plays of Hugo, Meilhac, Halévy, Dumas, Sardou, and most of the others owe their existence to the good application of the techniques created by Scribe; consequently they lent themselves readily to the particular kind of opera we call "grand." There were two possibilities of further development: either the intensification of the melodrama in the direction of Naturalism (Sardou's *Tosca*), or the apotheosizing of bourgeois ideals (Dumas's *La Dame aux camélias*, i.e., *La Traviata*). Thus arose a theatrical movement known as the "common-sense school," or *théâtre utile*. It pointed out ugly things to be avoided, and its characters were models of virtue and sound common sense. Above all, it tackled the vexing problem of the battle of the sexes with fine and high-minded bourgeois sensibility. In the preface to *La Dame aux camélias* Dumas maintains that love can be regulated and made perfect. In effect, it was held that every decent girl loves, or will learn to love, the first man who happens to ask her hand in marriage. The disappointments of married women are but to be expected. Eventually they discover that their husbands, whom before marriage they believed to be paragons of virtue, are far from it. Well, too bad; a good woman has absolutely no right to look elsewhere. Moreover, she is incapable of it. If, however, the impossible does take place, the husband has the right to avenge the social order and kill the erring wife. The marriage bond must be held sacred—by women—and the obnoxious element removed from society.

Nevertheless, the seamy side of life cannot altogether be ignored, and there are two grave problems to be dealt with fearlessly: the fallen virgin and the illegitimate child. The process is mandatory: rehabilitation and legalization, both of which are tricky. There was an entire school that advocated what it called *refaire la virginité,* a process difficult to translate and even more difficult to achieve. Others, led by Dumas, realizing the magnitude of the task, and seeing that such misadventures do happen in the best of families, proposed a much more practical and noble solution—withdrawal from society and renunciation. Marguérite-Violetta's self-sacrifice became the model for all such plays. Playwrights developed illegitimate children into characters of such distinction that their fathers usually rushed out of discreet retirement to adopt them with great solemnity and breast-beating just before their impending marriages were threatened by the discovery of their unenviable status. These plays are seldom the symbols of a fate; they are merely illustrations of a moral. Their form and content is theatrical technique, in which they resemble many a modern French, English, and American play; things happen comfortably and conveniently, and the comings and goings of the dramatis personae have little intellectual and spiritual justification.

Now the librettist steps into this situation with special instructions to provide opportunities for the composer to deploy his music. He must make room for secondary characters, such as the inevitable confidant, companion, prying servant, or faithful lieutenant; splice in the ballet and the chorus at appropriate places; and provide the necessary solos and ensembles. All this was done with almost mathematical precision according to a well-established system. The wonder of it is that masterpieces could be composed upon such miserable concoctions. But then this is the miracle of music. Perhaps Donizetti's statement that an opera libretto does not have to make sense is a little exaggerated, but in many instances he was not far from the truth.

Curiously enough, the great and lasting operas based on this literary school were composed by Italians, not Frenchmen, perhaps because they shared Donizetti's views, which were not really as absurd and anti-intellectual as they sound when taken out of context. The Italian opera composer wanted positive dramatic personalities and strong scenes upon which he could drape positive and strong music; he was not unduly inconvenienced by a lack of logic, causality, and good continuity. Not so the Frenchman. He wanted a good story, good continuity, and logic, but after the heroic days of the Meyerbeerian grand opera he could not muster strength. In Halévy's *La Juive* the heroine is boiled alive in a cauldron; that sort of thing called for strong nerves and was going out of fashion anyway, but the new bourgeois plays offered a new theme, an eternal theme that was the antithesis of the enervating heroics in the great religious dramas like *Le Prophète* or *Les Huguenots*. The days when Parsifal and Siegfried became aware that man is only half of a pair did not come so slowly to the French. Instead of waiting they started immediately with their novel idea, and they discovered a form of it in the eighteenth century which they found so universally true and enduring that they based their new opera on it. This eighteenth-century woman loved much and all the time; she called this "to follow nature nobly." Being a disciple of Rousseau, and like him readily using the word "nature," this wonderful creature failed to define the meaning of the term with any precision; she simply designated by it something which in effect was agreeable to her. The eternal Manon urged other young women of all stations to follow nature, "nobly," if possible, but at any rate to follow it. Now in the nineteenth century the common-sense school, aiming at boudoirism without a blot, made this adorable coquette a woman of moral strength; even Manon herself atones for her early mistakes in moving words and music. The Germans may have had their Wagner, the Italians their Verdi, but the French were not idle and produced a master of their own who dominated their music drama as did those two giants their respective worlds of opera.

In the preface to one of his musical essays, Romain Rolland says meditatively that if a Frenchman should draw the curtain from the innermost recess of his heart he would find there the portrait of Jules Massenet. It is a very penetrating remark by a great connoisseur of French music. Massenet was an able and cultivated musician, a fastidious operatic craftsman, but what endeared him to his compatriots was his facile, perfumed melody that miraculously seems to satisfy all manner of French listener from *midinette* to *maître*. This melody teeters on the dividing fence between salon music and romantic song, and though strictly a hothouse product, it is smooth, caressing, and well designed. Technical ingenuities brush surface curiosities as Massenet always seems to be saying, "You see how well I know this stuff," but there is no arrogance in this attitude—rather, a genuine satisfaction in the congenial accomplishment. Massenet earned more honors than could be garnered by all other latter-day French musicians put together. Why, he even became president of the French Academy! There was ample justification for those honors; this musical idol of the French was—and is—ever-present even in recent music. The other day I heard the unmistakable echoes of Massenet in Poulenc's *Les Mamelles de Tirésias*, and I am ready to wager that *Werther* lurks behind every tone row of the French dodecaphonists. And those operas! True, Massenet knew only one type of heroine, the beautiful repentant sinner, but then he presented her in many reincarnations. Manon, Thaïs, Hérodiade, Sapho, Cléopatre, Ariane—and all the others. It is perhaps a little disconcerting to discover that when the script calls for Mary Magdalen, or even the Blessed Virgin, we find exactly the same lavender-scented lovelies, but after all, melody is stronger than history.

This, then, is the so-called French lyric opera, the smooth and sentimental sets of romances of Gounod and Massenet, in which fluency of elegant expression was the main concern. The *romance* or *mélodie* just mentioned was the core of this lyric opera. The French equivalent of the German romantic song, these romances were sentimental and shallow salon pieces of uncertain ancestry. Next to Massenet, Gounod was the most notable representative of the style and the species. While most of his operas are no longer heard—and his church music, which is still heard, fills one with serious doubts about salvation—*Faust* is still very popular the world over, and rightfully so. It has many sweet *mélodies*, but also some fine ensembles, notably the quartet in the garden scene and the trio in the last act, and Gounod's musical prosody and general operatic technique are impeccable. What is missing is real dramatic force, but then we are doing an injustice to the Frenchman if we try to connect his *Faust* with Goethe, a trap almost every German critic falls into. Gounod did not set to music the great philosophical drama—only its love story—and what he created was altogether within the French concept of sentimental opera without the slightest metaphysical connotations. *Faust* has real opera music of the French romantic variety, especially the song about the King of Thule, the drinking songs, the soldiers' chorus, and Mephisto's great scenes. I might add that whatever we may think about this undramatic, lightweight, genteel, and elegant music, the best of it has a surprising staying power. Take, for instance, Gounod's *Romeo and Juliet;* it is the only one of the half a hundred operas composed on the subject that is still alive.

These French composers avoided real passion as the heroic grand opera was watered down to flaccidity. This is understandable. Middle-class virtues, common sense, and sobriety often characterize even the greatest French artists and are often paraded in their art. "The Italians," said Manet, "do bore one after a time with their allegories, their *Jerusalem Delivered,* their *Orlando furioso,* and all that rubbish." French opera, as exemplified by Massenet, wanted to present women with a reasonably flexible code of ethics. But there was one woman among these anemic creatures of conventional French opera who was totally unfettered by any code. Carmen is not a slut; she may be a come-hither hellion, but she has cunning and courage. A new Carmen is like a new Ophelia, eternally fascinating, for the role is inexhaustible in meaning and nuance, and a great artist can make us wonder whether we have ever before known this fateful gypsy. The role also eternally fascinates singers, and although it really fits a mezzo best, even high sopranos and low contraltos try their vocal cords at it. Their number would fill Leporello's famous catalogue: hopeful beginners and seasoned veterans, short plump sorceresses and tall willowy *femmes fatales,* blondes with dark wigs and brunettes with their own tresses, girls who never forget that singing must always be musical, and others (unfortunately quite a few) who believe that crooning below pitch excites the male animal.

Carmen is a difficult assignment for the critic, who is at a loss to convey the unashamed psychological truth of this opera and its lyric beauty, especially since at times one excludes the other. Bizet's objective was to reveal the *bétise humaine* in its infinite and terrible variety. Because of this, some of the delicacy and hidden truth of *Carmen* may be missed, but what no listener can fail to enjoy is the great charm of the musical invention. Even so Germanic a composer as Brahms was irresistibly attracted to it, while Nietzsche's praise of its southern passion is positively dithyrambic. *Carmen* is a prime example of what music can do to a libretto. Prosper Mérimée, from whose novel the libretto was derived, though a comrade in arms of the romantics, cannot be counted in their ranks; in fact, he belonged to no school at all. He was a romantic in that he loved exotic subjects and bloody, passionate stories, but his depictions of Spanish dramas of jealousy, Corsican vendettas, and so forth, while colorful and extremely well-written, are cold, impersonal, and lacking in lyricism. Mérimée reached back from the age of Romanticism to the classics while at the same time thrusting forward to the naturalists, but his style is classic in its crisp precision. Even in its expert dramatic reworking by Meilhac and Halévy, the opera is not so much the raw verismo that appeared toward the end of the century as the incursion into the lyric stage of the psychological realism of the French novel, the same quality that carried Stendhal and Balzac to fame. The dosage of rawness and delicately pointed art work in *Carmen* is exact and psychologically perfect. Carmen always reacts to the state of mind and character of the other protagonists. Don José is a simple soldier caught in a passion beyond his comprehension, and we witness the gradual disintegration of what was once a man of character. Carmen watches the vacillating, demoralized man and moves in for the kill at the right moment and with the right accents. The healthy brutality of Escamillo provokes entirely different reactions, for the very earthiness of the bullfighter is a calculated contrast to the character of Don José. Micaela's role is condemned by some critics as being too sentimental, but what a perfect foil it is to the fiery heroine. What could be more disturbing in a drama of wild passion than the imaginative interjection of wide-eyed innocence?

This opera is a red-hot music drama that, from the very first notes of the overture—which starts out with the frenzy of a carnival—does not have a limp moment, drawing relentlessly to its denouement. Such intense, hearty, credulous love of straightforward passion ending in murder is rare in the annals of opera, and the conductor must tear into this music, stoke the fires, though keeping an eye on the pressure gauges. Yet at the same time *Carmen* unites piquant cabaret music and popular Spanish dance rhythms with the highest art in a marvelous organic whole. The popular element is present everywhere but is always informed with tasteful, original, and attractive refinements that make the work one of the most sparkling scores ever conceived. The harmonies are astringent, the orchestra dazzling, and the tunes delectable. They are very French, the tunes, teetering, as I have said, on café music, but always maintaining their equilibrium by veritable strokes of genius. Bizet's mastery never falters; it satisfies the most exacting connoisseur as well as anyone who has a feeling for music. But this charm must not be allowed to blind us to the underlying seriousness of the work, for the characters of the drama are presented with great sureness and sympathy. It is this insight that is the special virtue of Bizet's opera.

This sort of thing was unheard of in French opera, and the directors of the Opéra Comique were fearful that *Carmen* would alienate some of the chief supporters of their theater, the marriage brokers, who conducted their business in the boxes. One does not entertain prospective couples with "murder and immorality." *Carmen* was indeed considered both indelicate in its subject and "Wagnerian," that is, too elaborately worked and orchestrated, in its music. Alas, Bizet was one of those artists who has died to live. If he has few literal disciples he has had many whom we may consider his spiritual progeny. *Carmen*—like *Pelléas*—is an opera *sui generis*. Its sophisticated yet powerful music, its etched, engraved, and enameled orchestration fill the most blasé, biased, and critical musician with joy. Yet it is also one of the most popular operas the world over—surely a unique case.

It was nothing less than a crime to turn *Carmen* into a grand opera by setting to music the spoken dialogues. The recitatives which Guiraud composed, and which we unfortunately must endure when the work is presented outside the French-speaking world, not only hurt the play but disrupt the fine dramatic balance of Bizet's music, which does not permit dilution by nondescript invention. The spoken dialogue is an essential element in the opéra comique, even if *Carmen* is like no other opéra comique.

Desiring to set to music Maurice Maeterlinck's *Pelléas et Mélisande*, Puccini requested permission from the Belgian poet to turn the play into a libretto, but he was told that the rights had already been granted—reluctantly—to Claude Debussy. One wonders what would have happened to this impersonal tragedy at the hands of one of the most subjective music dramatists? Maeterlinck's figures are noble and refined; they have all the means of life in their possession, yet they cannot live. They are afraid of touching one another, afraid of the sun and of the wind.

Maeterlinck carried onto the stage the dark mysticism of symbolism, its secret fears and unknown anxieties—his stage is almost always in semi-darkness. The symbolism was the rebellion of the spirit against the despotism of reality. Even when he depicts reality, the playwright is not inspired by it; his own work is more important, for it is the representation that matters—the words, the colors. One might almost say that the subject itself is determined by the requirements of style and color.

In all his plays Maeterlinck expressed a mystic concept of life according to which men's fates are directed by a secret power, the Unknown. This dramatic poet's world is the children's nursery into which the noise of the external world does not penetrate. It is in this sheltered atmosphere that his people live. They grope about but do not know; only a momentous turn of events can arouse them. Yet the soft resonance of human passion attracts the listener, for it reminds him of his own childhood, when the unreal was present and he constantly faced the Unknown. Maeterlinck's style is highly artificial, not unlike those modern plate glass windows that show no reflection and no shadow and suggest that there is nothing between the spectator and the goods in the store window. One can see the drama, but an exquisite unreality prevails, often enhanced by a decor that adds a mist of unreason. Even his love and death dramas, like *Pelléas et Mélisande* or *La Mort de Tintagiles*, contain unholy caves, doors that do not open or cannot be closed, swans, pigeons, and other requisites of the fairy world. Essentially, Maeterlinck's play negates the drama because his men are bereft of will, they are helpless, and their expressions are a form of resignation that is purely lyrical, favoring the soliloquy. This was, of course, what attracted both Puccini and Debussy to Maeterlinck. But Puccini would have had great difficulty with these lovers who meet and are separated by external circumstances so strong that no attempt is made to oppose them. They are being broken and ground up; only their feelings remain, and Maeterlinck analyzes neither the circumstances nor the characters. This is a profound turning away from Naturalism, because Maeterlinck's men are not really men, only possibilities for human revelation; they have no bodies, only feelings and thoughts, or, more precisely, they have bodies only to the extent that is absolutely necessary for the expression of their feelings. Maeterlinck himself calls them marionettes, and indeed they are extracts, symbols whose individual characters are not developed beyond the minimal requirements of the dramatic situation. Yet they are not the rigid figures that marionettes actuated by strings usually are; they vibrate, are nervously yet airily flexible, and they offer a constant if quiet and slow transition. But determinism so completely dominates everything in *Pelléas* that the tragic is almost entirely lyrical in nature, and this lyricism merely accompanies the drama. While neither Maeterlinck nor Debussy could create genuine poetic drama, their work is full of great beauty, the essence of this beauty being the blending of the psychological, lyrical, pictorial, and musical elements into individual scenes. It is here, in these scenic realizations, when the constant vibrations are caught in a decisive moment, that we see the kinship with pictorial Impressionism. When Pelléas and Mélisande meet for the last time, knowing that they are doomed, yet happy that this is the end, when Golaud stands before them with drawn sword and they spend with kisses what little life is left to them, we are spellbound. The situation is simple and believable, and yet it grows beyond the simple and the believable, becoming a symbol of the feelings which dominate it. The lovers' kisses grow into the symbol of all human happiness behind which hides the naked sword of retribution.

It is this mysterious, fragile, and muted mood that Debussy captured with unparalleled sensitivity in creating his pale, sickly, but beautiful flower of a decadent world. One could not find a more sensitive awareness in any musician of his time; he is subtle and he sees everything, though this subtlety does not mean that for him small events have large significance. He is quiet, sad, and emotionally tired, like his figures who vacillate between pity, desire, and dread. Unlike the great opera composers he refuses to interfere with what has been decreed. The concreteness of matter has been overcome by Debussy; everything becomes independent of matter because beauty transfigures and ennobles everything in its path. In Impressionism, beauty is not localized, nor does ugliness exist, for in this art everything becomes beautiful if properly viewed and heard. "I have never seen an ugly thing in my life," said Constable, one of the great ancestors of Impressionist painting. Impressionism was really a paradoxical movement both in painting and in music, requiring a discipline of imprecision to render exactitude.

But as we cast a critical eye on the score of *Pelléas et Mélisande* we discover that the musical substance of this opera is slight; sometimes flickering, sometimes dimmed almost to extinction, yet never dying completely, it asserts itself to any extent only in the instrumental preludes and interludes. At times Debussy seems to strike a pose, repeating without reason a pleasing, colorful harmonic turn, and he cannot forego playing with color patches, but all this suits him well. There are passages where the colors are not real, where atavistic medieval musical procedures gain magic light, and these passages are no less attractive. It is the orchestra that really creates the moods and carries whatever musical substance there is—with the aid of leitmotifs! Thus Debussy's vaunted anti-Wagnerism was subverted, and his music evidenced, if in an altogether different way, exactly what the French composer had wanted to avoid. His music is Impressionistic because it is dictated not by the magnificent symphonic planning of Wagner but by the feelings of the moment. His pictures are not designed but are made of torn and tangled lines. The composition is sketchy; it touches everything lightly, but it only floats past things; it is lyric, not dramatic.

This is indeed a strange musical language: expression hides behind the words, requiring constant alertness to the niceties of inflection and cadence. The orchestral part may follow its own rhythms, but the vocal line is purely word-begotten; the music almost completely abdicates its rights and privileges since the vocal lines have little or no musical substance. They follow Maeterlinck's words with absolute fidelity; that is, the notes merely second the rise and fall of the verbal cadence. It is held that Symbolism goes beyond Impressionism in trying to convey things that cannot be expressed in words, which of course brings it very close to music, and indeed the musical qualities in this French poetry are pronounced. But the Parnassiens worshipped the word, and the Symbolists could not shake it off either, even though Maeterlinck tells us that no sooner do we have something worthwhile to say than we are compelled to keep silent. In their vocal music the French always prized impeccable verbal rhythm, but nowhere was this preference carried out more consistently and with more complete abandon than in *Pelléas et Mélisande*. I remember an occasion when an excellent young American Pelléas permitted a heroic tinge in his baritone voice: the equilibrium was immediately disturbed because the scales were tipped in favor of a masculine musicality which robbed the words of their supremacy.

In fashioning a unity from the autonomous elements of this opera, the conductor is faced with a difficult task. He must catch the mimosa-like delicacy of the orchestral texture, the many fleeting pastel shades, the sudden illumination of a word or a gesture, because the unity of this work is not achieved by construction: it is the unity of a bouquet of flowers. *Pelléas* is not the result of the theme of the drama but the way the composer absorbed it and made it into an opera. We do not feel here the effective grouping and development of events, of a plot; the individual scenes simply coalesce into form, defying all analysis. Is it a fault that *Pelléas et Mélisande* is not a real opera? No, only a peculiarity. It was created by a composer to whom sensuous, hedonistic beauty is more important than the weight of utterances. Though esoteric, unreal, and highly stylized, this opera does catch the beauty of human relationship, and it is not less poised between immensities and eternities because its material limitation and power of expression are narrow.

Francis Poulenc was a very able musician, the epitome of the French composer who works with his brains and is convinced that wit, *esprit,* and a little ribaldry can take care of everything. In *Les Mamelles de Tirésias* Poulenc stakes his success on the Frenchman's proverbial ability to make a fine ragout from the most heterogeneous ingredients. The trouble is that in music there is no sauce to make the questionable elements palatable. Guillaume Apollinaire's libretto is a surrealist play. It goes beyond Expressionism, Futurism, and Dadaism, for while these have loosened the old restrictions upon form and expression, Surrealism permits really Freudian liberty in joining inorganic fragments of memories and thoughts in an association wholly free of logic or sentimental reason. A surrealist play is difficult enough, but how can automatic thoughts and memory reflexes be set to music? In truth, Poulenc's music is not schizophrenic, but neither is it opera, nor, I am afraid, music of any distinction; I find it banal and full of very ordinary clichés, though the vocal writing is very skillful.

If not taken seriously, the "opera" offers a modicum of rather low-grade entertainment, but it *is* taken seriously and even has a moral thesis. Whether, upon hearing it, the male population of France will perform its duty and raise the nation's birth rate is very much open to question. Or perhaps there is more to this loony symbolism? I would hate to speculate, though.

The picture changes altogether when we advance to Poulenc's last opera, *Les Dialogues des Carmélites,* composed on a libretto taken from the play of Georges Bernanos. The work was received with resounding success, and television brought it before vast American audiences.

Les Dialogues is based on one of the most powerful of affections, the religious, enhanced by the clash of the French Revolution with the established church. The setting and the topic virtually ensure success if the composer is at all able to provide good vocal texture to the protagonists, and Poulenc is a past master of that art. If we add to this the always effective use of Latin prayer sung by a choir, the sum total is considerable. Meyerbeer and Scribe realized that this sort of thing is a foolproof subject and, while much more delicate than *Les Huguenots* or *Le Prophète, Les Dialogues* is quite within the sphere of grand opera with a religious theme. And, its attractive nature notwithstanding, it is just as faulty both as religious drama and as opera.

Our duty is not to evaluate religious devotion, for we must judge a work of art. Once we pass into the domain of esthetics, entirely different criteria are needed, and the password of the most exalted sentiments will not be honored. There is only one artistic truth, that of imagination, and that truth may be in conflict with logic, religion, nature, and even life. Bernanos, the original author of the story made into the libretto, was an able and eminent man of letters, but large portions of the libretto in its present form are of the quality of a school drama, the kind an intelligent priest would write for performance in a Catholic girls' school. Its studied vagueness gives the work an odd flavor of impersonality, something that is in keeping with the spirit of the liturgy but not that of drama. The story is very simple. A young noblewoman, delicate and fragile, is unable to cope with the stern realities of life and becomes a nun. Her indecision haunts her even while she is leading the life of a religious, until in the final holocaust of the Revolution she finds through others the strength for martyrdom. This is a noble subject, but its realization is quite Meyerbeerian. Take as an example the final scene where the doomed nuns mount the scaffold, one after the other, singing the *Salve Regina*—"punctuated by the rumble of the guillotine," as the stage directions demands. This is perilously close to Grand Guignol. The device whereby the choral singing gradually fades out, as the execution of each nun diminishes the choral group until there is only one left, is too facile a theatrical trick and must be recognized as such in spite of the saintly character of the figures.

The libretto is wordy and abounds in homiletics which resist musical interpretation. The Mother Superior gives an address to her charges that is a little sermon on prayer as duty, whereupon one of the nuns exclaims: "My sisters, Her Reverence has explained to us clearly that our most important duty is to pray, let us obey." And once more the ineffable prayer is heard: "Ave Maria, gratia plena. . . ." Unfortunately, this is neither religion nor drama, it is once more the edifying school play. Even so, a true music drama could perhaps have been shaped from this libretto had Poulenc seized it with contemplative force, but he merely set it to music. This was done with great skill, with a remarkable ability to transform prose into musical declamation, but this faultless declamation remains prose and seldom rises to the level of dramatic musical poetry. The composer gives us effective, even moving, musical theater which, because of its universally revered subject, cannot fail and will perhaps be somewhat immune to criticism, but the transcendental ideas it intends to represent remain largely untouched. The nuns sing of holy things, of the glories of the spirit, but the pleasant and smoothly flowing music they sing is of the more secure world of earthly existence. This elegant and artistic music is not fired by sufficient genius to do justice to the subject; it owes more to the inspiration of Thespis than of Christ. By the middle of the first act the high vocal sound of women's voices unrelieved by men's becomes monotonous. The few perfunctory sentences sung by the Doctor upon his arrival only heighten the sensation. The heroine's father and brother, the principal male roles, are also vaguely drawn.

The theme of death and the fear of death has a special meaning for our time and must often have come close to Bernanos, who was active in the French Resistance, as was Father Raymond Brickbarger, who wrote the scenario. *Les Dialogues des Carmélites* is a slight work compared with this author's novels, but there is present an echo of his constant theological theme in the strong suggestion that the Prioress by her hard and unheroic death won for Blanche the courage to face her martyrdom with ease. The almost insurmountable difficulty faced by the composer with such a libretto is that the great mysteries of Catholic world outlook oppose nature and naturalism, as its metaphysical collectivism rejects the kind of subjectivism that is the animating force of the music drama. To rise to this region and to this task a composer must be the rare person in whom the wholeness of culture lives. This oneness with faith and culture has been achieved in countless religious works, but very seldom in opera, for the simple reason that liturgy when used as an accessory to the drama usually fails to sound convincing. The glorious hymns and other church songs that appear in various operas make for very effective numbers, but mere numbers they usually remain. Poulenc's opera has a whole string of these songs, and the simplest device he uses is "let us pray," whereupon those present kneel down and sing *Ave verum corpus* or *Ave Maria*. This is an old and legitimate operatic device and does not differ in nature and function from a drinking song or a soldiers' chorus. And, of course, in setting such pieces the composer cannot deny his musical personality; that is, if he composes spontaneously and does not deliberately resort to archaism or borrowing. It is very seldom that such an authentically dramatic scene is composed as the halting *Ave Maria* Desdemona sings in Verdi's *Otello*.

Poulenc, whose sincerity is unquestioned, did not escape these pitfalls. The composer of *Les Mamelles de Tirésias* appears here in new garments, but underneath is the amiable and resourceful hedonist. He composes old-fashioned recitatives, accompanied and unaccompanied, and melodic turns that are as sweet-scented as anything in Massenet, though perhaps a little less securely designed. Thus, the Chevalier and Mother Marie sing a scene that suspiciously resembles—musically speaking—a Wertherian love duet. At times there is a ballad-like tone that is quite attractive, though this, too, can become a little incongruous. When comforting her daughters in jail, the Mother Superior sings a song that is quite a fetching romance. All this is always theatrically effective and smoothly melodious without offering positive melodies. In this respect Poulenc reminds one of Umberto Giordano.

Behind all this is the fact that Poulenc is still strongly rooted in Impressionism, and Impressionism is the most profane of musical styles. This music is free of all bonds; it utilizes the whole of the subjective world, its instrumental colors, its piquant harmonies often transcending the esthetic and becoming a sensual narcotic. It is quite significant that jazz received its modern ingredients as hand-me-downs from Impressionism. However, the more transcendental the drama the more difficult it is for the Impressionist to create human character—the atmosphere soaks up everything. Even in *Pelléas et Mélisande*, the solitary masterpiece of the impressionist musical theater, there are no distinct contours, only air, bewitching atmosphere. Everything that modern life and musical technique offer for the intensification of feeling seems to enrich the atmosphere only, to the detriment of dramatic strength and composition.

It must be admitted that both Bernanos and Poulenc failed to establish the compelling feeling which saves the autonomy of a tragic human being. Bernanos's lofty concept of death and martyrdom must be verbalized, and that is futile in opera;

moreover, the attempt easily becomes frivolous. *Dialogues* is not free of frivolity because it is often merely hedonistic, not unlike the delightfully fluent music of the Rococo, which also treats exalted subjects without being aware of superhuman divinations, incomprehensible secrets, and insoluble problems.

Twelve

RUSSIAN OPERA

HE OPERAGOER used to the amiably decorous pagans of Ethiopia, Egypt, Babylon, and Druidic England may be shocked when he first encounters the real barbarians of old Russia, the real miseries of old Poland, and a czar whose insanity is uncomfortably real. When he has witnessed in *Boris Godunov* the greatest music drama that has emerged from the East of Europe, a powerful, disjointed, awkward, and withal profoundly human work, he also learns that the Russian composer par excellence is neither Rimsky-Korsakov, nor Tchaikovsky, nor Stravinsky, but Modest Mussorgsky. Tchaikovsky, the best known of the Russians, was a professional, trained in the ways of the West; Mussorgsky was a largely self-taught musician who had his troubles with harmony and orchestration. Nevertheless, he was the Dostoevsky of music, the interpreter of the vast mystery that is Russia, of the souls of the czars, peasants, and children of Russia. Dostoevsky in his novels does not describe the czar's realm but conveys the history of the lower strata of the soul. He does not really penetrate to the feelings that lie below consciousness; he simply abandons conventional conversations and acts, the clichés of social life. Literary and other conventions do not exist for Dostoevsky; the impulses that interest him arise from the meeting of man and idea. It is for this reason that he is so fantastically cloudy and moving. Mussorgsky's attitude is astonishingly similar. He simply ignores the musico-dramatic conventions and pays little attention to the niceties of the composer's métier. What he sees he renders with extraordinary force and fidelity, but for the world he does not care a whit. For him the composer's domain is a strange and particular world in which the rules of logic are valid only in modified form.

The musical language in *Boris Godunov* is new and original; everything here is invention rather than elaboration, the visions of genius, some tender, some overwhelming. But the visions are often disconnected, not only because Mussorgsky did not possess full command of the composer's craft, but because he could not—and perhaps would not—shape an organic dramatic structure in the Western manner. What he created is magnificent and somewhat chaotic, as was his own much-tried Russian soul, rent by pity, childlike wonderment, and unspeakable agony. Though based on known historical facts (as treated by Pushkin), Mussorgsky's *Boris Godunov* offers not only dramatized historical events but the manifestations of the more confused and hidden layers of humanity lit by the fire of suffering. And the fire gives off not only light but warmth, too, warmth that comes from the composer's own experiences with suffering. It is a form of self-confession that neither beautifies nor omits the ugly things, yet it is far removed from the sentimentalism that reigned in opera contemporary with *Boris*. Indeed, Mussorgsky was a romantic, but he did not participate in the Romantic movement.

Russia, immense, legendary, and inscrutable, is a land made for romance. Its people live with the sense of boundless horizons. The language also has poetry in it, a wealth of words still close to the primitive life that created them, words always expressive and musical. Having been isolated from the West and not nourished by ancient and settled traditions, the Russians made contact with European art music very late as the history of music goes. Mussorgsky could look back on perhaps a century of Western-style musical life in Moscow and St. Petersburg. How could such a poorly informed and equipped musician summon the melodic élan, the dramatic pathos, and above all the art of characterization in music that has the force of revelation? Where could he have learned all this? Surely not from his musical colleagues, most of whom were in need of professional polish themselves. The only explanation is that Mussorgsky imbibed his strength from living among the peasants. The Russian people were his teachers; it was from them that he learned the purity of expression, the force, rhythm, and melody of Russian life. It was thus that the untutored and inexperienced composer, whose incomplete music has so often been completed, refinished, arranged, edited, and polished, became the greatest musician of genius Russia produced in the nineteenth century.

No one who has seen Repin's portrait of the forty-two-year-old Mussorgsky will ever forget it. It shows a pitiful alcoholic whose contorted, tragic face shows that he understood his imminent fate, whose eyes are looking straight at death. This is the composer who ended one of his utterly charming nursery songs with "Please good Lord, guard Aunt Katja, Aunt Natasha, Aunt Ljuba . . ."; and this is also the composer whose dying Czar Boris leaves you with a lump in your throat. How is one to comprehend these Russian poets, writers, and composers, all of whom look at us from Repin's picture of Mussorgsky? Their souls are filled with sympathy and compassion for the people and the oppressed; they are mystic, brooding, humiliated, and addicted to self-inflicted misery. They are full of noble intentions but are unable to act; they do not know what their destiny on earth should be, and often they do not even know what they live for. This is Hamletism, but a Russian Hamletism, for these artists could not reach a concept of life; they were eternally searching but could not organize the results of their search. The Slavophile school, of which Mussorgsky was the outstanding example, was seeking the types and categories of a national culture and at the same time idealizing the Russian past; they hated their tyrants and everything they stood for, yet they were irresistibly attracted to the symbols of tyranny that were the czars. The culture of the West they tried to avoid, not infrequently hating, fearing, and despising it. But they also condemned pure art and believed that art should represent only real life, demanding "truth" even from the musician. (The "Socialist Realism" of Soviet art obviously is a continuation, if a pitiful one, of this old Russian doctrine.) The creative artist fretted and got deeper and deeper into his desperate dilemma because he could not make up his mind whether to fight for social and political improvement or acquiesce to eternal despotism; he would drown his sorrow in drink and create in lucid moments. This dualism accompanies him everywhere. Such an artist would start his mature life as a guards officer or a high government official. Then, haunted by the sight of the poor muzhik's suffering, he would turn his back on the privileged classes and try to make a living as a writer or composer, which, in his Russia, meant privation and humiliation. But he also hated and despised the obsequious middle classes, the little gray people who enjoy life because they have neither problems nor concerns beyond a warm home and a good meal. The artist found life a burden.

Mussorgsky went through all these stages, but he was sincerely devoted to music; however, devotion could not make up for a lack of self-discipline. He loved the great scenes and composed them magnificently, but he failed to connect them well; his harmonic imagination was original and prophetic, yet he constantly made elementary mistakes; his orchestral palette was full of color, but he assigned to the instruments awkward tasks that they could not always execute. Being an autodidact he shows all the shortcomings that usually go with this process, and though his great gifts were genuine and elemental, aside from the songs he could not create works of absolute artistic merit. The execution of deeply affecting scenes and pictures is not only insecure but often deliberately so, because he was not interested in shaping and organizing his material according to traditional Western artistic canons: he wanted only to communicate, communicate the secrets of human nature as he felt them, instantly, and without reflection. He wrote directly on the souls of the people, rather than on paper. Yet he succeeded in showing with vivid and penetrating eloquence how a criminal idea is conceived in a man's mind, how the idea develops into deed, and what the man's state of mind is after he commits his crime. A figure like Boris simply crushes us. Here is a proud tyrant racked by superstition, remorse, and fear, who in turn is tender and hesitant, haughty and demented, but always moving and convincing. One might ask why Mussorgsky deals so severely with Boris. But Mussorgsky was not sentimental; like the Greeks he knew where the storm of tragedy rages, where both the guilty and the innocent are swept away. No less impressive is the composer's ability to convey the feeling of doom sensed by Fyodor. All the other characters are also well drawn, except that the women's roles are less incisively individual; they seem to be accessories to the drama. On the other hand, the chorus, ever-present in the opera, is virtually the chief protagonist next to Boris.

This great and fascinating music drama is so full of alleged "crudities" that we never hear it in its original form; it is generally believed that without professional assistance, i.e., refurbishing of the score, it could not be presented. Mussorgsky himself made two versions of *Boris Godunov;* after his death, Rimsky-Korsakov made a radical revision of Mussorgsky's second version, with many cuts as well as additions of his own, and what was left of the original he thoroughly reworked. Ten years later he undertook still another revision— the fourth—restoring the cuts but keeping his own additions. This fourth variant is the form in which *Boris* has been performed until recent times.

Transcription and reworking of original compositions by other, later hands is a very old practice. Bach himself nicely disfigured a Palestrina Mass, Mozart recreated Handel to his own specifications, Wagner gave Gluck a life, Strauss committed mayhem on both Gluck and Mozart, while Berlioz and Mahler retailored Weber. In more recent times Stravinsky did some favors for Gesualdo. Now in view of this sad list of adult artistic delinquency, why should the radical revision of *Boris Godunov* be acceptable? All the above-mentioned composers reworked unquestioned masterpieces that represent stylistic and technical perfection from every point of view. The musician was not born who can improve on Palestrina's polyphony, Handel's choral splendor, or Mozart's operatic skill. What the arrangers did was to "modernize" these works to make them sound as if they had been composed in their own day. This is something unknown in the other arts. Would anyone seriously consider painting a Dior gown on the Sistine Madonna, or putting Colleoni in an armored car instead of on his charger? But Mussorgsky, an original genius and powerful dramatist, was not an accomplished craftsman; he never mastered the intricacies of the composer's métier. Rimsky, the naval officer turned composer, and the most versatile musician among the Russian amateurs, was the first to declare that the original *Boris* was not seaworthy and that to make it so mere caulking would not be sufficient. Unfortunately, what he did altogether changed the physiognomy of the work; his smooth and elegant Western ways considerably diminished Mussorgsky's barbarously powerful impact. Still another version was made by Karol Rathaus, who limited himself to spot-removing without materially changing the original score. This was regarded as a half-measure, and a few years ago Shostakovich decided to attempt a sixth reworking. Now for the first time *Boris* was redone from stem to stern by a superior musician with a personality of his own. (The subsequent destruction of this personality by present-day Russian "aesthetics" does not concern us here.)

A musician with a pronounced individuality cannot touch anything without leaving his imprint on it, nor can he withstand the temptation to meddle with the material he is manipulating. Shostakovich did not simply correct harmonic progressions and improve the orchestration of the old opera, he too reached into the innards of the score, often changing part-writing, harmony, and other very personal elements. Yet in a way he was more successful than his predecessors, and the reason for this is not difficult to find. Mussorgsky was a far more advanced composer than Rimsky; therefore his work could not be modernized by a less venturesome musician without creating a feeling of stylistic incongruity. Mussorgsky's harmonic writing in particular was far in advance of his times and beyond Rimsky's comprehension—even Debussy found it inspiring. Furthermore, unlike Rimsky, Shostakovich did not round the sharp edges of Mussorgsky's rough blocks; he retained the often violent accents, clothing them in orchestral sounds that appear quite appropriate. Only the splendid coronation scene seems to be overdone. The brass band the modern composer put on the stage lends it a Spontinian touch that is out of keeping with the spirit of the work. The scene is so impressive that it can do without the stentorian trumpets that overshadow the chief protagonist, the chorus.

It is questionable, however, whether even Shostakovich made *Boris Godunov* more viable and powerful; once again the opera seems to have lost something more than awkwardness in the process of retouching. This music does not offer soaring beauties of the Italian kind; on the contrary, it bears the marks of great and unresolved struggles. One feels that the composer's ideas piled up behind a fence that has a small gate—they block the way to one another. This richness of ideas leads to occasional distortion of what is being said. Since, unlike any other category of music, opera does require certain compromises and accommodations, a modicum of editing by knowledgeable but also discreet and pious hands is not to be rejected. Actually, there is a scholarly version of the score, edited by Paul Lamm and published as part of the Soviet edition of Mussorgsky's collected works, but it is virtually unobtainable in the West. I suppose it will take as long if not longer to hear *Boris Godunov* in the original version as it will take to hear *The Barber of Seville* as Rossini intended it to be heard. The Rimsky edition is in the library of every major opera house, and the Russians make no effort to acquaint the world with the unexpurgated score—indeed, they do not use it themselves—so the world will have to wait for the millennium.

The music of *Boris Godunov* may be ungrammatical, its harmonic writing at times bizarre, its modulations occasionally inept, and its orchestration gauche, but *Boris* is also the greatest musico-dramatic achievement of Eastern Europe and demands respect rather than generous assistance. Pushkin's original drama is more polished, more poetic, but Mussorgsky's opera goes far beyond that, for it is not only a tragedy of conscience but a musical folk drama, the musical tragedy of the Russian people.

As we turn to another Russian opera, this time by a musician who was a professional to his fingertips—as a matter of fact, the only full-fledged master-composer in his land until the advent of Prokofiev and Stravinsky—we wonder whether the amateur Mussorgsky's work should not be left altogether unretouched. *Eugene Onegin* is not a good opera—it is too pretty to be a good one. There are melodies galore and some really fine ones, but the industrious sparkling of Tchaikovsky's music, and the eclectic and unbalanced optimism of his operatic procedure ruffle any listener alive to the graver and sterner elements of music drama. For want of a stronger grasp of theatrical realities, despite all its sense of beauty, *Eugene Onegin* misses a well-meant aim.

Perhaps the most curious shortcoming of this opera is its lack of true vocal concept. This does not mean that the songs are not singable; they are very much so, but most of them, such as Lenski's big aria before the duel, are of the "Melody in F" variety—general-purpose elegant sob stuff, just as good for solo cello.

This opera reminds me of one of Saintsbury's pithy remarks about some novelist whose name escapes me. It can be paraphrased to read: "Tchaikovsky had every faculty for writing operas, except the faculty of opera writing." Still, for those who want to spend a pleasant evening listening to melting music and nicely staged and costumed production, *Eugene Onegin* will be no disappointment. There are many operas with the always grateful ballroom scene; this work has two— surely an unusual recompense for the absent music drama.

Thirteen

WAGNER

NEARLY everything that took place in music in the latter part of the nineteenth century was in some way connected with the lifework of two composers born in 1813, Verdi and Wagner. It has been frequently debated who was the greater composer, but quality in art is always *sui generis;* the great in the creative arts cannot be graded. Moreover, since in the flourishing productivity of opera the bloom of today so quickly becomes the leafmold of tomorrow, these two opera composers would not have held the boards with such remarkable consistency unless they showed an equally enduring greatness. Nevertheless, we are dealing here not only with diametrically opposed temperaments, but also with diametrically opposed esthetics which intruded into the works of art themselves, causing a controversy that has not yet been resolved.

One group of partisans maintains that Wagner's works represent the summit of opera and that Verdi's, with the exception of the last operas, are little more than hurdy-gurdy music. The other party sees in Verdi the culmination of almost three centuries of operatic history, allowing Wagner musical merits but deploring his operatic ideal. Wagner's extensive literary activity and the susceptibility of his theories to different interpretations account for part of the heated disagreement. There was a time when Wagner was considered musician, poet, philosopher, and cultural prophet, and of equal rank in all his capacities; what remains today is the unquestionably towering musician. Wagner wrote his own librettos and kept generations busy trying to extract concrete meanings from their allegorical symbols. The Germans saw in them the exaltation of their own ideals; Bernard Shaw was convinced that *Der Ring des Nibelungen* expressed social criticism, the curse of capitalism being represented by the gold of the Rhine; and more recently Robert Donington in his psychoanalytical dissertation deals with Wagner on a Freudian basis. Yet among the quarreling, grasping, and treacherous beings in these long dramatic poems, among the peculiar, passionate, incoherent, and unimaginable loves, temptations, and challenges, one can still discover the ambitions that seek satisfaction, the eternal desires that cannot be fulfilled, which make up the human situation. It is the sheer force and sweep of the music that makes this possible. This searing and soaring music can be bewildering because the most spiritual and the most carnal are often inextricably interlaced; this ambiguity surrounds the dramatic characters in all of Wagner's operas except *Die Meistersinger*.

Today we realize that in accepting and attempting to promulgate Wagner's esthetic and dramaturgical doctrines the mistake was made of basing an esthetic system on an exception; Wagner's theories, like his music, are altogether personal, inimitable, exclusive, and not transferable. He was convinced that neither the spoken theater nor the old opera, nor even pure instrumental music, but only his *Gesamtkunstwerk*, the "Universal Art Work," can lead to supreme art. This was, as it turned out, a flagrant misjudgment of the function and boundaries of the arts. But if this is true, what becomes of the Universal Art Work? The answer is that the question is invalidated by the music, for the music dominates here—the theory notwithstanding—as completely as in the despised Italian opera, the only difference being that the substance emanates from the pit rather than from the stage. What Wagner did was to change the riverbed of the symphony so that it would again flow in the opera pit whence it had emerged a hundred years before—a solution congenial to a nation whose heritage was symphonic. From the jumble of leitmotifs emerges a symphonic fabric of endless imagination and of a thousand hues. The singers on the stage are overwhelmed by it, their function often reduced to commentary, like the "ideal spectator," the chorus of the ancient Greek drama. This particular quality in the Wagnerian opera created a situation unshared by any other opera composer: until very recent times, Wagnerian excerpts were among the staples and unfailing favorites at "symphony" concerts. It is inconceivable that portions of *Figaro* or *Un Ballo* or any other bona fide opera should be given without the vocal parts, yet the *Liebestod*, the climactic scene in *Tristan und Isolde*, can be performed with the voice omitted, and it remains a powerful piece.

In one of his letters Verdi declared, rather laconically, that an opera is an opera and a symphony a symphony. Here, then, are two sharply opposed conceptions of musical dramaturgy, a comparison of which makes it clear why Wagner is such a frequent guest at symphony concerts while Verdi retains his primacy on the lyric stage. Opera has its own esthetic canons and cannot obey laws that come from extra-musical domains. That familiar quartet in *Rigoletto*, to quote an example, cannot be performed without the voices because the participants are living persons, pouring out their innermost thoughts and feelings. They sing simultaneously, in an ensemble, yet they remain individuals and they sing individual music. This is the great glory of opera, a unique feature that is not to be found in any other form of the theater. In the *Liebesnacht* there are likewise two protagonists involved in a palpably dramatic situation, and the music soars with irresistible élan. Tristan and Isolde are caught in a symphonic torrent and their voices are superimposed upon music the logic of which is little concerned with their individual personalities—both are singing the same musical substance. And this substance comes from the orchestra and remains its property from beginning to end.

No wonder, then, that such music is just as effective in the concert hall as in the theater—indeed, not infrequently more so, because the sweep and continuity of the symphonic process is not weakened by the often labored passages that connect these symphonic odes. This is the secret of Wagner's success in the concert hall, and a deserved success it is. One cannot help wondering what would have become of this extraordinary man had he not been possessed by the idea of erecting a dramatic monument for the glorification of Germandom. He might have become the greatest post-Beethovenian symphonist, for all his instincts drove him toward the "abstract" symphony; but Hegel, Nietzsche, Schopenhauer, and Gobineau proved to be more enticing to his mind, already filled with philosophical vapors. Somewhere in his many writings on Wagner, Ernest Newman makes a suggestion that would surely be the death sentence of opera. He advises the listener who may find Wagnerian dramaturgy a bit confusing to close his eyes, lean back in his seat, and simply abandon himself to the music. Yet there is a good deal of justification for such an untheatrical attitude in long stretches of, say, *Tristan*. This music does not equivocate, nor does it acknowledge conventions, restrictions, or obstacles of any sort. If you are tired of watching Isolde's death throes, close your eyes and the make-believe stage will disappear, while the music will carry you to paroxysmal heights. Perhaps it is best to abandon ourselves without trying to rationalize the stage business; but then what about Verdi's dictum that symphony and opera are two different things?

Admittedly, Wagner is a difficult proposition for us who are living on the downward slope of the twentieth century. Moreover, he is surrounded by legends, misconceptions, propaganda, and counterpropaganda that make a clear appraisal of the man and of his work very difficult. It is about time that a new, modern, and impartial study be made of both. Wagner became the representative of German Romanticism, if not of German music in general, the symbol of Germany's political and cultural aspirations. He was the defender and apostle of Germandom, worshipping and flailing it at the same time, always absorbed in great deeds and always lost in petty intrigues, but never permitting his own titanic work to suffer. He is either admired beyond bounds or despised, but uncritical adulation is as misplaced and ridiculous as is complete denial. Similarly, the setting up of the "music drama" as the supreme achievement compared to the "mere opera" is an untenable point of view. Wagner's *Weltanschauung* should not be the touchstone by which we judge his music. What he stood for is less important than how he invented and shaped his music. And if we put the Wagnerian theories through a critical sieve, a multitude of things that at first look important fall through, and we are left with great music.

The grandiosity, the horizonless proportions, and the ecstatic nature of Wagner's style were not due exclusively to his own personality; much of it was characteristic of the age. Böcklin, the painter, is a good parallel example. Wagner's nebulous and indigestible philosophy and his other writings, once considered the pride of German letters, are today read with dismay; with the exception of such excellent professional essays as *On Conducting*, they add a powerful deterrent to the appreciation of his art. The philosopher-composer proclaimed pure instrumental music to be no longer justified after Beethoven's Ninth Symphony, decreeing the same fate for the spoken theater; all other musicians and playwrights can pack up and go; only his Universal Art Work points to the future. And of course Italian opera, that low-grade and frivolous species by an inferior race, must be cremated; Wagner never forgave Mozart for writing Italian operas. He did not seem to have noticed that in his hour of triumph this defunct absolute music produced a Brahms and the cremated Italian opera a Verdi. But then he had little if any sense for all this, for his own grandiose world-view made him completely blind to everything else. He did not realize that his philosophy represented and elucidated only his personal art, that it had no universal significance. It is precisely for this reason that Wagner incarnates the subjectivism of the late- and post-Romantic era, because his complex personality is a unique and altogether inimitable phenomenon. These profound inner contradictions account for Wagner's tortured and eruptive nature, the waywardness of his spirit, his aberrations from the optimism of revolutionary materialism through the darkest Schopenhauerian pessimism to the muddled doctrine of "spiritual regeneration of Germany through the theater"—his theater. His unparalleled fame can be explained only by his century's attitude toward art, for to the late nineteenth century revelation was to come not from religion but from art; its prophet was the sorcerer, the magus, and such a sorcerer was Wagner.

Opera guides and popular histories of music inform us that Wagner returned to the ancient Germanic saga of the Nibelungen and that thus *Der Ring des Nibelungen* is really a form of the national epic. Actually, he created his own dramatized myth. The *Nibelungenlied*, as it exists in a number of manuscripts discovered in the latter part of the eighteenth century, represents a most complicated piece of literary history. Originally an early medieval Frankish poem, its final form (early thirteenth century) is a typical *chanson de geste,* which combined some elements of the Kriemhild, Brünhild, and other legends with concrete historical events occurring in Worms and similarly identifiable places. The poet to whom we owe the final version, probably a Bavarian or Austrian professional, an educated *Spielmann,* was demonstrably acquainted with Virgil, French chivalric poetry, and the Arthurian legends. The Nibelung are really the medieval Burgundians. The chief figure, Kriemhild, marries Siegfried, and after his death by treachery she again marries—none other than Attila the Hun. Brünhild fades out of the story before the grisly denouement. These figures are not mythological creatures but kings, queens, and courtiers, Burgundians, Huns, and Goths (Theodoric is also in the picture). The epic's events are courtly intrigues, female quarrels caused by jealousy, and passions aroused by chivalric fealty and rivalry. The Christian veneer is quite obvious; Siegfried is buried with all the pomp of medieval Catholicism, and Kriemhild, though vindictive and no mean hand with the broadsword, never misses morning Mass. Goethe had already warned the Germans not to consider this romantic poem a "naive mythological epic," for it is indeed a remarkable literary work with well-regulated rhyming verse, and not the result of autogenesis. A modern German translation was made available early in the nineteenth century, and Wagner also certainly knew Karl Lachmann's valuable, pioneering study of the *Nibelungenlied* that appeared in the 1830s. He realized that this is not the authentic Nordic and national saga but a fine example of the international chivalric romance of the age, so he proceeded to make what he wanted out of it. While retaining the oldest elements of the legends and adding elements from Norse legends, he removed every vestige of the medieval-Christian accretions, thus creating an entirely new Nordic saga, his own, overlaid with cloudy symbolism and cast in a language saturated with labored alliteration. Yet nothing proves more conclusively the power of his music than its ability to survive his librettos.

It was the disillusion following the failure of the Revolution of 1848 that turned the hearts of German poets away from the gods of Greece, of whom Goethe had been the high priest, to the setting up of a national religion based on a mystic interpretation of the old Germanic mythology. But these were the dark and joyless gods of the north; they were no longer masters of their souls, but rather reflected the skeptical, political, and materialistic period that superseded genuine Romanticism. The figures of Wagner's mythological world were singularly favored in being allowed the advantages of the human form without suffering its everyday drawbacks: they had no souls and no common colds. The subdivinity—and subhumanity—of their characters can rob the narrative of its significance. They are unhappy, greedy, suspicious; they torture one another, the powerful are helpless and the helpless wield great power; no one acts as he would like to. It is a ghostly world where lance-bearing amazons ride on steeds with corpses slung across the saddle and the women sleep in full armor, unapproachable and untouchable. This new mythology as concocted by Wagner is not anthropocentric; it denies man's exceptional place in creation. The great gestures and the great words do not mean much because the deeds and the men are not one and the same. It must be said, though, that when Wagner uses a palette with clear colors, the wonderful symphonic arabesques coalesce into true drama and the quarreling and double-dealing gods become, for the time being, believable human figures. In these moments the demigoddesses can be women with hearts, the gods stop their eternal bickering, and the men pause in their weird plottings to act like plausible dramatic figures. It is very important to catch them in their moods of human impersonation to provide a balance for the somewhat trying heroics that dominate the *Ring*.

Now let us take one aspect of this curious Wagnerian dramatic poetry, the one that usually decides the fate of the drama: love. Wagner's heroines, with the exception of Eva in *Die Meistersinger*, are not girls but women; to him girlhood is not a definite station in life but a mere preparation. And when these women make their debut they are instantly involved in some sort of adultery, actual or mental. They only dream of love and do not live it. When a somewhat plausible amorous situation arises, a love potion reverses the inclinations and an entirely new, implausible dramatic conflict is created. If it is not a magic potion, some other sort of black magic claims them, whether Elsa, or Elisabeth, Isolde, Kundry, or Brünnhilde. All of them perish, consumed by internal or external fire, but love is never blessed because all of them are inflicted with death worship. In such a state love cannot become itself; the love of these heroines is not an unexpected secret, a disquieting miracle, but a violently and artificially contrived conflict in which it is not uncommon for at least one of the participants to be drugged or otherwise rendered incapable of experiencing compellingly deep feelings. With the exception of Eva and Walther von Stolzing, Wagnerian lovers cannot seem to conceive of a simple, non-pathological relationship. Though imposing in stature, placed in a severely grandiose decor, and singing powerful music, these women are but butterflies helplessly impaled on pins, their beautiful natural colors wasted. Their sad and fruitless lives, whose high emotions are dependent on magic herbs, negate the essence of drama, and one cannot help wondering whether their creator, the same man who gave us the sunny characters of *Die Meister-*

singer, was really able to use the magic wand of the poet. Here was a musician whose exceptional powers gave his creatures all the attributes of life, and they cannot live. Wagner possessed the composer's gifts in abundance, and his erotic suggestivity was unparalleled, yet his heroines cannot love, they can only perish. This is not, and cannot be, true drama. But the music itself, or much of it, is still of the kind that can deliver us from our puny existences.

Looking back on Wagner's career as a composer, we see that at first he was altogether in the mainstream of opera, combining the French grand opera of Meyerbeer and Spontini, and the Italian opera of Donizetti and Bellini, with the early German Romantic opera of Marschner and Weber. In *Tannhäuser* the Italians are largely abandoned, and the mixture is restricted to French and German Romantic opera. Then with *Lohengrin* the personal Wagnerian synthesis is arrived at. Following this opera, Wagner's grand plan for the creation of a national musico-dramatic epic was progressing satisfactorily, and he had reached the middle of the second act of *Siegfried*, with everything so far well ordered if somewhat sprawling, the texture diatonic and under excellent symphonic control. Then suddenly something happens; his brain is seized with convulsions and his blood boils. The pictures turn into visions, the visions into yearning, and yearning into lust; the flesh is tormented, for this is the all-consuming passion of an aging man, more intense and dangerous than that of youth.

Biographers have shown Wagner as a rather promiscuous person; as a matter of fact, he was completely amoral in sexual matters. Many of his affairs were simple, some scandalous. He was not at all reticent about his views on a "liberal" concept of the relationship between men and women, but he put them in nebulous philosophical terms. There can be no question that Wagner exerted great attraction on women, young or old, aristocrat or commoner, single or married. Even those who managed to keep their distance, like the Princess Metternich, went out of their way to help him, though sorely tried by his eternal borrowing of money. There were two women in

Wagner's life, however, who were in a separate category. One was Mathilde Wesendonk, the immediate inspiration for *Tristan und Isolde*, the other Cosima Liszt von Bülow, his second wife, who proved to be his match and who kept him in line—or almost—for the rest of his life.

The story of his passionate if idealized love for Mathilde Wesendonk is well known, but the key to the particular mental state that resulted in *Tristan* can be explained only if we refer to Wagner's writings, where there is a passage that sheds light on the situation. "To seek a pure, chaste, virgin love, sprung from the soil of fullest sensuousness, but which sensuousness as understood in modern society could not satisfy." This is not really as cryptic as it may seem. Social and moral obstacles acted as a tonic on Wagner's imagination. Already under the spell of Schopenhauer's pessimistic philosophy, and gathering new ideas from Buddhism, he formed his own chaotic and mystic theory of catastrophe, of the oneness of highest rapture with death. What he needed was a catalyst, and this he found in Mathilde Wesendonk, an attractive and highly cultured woman. The vapors in Wagner's mind began to billow, and in *Tristan* an entirely new composer is before us. The diatonicism of the *Ring* gives way to an agitated, gnawing, inflammatory, and seditious chromaticism that carries Western harmony to its limits. But after a while this music, this frenetic, tumultuous tangle of motifs and instruments, harmonies and counterpoints, becomes so complicated and overwrought that one is reminded of the battle pictures on old tapestries, with an inextricable maze of horses' hooves and warriors' legs trampling the flowers of the meadow. Wagner will not omit anything he sees or feels; everything is retained in an intoxicating richness. It is almost impossible to follow *Tristan* throughout—one gets lost in this Nirvana. Wagner, entirely possessed, was incapable of gauging the total effect of this work; nevertheless, most of the individual scenes, even the very long ones, remain overwhelmingly exciting.

Yet this paean of rapture and death, rich as it is, leads nowhere. All this beauty is fundamentally aimless because it does not merge into a dramatic synthesis. Wagner's overheated

imagination, surging into the infinite, violently thirsted for
the unheard-of and the unutterable, and these are not the
ingredients of drama. Dramatic unity and ideas are not so
much replaced by the music as they are drowned by the sheer
power of it. Instead of great dramatic conflicts the music gives
lyric ecstasies, and those cannot be sustained through three
tremendous acts. Somewhere and somehow the fate of
Wagner's work is connected by secret and invisible threads
with the entire fate of his century. It is for this reason that so
many rose in protest against him, and that all this protest
proved to be futile. The more he was victorious before the
public and the more he lived for the public, the more he lost
whatever sincerity was left in him. No artist ever addressed
his public with such a number of manifestoes and open letters,
pamphlets, and books as this embattled would-be philosopher,
but while he could hide his real nature in his writings, the
composer could not hide the truth. *Tristan* embraces all the
sins of the era: its nebulousness, loud-mouthed pessimism,
convulsive swooning, overwhelming and irrational passion,
intoxication, and hysteria. The world of the senses is liberated
from all restraint; it is lost in its excesses and rushes, albeit
willingly, into destruction, for death is considered a natural
culmination. The hypertrophy of chromaticism in *Tristan*,
crowding the limits of harmonic intelligibility, the fantastic
tangle of orchestral polyphony or pseudo-polyphony express
all this faithfully—it cannot be concealed as in the printed
word.

When the madness departed—it was to return once more,
though diminished, in *Parsifal*, now caused by the young and
voluptuous Judith Gautier-Mendès—this incredible man had
to turn back. And he returned to something so different, so far removed from the lethal voluptuousness of
Tristan that one is entirely at a loss to fathom his power of
regeneration. *Die Meistersinger* is an opera—sacrilegious as the
designation may seem in view of the careful distinction that is
made between Wagnerian "music drama" and Italian "tinsel
opera." That Wagner was able to return from the orgiastic
world of *Tristan* to life as it is lived by men in this world,

from the murky shadows of a distended chromaticism to the clear and brave light of diatonicism, from the shrieks of "highest rapture" to well-turned melody; that he was able to overcome the irresistible attraction of "consuming fire-death" in favor of the living humanism of the medieval artisan-poets—this remains one of the incomparable feats in the history of the arts. This opera has to be sung, like an Italian opera; it has real songs for the singers and honest ensembles such as only a true opera would have. It cannot be excerpted for the concert hall—only its preludes are detachable; it must be sung on the stage. But his demon would not let Wagner take leave of life in such a sympathetic mood. A real hero does not die peacefully; he has to fall, like the stabbed Siegfried. The sunny landscape again changes into the forbidding caves of the Nibelung and the cold reaches of Valhalla as Wagner takes up the unfinished scores of the *Ring*. We are back in the symphonic apotheoses that never cease to exert their sorcery on spellbound audiences whether in the theater or in the concert hall.

Samuel Shellabarger's comment on Lord Chesterfield applies with even more justice to Wagner. "Under the pagan dispensation his rank would be high; judged by the real, not conventional Christian practice, he would have no rank at all." What made this arch pagan who had finished the immense scores apotheosizing the ancient Germanic saga turn in *Parsifal* to a "Christian" theme, seemingly disavowing everything he had done before?

The French prize and overprize reason. Their world is an elaborate pattern of words in which the literal references are consistent. At the other extreme, the Germans surrender themselves to feelings; they move in a very mysterious world, a world that is not what it seems and never was. They are most themselves when romantically nostalgic. Though seemingly different, Parsifal is no less the prototype of the national hero than Siegfried. Thus, appearances notwithstanding, Wagner did not stray far from his accustomed bailiwick, and *Parsifal* has nothing to do with credal religion. Wagner was not a believer; neither does he belong among the great seekers after

God. To him Christ was only a symbol. It is true, of course, that in order to represent this symbol artistically he had to resort to well-known religious rites and figures, but God, the fount of every metaphysical religion, is nowhere mentioned in *Parsifal*.

Wagner, as was his wont, studied the literature on the subject he planned to work up into a libretto, in this case the complicated Perceval-Grail legend already touched upon in *Lohengrin*. The story goes back to a folk tale long antedating the medieval romances, and was curiously widespread in the West. His main source was Wolfram von Eschenbach, the great German epic poet of the early thirteenth century, whose work was available to him in a modern edition of 1833. But if we read the old poem we would not recognize the Wagnerian tale. It is quite important to realize that Wolfram, like other noble Minnesinger, could neither read nor write; he dictated his poetry to a scribe. Lacking the tutelage of clerics, who in that age were the sole dispensers of literacy, with the inevitable religious influence upon their students, he was a pronouncedly secular poet. A knight and a member of the Minnesinger group at the Wartburg, Wolfram was the poetic interpreter of Western medieval chivalry. His epic poem *Parzival* is infused with all the vigor of his own personality and that of the spirit of his age, for he had a living knowledge of its ways; his story is that of the education of the "verray, parfit, gentil knight" of the Middle Ages. The Bavarian knight-poet describes with enormous gusto tournaments and festivities, with minute attention to such details as costumes and decorations. His ideal was not asceticism; indeed, he extolled marriage as the highest good and loyalty to the spouse the highest virtue. Neither was the Grail itself what it became in later versions of the story. In Wolfram's poem it is a precious stone, the symbol of eternal youth, and it supplied its guardians with food and drink; there is no identification with the chalice of the Last Supper. In order to make a Christian drama of redemption from this secular epic, Wagner drew on Chrétien de Troyes's earlier version of the legend (which was also Wolfram's source, but which he used very selectively), and sundry other writings, and then applied his own imagination. The result was a typical Wagnerian tableau: a hero blameless and ascetic, but subjected to the raptures of temptation, and the sensual temptress who falls dead at the moment of her redemption.

Today we recognize in Wagner's philosophy the bankruptcy of the Romanticism of the latter part of the nineteenth century. As a poet and playwright he failed in his attempt to "recreate German mythology" for want of a real poetic language and a reasonable sense of proportion. As a writer on esthetics he dominated musical thought into the twentieth century, but his dramaturgy is now pretty well restricted to his own works; he had no real successors. But we must always remember that this extraordinary man was first of all a composer, and whatever he proclaimed about the "secondary role" music must play in the drama, it was as a musician that he triumphed. When the creative urge fired his imagination the musician in him gained supremacy over the poet and esthetician and the theories were largely forgotten. Unfortunately, it was the theoretician who not infrequently gained the upper hand. Many an act or scene in Wagner starts out with impetuously inspired music that runs its course guided by the musician's instinct until the philosopher-poet-dramatist's intellect recovers from the ecstasy of sheer creation and begins to interfere by enforcing the dramaturgical doctrine. Then the leitmotifs meander hither and yon, called upon to tell a tale which they are scarcely capable of telling.

Many writers have seen in the Wagnerian music drama a minutely organized and developed achitectural entity, indeed, one so logically and seamlessly organized that the construction has been graphically reproduced in analyses. They also cite the unifying force of what is called Wagner's "endless melody." This endless melody echoes the nineteenth-century composer's desire to break away from the "number opera" and assure an uninterrupted flow of the *melos*. We shall not attempt here to dispute the contention that the "numbers" with their double bars at the end of arias interrupt continuity, except to say that it was a perfectly valid concept and that countless masterpieces were based on it. After all, recitative and aria did not disappear altogether; they were merely absorbed into the general texture, with the sutures often in evidence. The cadencing did decrease, but on the other hand, the eternal avoidance of positive cadences, as in *Tristan*, can become tiresome. The idea of this new form of continuity is once more of literary origin; Wagner wanted to have the same continuity that is achieved verbally in the spoken drama. Actually, these operas are made up of individual scenes, large and small, not unlike the old opera; they are dramatic ballads in music, as it were. The climactic scenes have very little to do with Wagner's complicated theories; they are almost purely emotionally musical. Their significance is neither consummated nor necessarily helped by the scenic realization; they live and are understood through the music. And these scenes are well constructed even when the opera itself is sprawling, even when the mortar that binds them crumbles, indeed, even when this musical construction does not agree with the dramatic-scenic plan. They are built on certain corresponding motif groups, governed by harmonic progression and tonal concordance as well as by orchestral color. The molecules of this organization are the leitmotifs which are symphonically combined, developed, and built into larger units. It is the compelling logic of this symphonic procedure rather than that of the libretto that binds the individual scenes together, but the connections are not always successful; the ballads remain units, episodes, however large and significant. Every detail presents a new difficulty that must be overcome; every connection achieved is a new triumph. Such a procedure is complicated and may lead to dense textures. The danger points are before or after a magnificent "ballad," when the dramatic poet takes over from the musician and makes the figures orate and declaim. Here the music, the chief agent of coherence, loses its sweep, and Wagner just manipulates his leitmotifs as well as he can until the verbal exchange subsides, and the musician recovers and takes command again. On such occasions the conceptual meaning of the sharply profiled leitmotifs is supposed to assist the listener. This may work, but in many instances the actual conditions of observation are seldom so favorable—given a rapidly changing polyphonic texture—as to allow the formulated conceptual association to be actually heard and grasped. But we must beware of underestimating Wagner's genius at making the most of this difficult situation, for he often succeeds admirably in going from scene to scene.

The listener may be bored by the often extended recitation or surfeited by the alliterations that fill the singers' mouths, but when those scenes come along he is roused and is carried away irresistibly by the sheer power of the music, for this insufferable philosopher and second-rate poet-playwright was a supreme musician. If many have grown disenchanted with this formidable man and his formidable creations, they should remember that he must be comprehended emotionally or not at all; then in spite of their reservations—even hostility—they will be overwhelmed if not convinced.

The Flying Dutchman is a nice, melodious opera, roughly corresponding to those of Verdi's middle period. It has fine arias, choruses, ensembles, and good tunes. The fact that it was composed by the creator of *Der Ring des Nibelungen* should lead no one to false conclusions; this is almost an Italian opera, though besides the clear influence of Bellini and Spontini, it also contains traces of Auber and Weber. The *Dutchman* is not juvenile or substandard Wagner but the work of an already seasoned and clear-thinking opera composer thoroughly familiar with all aspects of his trade and never wanting in inventiveness. After a big, garish grand opera, *Rienzi*, Wagner turned to myth and legend, never to abandon them (with the exception of *Die Meistersinger*) for the rest of his life. Whatever we may think of Wagner's other librettos, the *Dutchman* has a good one; it is good theater and good opera. The dialogue, pleasantly naive, is not yet artificial, the conflict is simply and operatically effective, and the scenes offer considerable variety. Interestingly, this first of his viable operas already shows Wagner's obsession with the unconsummated love affair, Senta being the first of those heroines who perish, sacrificing themselves for the redemption of their lovers. The cast is dominated by the Dutchman. This is a deeply felt and carefully thought out role, his every move compelling and strange, and his general tone and behavior tragic rather than sinister. Senta's music is characteristic, especially in the ballad, where wild outbursts alternate with dreamy Weberian cantilena. It is unfortunate that conductors often misrepresent the nature of this opera; the gentleness and mystery escape them because they are too much concerned with the violence of the storm.

Under the best of circumstances, and even with liberal cuts, *Tannhäuser* is something of a bore. The first singing is heard long after the big overture and the subsequent Venusberg ballet, and when it does come (in the Paris version) we feel sorry to have exchanged the lively symphony for it, especially since this swift and brilliantly orchestrated music is a later addition by the mature master's hand. The libretto, with its ponderous opposition of idealized medieval chastity and pagan lust, is at times hard to bear. Wagner was naturally attracted to the sensual, but on the other hand he was fascinated by the idea of redemption; therefore Tannhäuser, a man entangled in the pleasures of the flesh, must be redeemed by Elisabeth's piety. All this takes place in a slow-moving and densely verbose text, thoroughly pedantic in its heavy-handed mysticism and contrived historical setting. On the whole, this is still a "grand opera," with its set pieces, solos, duets, and ensembles. The pilgrims' choir, the shepherd's piping, the hunt music, the grand march are all standard ingredients. The opera is weak dramatically, the Landgrave's orations being especially trying and much of the recitation seeming interminable. The whole scene of the singing contest offers nothing but dull music, though it picks up somewhat when Elisabeth stops the enraged knights and the protagonists unite in a large ensemble. Never again would Wagner be guilty of such a sentimental romance as Wolfram's song to the evening star; but Tannhäuser's "Rome Narrative" is a fine dramatic piece. *Tannhäuser* does contain some good music, and the principal characters, though long-winded and inclined to preach, are recognizable individuals.

Beginning with *Lohengrin*, Wagner's operas can no longer be judged by grand opera standards. Here we have the first, though not yet fully evolved, realization of a conscious musico-dramatic plan; with this work German Romantic opera reaches its apogee. The brevity of its development (Weber, Marschner, and Spohr are the outstanding composers) only enhances Wagner's achievement. But *Lohengrin* is not only a culmination, it is also the starting point for a rich future; Wagner lived through all phases of Romanticism and decisively influenced all of them. This opera still has many of the traditional forms and formulas, yet the musical development of its composer is momentous. The difference between arioso and accompanied recitative is considerably minimized by the lengthened stretches of through-composed music; the set pieces, like the "Bridal Chorus," are still with us (as in essence they always will be), and Wagner handles them in true operatic fashion. It is interesting to observe how the musician has grown—and how he dominates the *Gesamtkunstwerk*! The tonalities are well organized symbolically and structurally, recalling the procedure employed by Mozart in *The Magic Flute*. C-major represents the King's earthiness, A-major the world of the Grail, the dusky F-sharp minor mirrors Ortrud's character, the gentle B-flat major is reserved for Elsa, and so forth. And these keys have a logical relationship (musical logic, that is) to one another. A similar attractive symbolism is carried out in the orchestration, in which certain instruments, or groups of instruments, and registers are associated with particular figures and ideas of the drama. The use of motifs of reminiscence, which Wagner learned from Méhul, Cherubini, and Spohr, now changes from simple reiteration to symphonic-dramatic development, already manipulated with great skill. The role of the overture is changed, as Wagner avoids any concentration on a quasi-independent formal piece; the curtain-raiser becomes a "prelude," a symphonic synthesis of the basic ideas of the drama, and hence one of its integral parts. But we also notice the beginning of a turning away from the songlike toward recitation, the increasing preoccupation with the redemption theme, and the first intrusion of cognitive elements into the music. In *Lohengrin* Wagner also makes his first attempt at dealing with nebulous Christian mysticism by drawing on the Parsifal-Grail legend, awkwardly combining it with German history. The result, especially the "Gralserzählung," is nothing but theatricalism. These are not real depths, not real confrontations, but exotic and misty rhetorical effusions—the myth as the nineteenth century conceived it. But *Lohengrin* is a good opera, its music much more convincing than its dramaturgy.

The first thing that strikes the listener in the four operas that make up *Der Ring des Nibelungen* is the archaic quality of the language. Wagner, no mean researcher, devised a special language that is supposed to resemble old German. This language does not destroy one's enjoyment of the operas, but in the long soliloquies, especially when the forced alliterations cascade endlessly from the singers' mouths, it can be trying. On the other hand, the special orchestra that Wagner uses only in the tetralogy—which, in addition to the large ensemble employed in *Tristan* and *Die Meistersinger*, includes another quartet of horns (interchangeable with tubas), bass trumpet, contrabass trombone and tuba, and several harps—is always fascinating, with its myriad colors and its tremendous power. This orchestra has a splendor of its own, brassy but also esoteric, especially with Wagner's noticeable interest in the deep regions.

Das Rheingold is the "prologue" to the great trilogy, and being a prologue it has the modest dimensions of an ordinary opera. It is heard only when the entire *Ring* cycle is produced, but this restriction is altogether unjustified. To be sure, the story and plot are weird, but there is plenty to watch on the stage.

As the curtain parts, we behold an underwater scene with the Rhine-maidens swimming gracefully about, usually manipulated by invisible wires. They do not sing; the singers, being

less athletic than the shapely ballet dancers, are concealed.
Nevertheless, the illusion thus created is very agreeable. Then
Alberich, the Nibelung, steals the famous gold of the Rhine
from the maidens, for, the legend says, whoever makes a ring
from it acquires magic powers. The ensuing action involves
sundry gods, goddesses, gnomes, and giants in episodes of
elaborate plotting and violence, ending with the forcible
seizure of the ring from Alberich and his curse on the ring and
all who wear it. It is quite a story for such a short opera, but it
has a nice fairy-tale quality, and the comings and goings of
those fantastic denizens of the deep and of the heights are
entertaining. In the end, however, all this is of little account
as we listen to the fine music. The first few dozen measures
alone are worth the price of the ticket. The basses settle on
a deep E-flat; the sound gradually swells as more and more
instruments join in the tremendous chord, until it acquires such
elemental force as to convince the listener that the Rhine is
flooding into the auditorium. It is relieved by the fresh and
melodious song of the Rhine-maidens, and all the leitmotifs,
especially since they are new at this stage of the cycle, are of
pure gold. But what is most admirable is Wagner's skill and
inventiveness in developing and combining them until he
stuns us with the scintillating tapestry. There are some good
melodies in this work, which is full of warm romantic accents.
Das Rheingold sags a little toward the middle, and I do not see
why a brave opera house could not break the tradition and
insert an intermission that would take care of both the music's
and the listener's momentary fatigue. It can be done; two and
a half hours of opera is too much for one sitting, and I
venture to say that with a sensible pause somewhere, this
opera could be made a popular repertory item.

The story of *Die Walküre*, the second opera in the *Ring*
cycle, is well known; it is not necessary to dwell on it.
Although unquestionably overextended, this is a tremendous
opera. The music's symphonic logic is compelling, yet there
are many instantaneous—even capricious—inspirations that are
purely musical; that is, they do not represent the "system."

And whatever Wagner and his eulogists say, there are many welcome remnants of the old and despised opera in this great score. There are also stretches where Wagner plays dominoes with his leitmotifs, but that is mainly because domestic matters, even of the gods, did not really interest him. It is these scenes between husband and wife, father and daughter that slow down the opera in the middle, where Wotan has endless tirades. But when Brünnhilde puts down that wicked lance, she becomes a woman, compassionate and tender, melting in turn the pomposity of Wotan, who becomes warmly lyrical. There are some corny moments too, chief among them the "Ride of the Valkyries." On the other hand, the large compound scenes are phenomenally well constructed, absorbing, and moving, the sound of the orchestra is glorious, and the wizard of Bayreuth always manages to end with a blazing peroration that makes us swallow our petty grievances.

Siegfried is the one opera in the Ring that has no woman in it until practically the end of the third act, which is approximately at midnight. The all-male cast is a pretty lugubrious affair, and one that affected Wagner himself; without women the world was bleak to him. More and more as *Siegfried* unfolds one wonders how even the broad embrace of Romanticism can be wide enough to contain Wagner's strenuous idiosyncrasies. This is the talkiest opera in the tetralogy, forcing Wagner to a rather fretful play with the leitmotifs through a series of developments. The ponderous neatness, the jolly gravity, the expository philosophizing are at their worst in the first act, which mixes tortuous allegory with a kind of elementary instruction in the facts of life dispensed by Mime to the innocent Siegfried. Being a boy of nature, the latter should be familiar with the behavior of the little animals which constitute Mime's biological exhibits. At the end of the interminable dialogue. Siegfried seems to be as ready for life as the little boy who has been prepared for confirmation. Another dramaturgical miscalculation in this act is the question-and-answer game between Mime and Wotan, which elicits a recapitulation of the preliminaries leading up to this point in the *Ring*. This was undoubtedly deliberate on Wagner's part, but it detracts from both dramatic and musical interest. This act takes well over an hour, but no more than half of the music is really solid material. Throughout long stretches Wagner just doodles with his motifs; the music is diffuse and unconnected stop-and-go.

Then in the second act there are many magnificent moments. The nature scenes are superb and the sound delectable, though elsewhere the absence of "human interest" shackles Wagner's imagination. The myth, the story-telling, and the scenic realization are so atrocious that one feels embarrassed. The stage director officiating at this opera is foredoomed to defeat. What can he do with a papier-mâché monster that sings while blowing steam from its nostrils, and with a Nietzschean super-man who leads a wild bear on a leash, all the while brandishing his sword, ready to slay anything within sight? Still, those who can last it out cannot help experiencing the exhilaration that invariably comes at the end of these operas.

Even though Wagner's ability to pick up the thread and style where he had dropped them years before in the middle of *Siegfried* is an artistic achievement and tour de force of un-paralleled magnitude, the experiences gained in composing *Tristan* and *Die Meistersinger* could not help being brought to bear on the continuation of the tetralogy. The third act of *Siegfried* shows this plainly when compared with the previous two; the texture is tighter and the continuity firmer. Wagner never ends on a dubious tone, and, especially in this opera, the warm and the interesting music comes toward the end, when Siegfried first meets a woman. Brünnhilde's ecstasy upon awakening is one of the finest scenes in the *Ring*.

When *Götterdämmerung* begins one soon senses that it is going to be an enjoyable evening—if a long one. A warm romantic ardor suffuses the house, showing that this is indeed a Romantic opera in which Wagner's mythological and philo-sophical musings are largely dominated by carefully worked out yet spontaneous symphonic music-making. One marvels at the sustained power of this music, the crowning glory of the

Ring. After a while the opera—or perhaps the overtaxed listener—sags a little, but Wagner picks it up before any real damage takes place, and the climactic scenes are simply overwhelming.

Götterdämmerung gets under way with a somewhat benumbing recitation of the Norns spinning the thread of fate. This is in fact an extended prologue, again satisfying the needs of the verbose dramatic poet at the expenses of the composer. And after the surprisingly conventional duet, Wagner, who so far has used only such portions of the saga as deal with mythological and supernatural creatures and events, draws on the historical element in the *Nibelungenlied;* King Gunther sits on his earthly throne in Worms. Yet he is attended by Hagen, Alberich's son, so henceforth men and demigods are mixed in a tenuous tangle. Some of the weakest devices of the Wagnerian dramaturgy are present, including dependence on a magic potion to create dramatic conflict. The minute Siegfried downs his charmed dose he is completely smitten by Gutrune and forgets Brünnhilde altogether. Later he takes an antidote which instantly restores his amorous inclinations toward his first love. Yet most of the second act is bona fide opera; we can even spot Spontini and Meyerbeer in the wings. Though the orchestra lords it over all, there are dramatic situations, such as the confrontation of Siegfried and Brünnhilde, that are as genuinely operatic as anything in the repertory. And Wagner knows how to deal with them, even though it may cost him some of his cherished theories. If the immensity of the opera, the longest in the *Ring*, seems forbidding, no one begrudges its length because Wagner gives us marvelous pictures of sudden decisive power, or by contrast exhibits a sensitivity on the edge of tears against a background charged with doom. Even Brünnhilde is not merely a deposed Valkyrie, but a woman torn between love, humiliation, resignation, and pride. The enchanting nature scenes we admired in *Siegfried* are continued here—the sunrise is sheer magic. Such scenes are of unique charm and persuasiveness, yet this music is poetic, not descriptive. Well, perhaps the story is a bit primitive and verbose, but who cares? When Siegfried is killed, Brünnhilde is immolated, and the walls of Valhalla totter, the old Prospero of music masters a power that is absolutely devastating.

Tristan und Isolde is in a class by itself. Wagner himself felt that this opera would be the most difficult for posterity to accept; for "if well performed, it will render the listener insane." Indeed, more torrid, erotic, intoxicating music has never been composed. Yet while the musical language holds our attention for long stretches with its scorching and searing power, and the orchestra fascinates with its ever-changing color, there is an undeniable hypertrophy of all this, and there are passages that are wearisome. Attempts have been made to remedy this through judicious cuts, but they help little; Wagner as dramatist had a strong epic streak in him, a penchant for leaving nothing unsaid. This overelaboration cannot be edited out of his music, for it is ever present. Still, when the fire really catches, when the music cascades in a symphonic torrent, there is real passion to contend with, and we listen, almost paralyzed, to this unbridled, all-consuming ardor, this surging, searing pagan eroticism.

The conductor in *Tristan* cannot relax for a moment, and during long stretches he is at the focal point of unprecedented turmoil which he must control. The music rages and flows uninhibited even when little happens on the stage; in fact, there are scenes where theatrical values cease altogether. The stage director's job is to see to it that if a semblance of theater cannot be maintained, at least some visual justification for a stage production of this gigantic symphonic poem is offered. *Tristan und Isolde* is more a dream than a libretto. The dream moves in a no man's land between the temporal, which is sustained by the tide of physical acts, and that state of spiritual being in which persons ride above all conditions of time and timelessness. It cannot be said that Wagner brings his heroes and himself clearly out of this time-lost and self-lost state into one in which the temporal and the eternal are reconciled, but his *music* reveals a knowledge of the disabilities of such a state, and of the evasions by which its victims defer a true solution of it.

The drama is subverted and devitalized by the fact that the

lovers owe their ardor to the aphrodisiac potion administered by Brangäne; the use of this external means interferes with the realization of Isolde's character. She is not a sort of medieval Iphigenia, but a kinswoman of Penthesilea, who tore Achilles with her teeth and then tore herself. To remove this rawness from the "music drama," which is supposed to be a lofty improvement on frivolous Italian opera, the protagonists had to be considerably sentimentalized. But sentimentalism is the weakness of Wagner's psychology; it always wraps his heroes in helpless, drifting doom, rendering them equally incapable of life and of death. His treatment of the theme is made all the more elusive by an evident wavering between realistic psychology and moral allegory. Poor King Marke is a veritable professor of moral philosophy, holding forth with annoying nobility and perseverance while the drama is held in abeyance and everyone just stands around. Again, this weighs heavily on the stage director's shoulders; soliloquies can hardly be staged. Moreover—and this is the stage director's greatest dilemma—the music often contradicts the libretto. Indeed, Wagner does to himself what opera composers have been doing to their librettists since the origin of the species, thus revealing that for the composer to take command is a natural operatic law.

The overwhelming concern of the music is Isolde's passion; everything else, including Tristan himself, is only a foil. Her part demands extremes of both the vocal and the emotional gamut. Impatient and moody in the first act—a most difficult assignment, because the singer has to sustain it for a long time, and largely without help—she is both passionate and poetic in the second. The seething, consuming eroticism is present from the beginning of the great prelude, and is relaxed only during the bewitching, caressing love music of that part of the second act where the lovers—and Wagner—exhausted by their frenzy, subside, benumbed, into a wondrous nocturne. Only once more, in *Parsifal*, did Wagner find such accents.

Tristan und Isolde is undoubtedly the summation of all the virtues and sins of an entire age. It is compounded of overweening pessimism, convulsive delirium, an all-pervading and all-dissolving chromaticism which carried romantic harmony to its crisis, and a fantastic tangle of orchestral polyphony ablaze with color, all topped off by mad passion, orgiastic revelry, intoxication, and hysteria. A liberated instinct lost in its own excesses but artistic to the core runs willingly into death, the only natural denouement.

Die Meistersinger, full of song and whimsical comedy, is opera as we understand it: lyric drama, a play in song. In this, his most human work, Wagner divests himself of all pretense. He finds a home in the houses of the ancient Nuremberg burghers and rejoices in their quaint music-making; he shares in the sorrows of the cobbler-poet, Hans Sachs, in the jubilation of the people, in the enchantment of St. John's night and the dreamy summer morning. The old wizard of bottomless passions and searing voluptuousness makes peace with fate and genuflects before the orderliness of life. All this finds substance and shape in the old and indestructible operatic forms, those ariosos and arias, ensembles and finales, and even set choral pieces that Wagner avoided and despised in his other mature works. *Die Meistersinger* is a sunny, spectacular grand opera even though it is usually classified as a comic opera. Wagner could not write an opera without a thesis, and *Die Meistersinger* also has one: the age-old conflict between genius and the petty pedant. In this particular case the thesis also has autobiographical significance, which need not be restricted to Beckmesser, the caricature of the famous Viennese critic Eduard Hanslick, for the whole work is permeated by Wagner's experiences and the memory of his own lost innocence.

Wagner studied the works of the old Meistersinger as well as the scholarly literature about them, and Hans Sachs, the central figure in the opera, was a known historical person, a man of very modest poetical qualities but of a pure and honest heart. Since Wagner's own character was the exact opposite, and since hitherto he had created rather implausible figures, it is astonishing that he could draw with such fidelity and with such warmth the picture of a simple man at peace with humanity. The old Schopenhauerian doctrine of renunciation, Wagner's favorite, is still here, but Sachs is a human figure and not the mouthpiece of some nebulous mythus. Thus his renunciation is not the promulgation of a dogma but an engaging human conflict. Sachs is a man who, though well past his noon, is still very much attracted to feminine charms. Wagner wonderfully pictures the love of an aging man, but this love is more complicated than a young man's, and it is filled with doubt. Wagner, usually a sensualist, somehow divined that love in age, if rarer than in youth, is not less precious, and what it has lost in fire it gains in serenity and depth. Sachs is the symbol of what Wagner was not but wanted to be. That he could convey such noble and gentle resignation with the truest accents is another instance of the unbelievable extent of his chameleon-like creative range.

Walther von Stolzing is a very unusual Wagnerian hero, in that he neither kills, threatens, nor cheats, and is a fine specimen of a normal young man who is in love as a young man should be. Since he wants to win his love by the unusual—for Wagner —means of just wooing her with persuasion, he does what no other Wagnerian tenor ever does: he gets up and sings songs, real songs. Here again we have Wagner as he saw himself in his youth. In Beckmesser's role, tradition demands a certain amount of clowning, which usually is carried beyond the proper bounds. This is an excellent character study, and the composer himself warned that Beckmesser "does not have to be too foppish; the role makes the character." Eva is an altogether believable figure, a sweet. wholesome German *Jungfrau* who is not calculated to make her beloved lose his head.

In this opera Wagner substituted action for description, and now his heart warms to the old and rejected operatic conventions. Why, the final scene would have been approved by Spontini and Meyerbeer, and indeed both had something to do with it. Nowhere does the complete about-face from *Tristan* in conception and even in technique show more convincingly than in the first act tableau: the amiable, decent, unimaginative, and thoroughly Germanic artisans turned poet-composers casually seated around a big table. The easy conversational tone of the relaxed burghers hides a fabulous feat of ensemble writing, something Wagner had never done before and yet accomplishes here with a larger number of participants than any other composer ever attempted. Then in the third act he does something that belies all the million words he wrote about the true "music drama," as opposed to the "Latin tinsel" of the Italians. He stops the action and like any benighted Italian makes his protagonists sing a ravishing "formal" quintet that is all music, glorious music.

Tradition has honored Wagner's designation of *Parsifal* as a "consecrational festival play." The public was from the first willing to accept the thesis that when *Parsifal* is performed the stage is consecrated. Wagner contributed to the cultic concept by restricting this opera to Bayreuth, which was an excellent way to fill his coffers, but after the copyright expired the ritual was carried to other countries and opera houses. In New York's Metropolitan Opera House, the audience—though presumably largely the same subscribers who on all other occasions noisily glory in applause at the beginning, in the middle, and before the end of the arias—is completely subdued, and I am sure that if the management provided *prie-dieux* they would kneel down. In its "religious" portions this music evokes in the listener vague churchly memories, but Wagnerian music, like much such Romantic music, paints only superficial religious moods. For this purpose *Parsifal* employs old, codified liturgic melodies and archaic-sounding harmonies and counterpoints, as well as the always effective theatrical device of "voices from above." Yet this sleight of hand, this pious fraud, seems to be considered almost a form of religious observance.

It would be nearer to the truth to say that with *Parsifal* Wagner tried to replace religion with art, for he was completely blind to any other truth than his own art, which he served unstintingly, defying every obstacle. His cardinal thought was that humanity's redemption lay in art only, but since to Wagner redemption was earth-bound, Christianity was a mere mythus such as he used in the *Ring*. The Germanic saga had been exhausted in four tremendous music dramas, and at the same time, the religious theme was more appropriate to the new Second Reich—Wagner was a realist in such matters. It is significant that it is in the second act, dominated by sorcery and seduction, that Wagner's creative powers, stagnant during a good part of the first act, again rise to the summit. When Kundry, reclining on her couch, offers her outstretched arms to the innocent youth Parsifal, the searingly erotic music takes us back to Wagner's true world of Venus.

Kundry is the typical Wagnerian heroine: voluptuous and untouchable. Parsifal is a "nature boy," like Siegfried, but his natural instincts are thwarted by the complicated role assigned to him by Wagner. If he is another child of the German forest, how can he be so completely insensitive to the strongest instinct in man? Once Siegfried learns that a woman is different from a man, there is no doubt in his mind what his role should be, but Parsifal, the "guileless fool," is forced into a one-dimensioned role which, typically, is realized through sensual rapture or temptation. The kinghts of the Holy Grail are not well-drawn characters either; they, especially Gurnemanz, are long-winded and given to soliloquies compared to which Wotan's farewell is an epigram. Then, when we come to Klingsor, we are dealing with a man of Wagner's own taste and cast; he is crafty, resourceful, and has very definite objectives.

Yet though we question the spirit of this enormous work, aptly called by Nietzsche "Christianity arranged for Wagnerians," nevertheless it shows Wagner at the summit of his powers—if only intermittently. As a whole, the opera demonstrates a remarkable absence of sense of proportion; it is nearly interminable, with long passages that drag on without anything happening on stage or in the pit. On the other hand, the instrumental numbers, serene, translucent, and bewitching, are uniformly excellent, and almost the entire second act is magnificent. The leitmotif technique is noticeably less enforced than in the *Ring;* it is of course still present all the time, but used with obvious care for essentials. The employment and quality of the orchestra is so different from the previous operas that one might almost speak of a *Parsifal* orchestra. Whereas in the

Ring the winds, notably the brasses, dominate, in *Parsifal* it is the strings and woodwinds which create a velvety sonority. When the whole string body is set arpeggiating, the effect is truly incandescent.

In order to make this work what it should be—a great Romantic opera—two things are necessary. First of all, it must be trimmed to reasonable proportions—half of this opera would be greater than the whole. Second, it must be realized that for Wagner—as for his time—it was art, not religion, that provided revelation and redemption; it was this very idea that led him to offer a "religious" subject on the stage. His attitude has nothing in common with that of the musicians of the seventeenth and eighteenth centuries who composed "religious operas," i.e., oratorios and Passions, for the works of Schütz and Bach are firmly connected with established Christianity and were used liturgically. *Parsifal* stands for an independent Wagnerian religion, a religion of art essentially alien to Christianity, even though the opera seems to suggest a Christian milieu. This religion is devoid of metaphysical experience; it offers only artistic experience, and at best the stage lights illuminate certain ethical symbols in *Parsifal*, not religious ones.

But even the ethical aspects of the opera and its music must be critically examined. Art is ethical when it is good art. The spiritual aura hovering above a work of art does emanate from it, but it cannot be its substance. All art creates an ethical effect; it is not, however, its subject that does so, but its esthetic value. If *Parsifal* depended only on its subject for its effect it would not have artistic value. But it does succeed as art, though it fails both as religion and as ethics. Indeed, though Wagner is no longer the apostle he was held to be a generation or two ago, art, great art always lives, and *Parsifal* will also live. If we could see the work as an opera and not as a ritual, I really believe that *Parsifal* could be made *enjoyable*, and after all, operas are made to be enjoyable.

Can we draw a parallel between Wagner and Verdi? The biography of a creative artist should always proceed and be understood from his works, but there is no composer whose works are so far removed from his life as Wagner's. Still, this divorce is only seeming, for an artist must draw upon his inner life; he cannot completely step out of himself.

Wagner was a man untrammeled by worldly circumstance, spiritually endowed above most human levels, yet often possessed by a devil. Hard, capricious, scheming, inordinately vain, contemptuous of ordinary beings, amoral, yet absolutely devoted to his art and sincere in his inner life as a musician. Verdi's character, on the contrary, will always puzzle psychologists in search of subtleties, for it had none. It was founded on a few simple principles, formed by a strict conscience, and strengthened by great power of self-control. In everything he did we find truthfulness, a strong sense of duty, and an indomitable energy.

In the case of Verdi, who was a retiring person, even small external events could call forth great emotional reactions, but for Wagner as composer the outside world scarcely existed; he lived in his self-made myths. There is no greater contrast than the lyricism of the two great dramatists. Verdi's is nourished by human conflict and contrast, his dramatic scenes are realistic and earthbound. Wagner uses for his texts a poetic style that is lyrical in intent but most of the time succeeds only in being pretentious. He is dominated by fierce instincts that he mistakes for principles, but it is precisely at those moments when instinct overpowers reason and theory that his music is most convincing. Though a countryman and close to the soil, as a dramatist Verdi does not see nature, or whatever he sees only serves him as expressive means for a background or human characterization. Like Mozart, only living human beings interested him; among the few nature pictures he ever painted in music is the exquisite, almost impressionistic Nile scene in *Aïda*. Wagner worships nature—think of the magnificent riverine beginning of *Rheingold*, or the bewitching forest music in *Siegfried*—but man does not figure in this nature. His place is in the mythus; he is imaginary. Such exclusive reliance on imagination leads to pessimism, to a distrust of the real world, a quality that in Wagner was fortified by his reading of Schopenhauer. To Wagner the absolute goal of life became erotic rapture, the intoxicated bliss of love being consumed in death. Here the outside world disappears altogether, and in the supreme moments eroticism is transfigured into pure passion.

Transfigured eroticism, its emancipation from the bonds of mortality, is the basic motif of Wagner, and for such a man love is also sublimated; the feelings of his heroines do not develop, they merely overflow. As to the other characters, they are often merely observed and recorded, not creatively manipulated. Compared with Wagner's overwhelming and consuming imagination Verdi at first seems limited, perhaps even poor, but though he is less intense, he is much more persuasive. His imagination is all light and little color; his musical language is far less burning than Wagner's, but it is more direct, plastic, and realistic. Only under the influence of certain moods, in Verdi's early operas, do we encounter coarser accents. Verdi's spiritual development is steady and organic; his themes, his ideas, his style are all faithful reflections of an inner growth. A tetralogy would have been totally uncongenial to him because he moved from character to character, from situation to situation. He could not be attracted by myth, for he sought the painful truths of life to raise them to the tragic. He could not follow a system, a stated esthetic creed, or theoretical dramaturgy; he had to be unsystematic because there is no system in the life of men.

Wagner was a revolutionary, Verdi a conservative and, as he himself jokingly said, not afraid of the traditional commonplace; to him the great traditions of Italian opera were sacred. Nor did he show any interest in verbalizing his artistic ideas, whereas Wagner accompanied his works with philosophical dissertations and manifestoes. Wagner sought his heroes' ideas, Verdi the feelings that hide behind these ideas. Verdi is clear, simple, and transparent, and his realism is self-evident; Wagner's tremendous symphonic poems and ballads, which add up to his operas, are overpowering, but they are complicated and at times lack proportion. Verdi always shows a steady growth in maturity and wisdom; Wagner, the esthetic hypochondriac, changes from style to style, but always with a security that is as baffling as it is admirably consequent.

To Verdi, Wagner's artistic apparatus appeared too involved

and cumbersome, but he admired Wagner, a feeling that was not reciprocated. Though this admiration was qualified—for Verdi conceded the validity of Wagner's concept of opera only for Germans—it was genuine. This is the more remarkable because, although since the seventeenth century opera has been a world genre, its essence, the most profound characteristics that infuse it down to grammar and syntax, remain Italian. So it was to Handel, Hasse, Christian Bach, Gluck, Haydn, and Mozart, all of them Germans who composed Italian operas. But Verdi was right when he did not rule out other forms of the lyric stage for those differently oriented. Indeed, Wagner was the natural German complement to Verdi, and his self-styled "music drama" the other great and legitimate possibility of the lyric stage. We should look at the two composers forgetful of the old rivalry. Both have been idolized and both have been damned, if usually for the wrong reasons. Both took their art very seriously, and their opposing operatic esthetics demand equal understanding and respect. We can no more ask Verdi to sound like Wagner than vice versa, but it is clear that both have a just claim to immortality. We must be thankful that the century gave us both giants.

Fourteen

STRAUSS

THERE can be no question that Richard Strauss's most popular opera is the one in which he abandoned his avant-gardism and, calling on his phenomenal sense of the theater, recreated the spirit of the sparkling eighteenth-century opera. *Der Rosenkavalier* is a delight. But *Salome* and *Elektra*, immediately preceding it, demonstrate that there was a much bolder and original Strauss who actually carried the Wagnerian precepts to their culmination. Both of these operas are now fading, though even after more than half a century their power is of such violence that many are repelled by them. Yet both works are in their way more notable achievements than the glittering but somewhat conventional comic operas that followed.

The story of Salome has long attracted artists and writers; writers because of the subject's dramatic qualities, painters by the stark contrast of the bloody act and the dance, the severed head of the saint and the young girl. John the Baptist was of course a universally honored saint throughout the Christian world, and his martyrdom was widely celebrated. Many of the medieval cathedrals contain sculptures of Salome, usually holding John's head, though the dance scene was also popular. On the portal of the Cathedral of Rouen she dances on her hands, with legs held high. Perhaps the finest Salome bas relief is Donatello's in Siena, on a baptismal fount. Among the many painters of Salome one finds Giotto, Fra Filippo Lippi, Ghirlandaio, Andrea del Sarto, Botticelli, and Titian. But all these portraits present Italian beauties; there is nothing disturbing about these refined Latin Salomes—Carlo Dolci's seventeenth-century princess is downright sweet. Rubens's *Herodias's Daughter* is another matter; she is both woman and demon. This conception was followed by many others all the way to Beardsley, whose illustrations to Wilde's book once more catch the quality that made Salome irresistible to Narraboth. In literature, many writers, beginning with Josephus Flavius, used the theme in various interpretations and in elaborations such as Oscar Wilde's.

Though wholly persuasive in execution, the books of Strauss's *Salome* and *Elektra* are melodramatic in form, and melodrama is not the representation but misrepresentation of truth. Something more than violent incident is needed to make drama, something more than gruesomeness to make the macabre in opera. In Wilde's *Salome* and Hofmansthal's *Elektra*, which became the librettos of Strauss's operas, the longing to escape the bourgeois world, the gray existence of everyday life, becomes so strong that it ends by being morbid and aggressive. It brings with it a world in which the sexes are engaged in a desperate struggle, in which human instincts rebel against the intellect and demand uncontrolled freedom, in which sin is rampant. Men and women in these plays are unrestrained by sober judgment; they are pathologically erotic; they must destroy others and themselves too. All this weakens the drama, for it loses its ethical significance, and the violence which infects almost every emotional relationship, whether love or hatred, makes the dramatic figures seem to be case histories from an analyst's files expressed in lyric monologues approaching the operatic. Consequently, they are less than fully, or at any rate less than representatively, human. The external events are so gross as not to permit the internal drama to find expression, and for this reason the catastrophes must be wild and garish in order to create tension and dissonance. The protagonists are gripped by unnatural, fanatical passions free from thought and reason, and, having lost their ability to act independently, become no more than puppets. Men do not consort with one another in these dramas; each is merely a possible source of experience for the others, and therefore there can be no real struggle among them, nor can the external world become a dramatic factor. The protagonists appear on the scene as characters fully formed, they cannot develop, they await the fulfillment of their fate. These plays were musicless operas even before they were given to the composer, because only music could endow them with continuity, and only music could do away with the incongruity created by brutally naturalistic scenes expressed in a highly stylized, poetic language.

Strauss, attracted to Salome as Monet was to the banks of the Seine, stepped in and solved these problems with a virtuosity that far surpasses the consummate elegance of *Der Rosenkavalier*. What in Wilde and Hoffmansthal was weak drama drowning in beautiful words became raging, all-devouring erotic adventure. By applying Wagner's method of carrying through the expressive possibilities with symphonic means, thus seemingly relegating the words to the peripheries of the listener's consciousness, Strauss gave the impressionistic scenes continuity and logic; the quasi-opera became the real thing.

Reading Oscar Wilde's *Salome*, one gets the impression of scenes, morbid perhaps, but more decorative than really fearsome. As is often the case, a really skillful opera composer can transform the same scenes and words into something altogether different. Indeed, Strauss created a sordid splendor of extraordinary intensity. *Salome* is not a long opera, but by the time the soldiers crush the life out of that infamously fascinating princess, the listener is in need of a little tranquillity. The protagonists in both operas are deliberately primitive figures, nothing complicated about them, but they are filled with one consuming pathological passion, and this one searing experience completely fulfils them. When translated into music, such single-minded passions become overwhelming in intensity, and Strauss caught the intoxication, the madness, the narcosis, the complete dissolution into frenetic lust for murder, with terrifying fidelity.

Strauss had a very sharp eye for theatrical values and an excellent instinct; he spotted the essentially operatic possibilities in Oscar Wilde's play. Wilde was not a genuine dramatist; he was interested in decorative beauty and in the play of words, not in dramatic conflicts. But Salome intrigued him, and we know from the memoirs of his Parisian friends that her figure, character, and environment changed, almost day by day, as under the influence of some new book or painting, Wilde saw her in new and different pictorial tableaux. In a word, Salome was almost purely decorative to him. This is not unlike Maeterlinck's decorative dramaticism; indeed, Wilde was strongly influenced by the Belgian, but his language is broader and more vehement, for, though an eclectic, he was rooted in the English tradition, and the sensuous quality of his pictures is much stronger than Maeterlinck's. But these pictures require musical articulation even more than Maeterlinck's, for they are incomplete, almost impressionistic descriptions, in very brilliant and colorful language that threatens to drown the drama in undulating words.

The plan of Wilde's play is a surprisingly Wagnerian one, the difference being that the execution is by a genuine literary artist and not by a clumsy, make-believe dramatic poet. On the other hand, Wagner the poetaster yields to the supreme musician, whereas the elegant word artist Wilde is left up in the air; the music in the words was not enough to make the drama. Strauss fully appreciated the decorative and lyric opportunities offered by the play and it is astonishing what he did with them. The themes and motifs he invented are mostly banal—even vulgar—yet the intarsia technique is telling because the musical decoration added to Wilde's decorative language deliberately avoids beauty for its own sake. The composer was able to create genuine pathos and fearful dramatic tension, both of which are missing in the play. Strauss quested for sensational dramatic expressiveness, and most of the time he was successful. This music is not stylized, it is exceedingly receptive to nervous stimuli. The merely artistic dialogues of the playwright are invested with power, and the symptoms become facts. The shadow of death falls on the stage the very minute Narraboth lays eyes on Salome in the opening measures, and this shadow never departs. A more viciously obsessed *demi-vierge* of a heroine has never adorned opera, and the terrible saint imprisoned in a cistern, the loathsome lecher, Herod, and his murderous queen add up to a nightmare cast. When Salome tempts the captain of the guard, in that brief moment the young man's tragedy is illuminated. When Herod offers her half his kingdom, the monotonous repetition of her demand for the head of Jokanaan only enhances the constantly mounting excitement as Herod's catalogue of bribes is recited. Hysterically perverse, she stalks Jokanaan relentlessly, while at the end, writhing on the floor, her bosom heaving, and kissing the severed head of her victim, she reaches an orgiastic peak never before seen in opera. Herod's vacillation between lust and caution is as fascinating as it is repellent, and when Jokanaan emerges from the cistern one cannot take one's eyes from the tattered figure of the prophet, who is the very voice of doom.

The large orchestra is often employed like a chamber music ensemble, but in the climatic scenes all reserve is cast aside; these scenes are sheer madness and savagery even though from the masterly bedlam there emerge extraordinary visions of sound. And there is something else about this brilliant orchestra that is worth noting.

Some time ago I attended a curiously miscalculated performance of *Salome* in which not a singer could be heard above the din of the orchestra, an experience that shook my belief in some long-held critical opinions. It has always been agreed that Strauss carried the Wagnerian system to its limits. Commenting on the *Gesamtkunstwerk*, Strauss remarked that the modern orchestra not only paints, explains, and reminds, it gives the content itself, unveils the original picture, and gives the whole truth. In fact, the composer himself called *Salome* and *Elektra* "orchestra operas," while others called them "symphonic poems with vocal parts added." And so they seem to be, leitmotifs and all, yet when the singing was not heard in *Salome*, the opera's very *raison d'être* was seriously threatened. Obviously, the designation "orchestra opera" cannot be literally applied to *Salome*. The interesting discovery was that the magnificent orchestra alone cannot carry this opera as it might have been expected to do. Without fully audible singing at all times the reverse of Wilde's predicament becomes operative: the verbal wizardry of the poet is merely pictorial, it now gives way to the orchestral painting of the composer, and this too is incomplete. Whatever Strauss's original intention, the orchestra cannot represent the drama unaided; the dramatic figures must express themselves in singing that is powerful and soaring, but also intelligible. This is the more interesting because when Strauss wrote his symphonic poems—that is, before *Salome* and *Elektra*—he himself gloried in the omnipotence of the orchestra: "One does not have to bother with singers and can express his turmoil with the instruments alone."

Everything in this score is minutely calculated and actuated by springs, with the tensions calibrated; the singers must pull the springs exactly as required. What is sung on the stage cannot be expressed by the orchestra alone, though the musical substance is consistently allotted to it. So in the end *Salome* is a true opera that calls for a competent and powerful singing cast as much as does any Italian opera. Strauss always proceeds with conscious and well-thought-out artistry. Thus, since Jokanaan represents the ethical moment in the drama, his motifs are diatonic, chant-like, in the midst of a prevailingly chromatic texture, and they are never altered or distorted by rhythmic or harmonic devices as are all other motifs in the opera. Similarly, the many cross-relations in Herod's part depict his unsteady and degenerate character. In those days polytonality must have been as shocking as the subject itself. To mention an example, when Herod sings in A-minor while the two Nazarenes hold forth in A-flat on the miracles caused by Jesus, Strauss evidently wanted to contrast the two worlds. The melody is generally restless, the chords constantly merging, the rhythm and the tonality eternally changing and offering many surprises. His themes are usually very short, only in a few spots do we hear developed melodies as in Jokanaan's scene or Salome's dance. But in this music it is not the motif that is important, the elaboration is what counts as Strauss constantly strives for the maximum intensity of physical effect.

Hofmansthal's *Elektra* was based on Sophocles's tragedy, though Euripides was also drawn upon. Strauss heard Hofmansthal's play and immediately became convinced that as in *Salome*, only music could do full justice to such unutterable emotional forces. He asked the poet to convert his play into a libretto. The correspondence between the two men has been published and makes interesting reading. Strauss was very demanding, for his sure musico-dramatic instinct spotted the weaknesses in Hofmansthal's play. Characters were moved and reinstated, emphases and motives shifted and changed, and the action tightened, the result being still another version of the original Electra legend. Now all sorts of new, modern elements joined the classical myth, recalling the annoyed words of Jules Lemaître, the French literary critic: "My Lord, how exasperating it is when one is part of antiquity to have modern ideas."

What in the Sophoclean tragedy is wrought by fate and is carried into the superhuman was changed by Hofmansthal into a horrible act of raw human nerves. At that, Hofmansthal was essentially a lyricist—*Elektra* is a ballad drama (in the literary sense)—but this suited Strauss's particular talents, and the opera is a logical continuation of the Wagnerian ballad drama, though with important differences and a considerable lessening of sheer musical invention. Strauss was a great connoisseur of the stage, and he clearly saw the limitations of Hofmansthal's version of Sophocles's tragedy, for in the libretto everything genuinely human is dead; only pathological compulsion is alive. To compensate for this, Strauss attempts to break down the barriers between the conscious and unconscious levels of life, with special reference to the release of all those passions which are dormant in the unconscious. It is an achievement to have brought so original a solution to a familiar tale. This music is distinctive because Strauss strove consistently to bring librettist Hofmansthal's somewhat esoteric poetic language to earth without destroying its wings, though the very earnestness of the struggle at times makes for difficult and even ungainly musical utterance.

Strauss had a great gift for creating an atmosphere and mood at once sordid and highly dramatic, and the atmosphere is heightened by the fantastic realism of his brilliant orchestra. *Elektra* is a shocker, a reminder—badly needed at the opening of the twentieth century—that opera has something to do with drama and theater beyond placing tenors and coloratura sopranos before the footlights to entertain with mellifluous sounds. This opera is a gripping tragedy whose most obvious characteristic is violence of plot and style. When the performance is good and the singers strong-voiced, audiences do not budge until the final curtain, for the fearful tension is never permitted to slacken; one just sits there transfixed, waiting for the inevitable.

Elektra, the chief figure in the drama, has only one experience, the murder of her father, and she has only one feeling, revenge, which is the content of her life. Pacing up and down like a restless animal, she waits for the murder of her mother to take place inside the palace. Klytemnestra's agonized cry is heard—"stab her once more," screams her daughter—and the palms of our hands become moist. Klytemnestra, though important in the plot, is not really a mover in the drama; she is only the object of Elektra's revenge. Her character has only psychological interest because Hofmansthal changed Sophocles's version by taking away the moral basis of the drama, and made her a hideous creature. The pathological bent in his *Elektra* is even stronger than in *Salome;* the lines of the drama more rigidly drawn, because Klytemnestra is another creature of desolation and insanity. Though mortal enemies, she and Elektra are not in real conflict; their rhythm is too similar, because both are demented. Both of them are monumental, but bizarrely, decoratively, so. They are picturesque in a perverted way, though not really tragic. But Strauss turned their pitiful pathos into musical mood scenes of devastating power and horror. If there was a similarity of rhythm in their literary language, he changed that with his musical rhythm; if there were no force whatever in Orestes, who simply appears in the play to be Elektra's weapon of revenge, he makes his brief appearance on the stage into a breathtaking calm in the bedlam that reigns about the two tortured women. But only for a momentary spell, for the recognition scene between brother and sister once more whips up pathological frenzy.

Chrysosthemis is also taken from Sophocles. As a "confidante" or "companion" of some sort she fulfills a basic need in the sung drama; few operas are without such a part. In this case the gentle sister was needed as a foil for Elektra's violent character, as Micaela is for Carmen. The men have little to do in this opera but to kill, but their masculine appearance provides a marvelous contrast with the delirium of the women. After the brief calm, affording a respite in the unfolding drama, the assault on our nerves continues with renewed ferocity. The orchestra is even larger than in *Salome;* the symphonic-motivic elaboration is carried out with relentless logic and skill to a degree of complication where one can scarcely follow it without the score. The ranting and moaning, shrieking and screeching, this masterfully engineered chaos of unimaginable sound is relieved with equal mastery of dramaturgical strategy by the sober deliberation of Orestes's scene.

There is no romance in this opera, only hatred and violence. It must have shaken audiences half a century ago—it still does. While today some of its musical banalities are perhaps a little too much in evidence, *Elektra* is still very much alive, for it is a great score, the unsurpassed final orgiastic opera issuing from the Wagnerian heritage. The great recognition scene dwarfs everything in its incestuous erotic intensity. And to think that some chaste souls found *Wozzeck* unsuitable for upright Americans! You cannot revisit Elektra time after time, as you do *Don Giovanni*—its morbid ecstasy is too devastating—but an occasional hearing is exhilarating. Few composers of note during the last half-century have failed to be fascinated by the unholy power of *Elektra*, and the fascination continues unabated even though we realize that in order to achieve this power, the terrible and terrifying opera had to destroy certain values we hold dear. Strauss was perhaps frightened by the savage questions raised in these two operas, for he himself fled from them into the charm, elegance, and wit of aristocratic comedy.

Strauss's incomparable skill with the orchestra reached a new high with *Der Rosenkavalier*. The previous operas, heavy with orgiastic revelry, did not have the charm of whisper, insinuation, and make-believe that this one has. Strauss waded into the Freudian world and stirred it up with insatiable realism. But now he was after something else: *Der Rosenkavalier* is an attempt at pure music-making. The composer wanted to recapture the spirit of Mozart's—and the other Strauss's—Vienna, and he almost succeeded; almost, because the charm is a bit faded and the gracefulness a bit insistent. Yet he gave us an unquestioned masterpiece. Clearly, we are still dealing with a musical conqueror, even though his shining armor may be a little tarnished and may show a few scratches. This opera calls for real character actor-singers. There is the Marschallin, taking a last fling at love before it is over forever. And, as sometimes happens, the lady becomes enamored of an adolescent. Here are two roles that demand sensitive impersonation without which the situation can become ridiculous. By tradition the Marschallin is supposed to be a somewhat mature woman, yet still charming—although the tradition is largely a result of the maturity of the sopranos who venture to sing this exacting role. Though variously interpreted as a beauty and a seductress, as a noblewoman whose attractiveness is beginning to decline, and even as a magnificent courtesan, the Field Marshal's wife is not a promiscuous aristocrat, a titled harlot, but rather a *femme incomprise*. She is even noble and tragic, for, with the veiled resignation of a woman wise in the ways of the world, she knows that her lover will eventually discover that young women have more charm for him. The Marschallin's disillusionment, gradual but inevitable, is attractively realized by librettist and composer, reaching the height of introspective renunciation. Octavian, the young cavalier, is a charmer, and his rather rapid conversion from a tentative explorer of life's secrets to an ardent and chivalrous lover is delightful. Baron Ochs is a cynical old go-getter who hums waltzes while trying to make a living by pulling rank on parvenus. Sophie, Octavian's newly found flame, is a difficult role too, a mixture of soubrette and ingénue, both innocent and knowledgeable.

The surprising thing about this music is that while it is impetuous it is also conventional. The themes are mediocre, even a little trite, but they are well developed and manipulated, and, especially with Strauss's superlative orchestral imagination and technique, they acquire almost emotional force. But the qualification is important. Strauss uses in *Der Rosenkavalier* a "foreign" musical style, a deliberate archaism richly peppered with sophisticated harmonies and bedecked with sumptuous color. A certain deliberate parody of *Tristan und Isolde* in Octavian's monologues has been noted. The irony and parody are gently and cleverly suggested by fleeting quotations and metamorphoses of the Tristan motif in the orchestra. Indeed, all of this opera seems to be a parody, but perhaps it is also a secret and unspoken longing for another, bygone, world. Strauss was always attracted to the Rococo, to its elegance and delicate tinkling sound. But he was also strongly attracted to the incarnation of elegance as raised to the summit of art by Mozart. In the end, however, Strauss's evocation produces only a Mozart in costume.

The time of *Der Rosenkavalier* is Maria Theresa's and Mozart's time, but then why Johann Strauss in the middle of it? Richard Strauss said about Mozart that "he solved all problems even before they are posed," but surely here the problems are created after the fact and remain unsolved. Still, the workmanship—like the symbolism—is very, very *soigné:* no melodies and harmonies that are characteristic of Octavian's music are to be found in the Marschallin's part, and vice versa. *Der Rosenkavalier* is a brilliant and sophisticated work that can be properly presented only in a big house and with top-drawer forces. It needs all the trimmings of the court opera of old, because the indulgence in wit and caprice to the neglect of solid musical substance can be justified only by success.

Nowhere did Strauss manipulate his forces with more skill and refinement, nor write ensembles more exquisitely than in the comic scenes of *Ariadne auf Naxos*. Yet in the end *Ariadne* is a strangely miscalculated opera. It is too studied and deliberate, an elaborate portraiture, consistent and often merely vivid rather than glowing with humanity. In its final version the opera begins with a prologue, in which a group of actors and singers are preparing, respectively, a comedy and an opera seria, to be performed in a palace. Word comes to them that in order not to delay the concluding fireworks display, the master of the palace wishes both plays to be performed simultaneously. After an intermission, the combined comedy-tragedy begins as the opera proper, and we witness the classic legend of Ariadne and Bacchus entwined with the Harlequin comedy of the popular stage.

Hugo von Hofmansthal's libretto is precious and overloaded with classical learning combined with stilted *commedia dell'arte*. Between his dramatic poetry and life there is no bridge, for his vision is an avoidance of life by immersion in the negative experiences of aristocratic aloofness. This is the typical product of Vienna at the turn of the century—Vienna, the last European metropolis to maintain a semblance of an earlier Eden before the great catastrophe of the first World War extinguished even the semblance. The form of *Ariadne* is that of the Baroque, but without the Baroque's wondrous emotional vitality, true pathos, and genuine humor, for Hofmansthal's theater is only a frame; his form is a mask, his dialogue fictitious, and his heroes but mouthpieces for an artificial lyricism.

The composer who set this text to music was a man in whom by that time passion had turned to virtuosity. Strauss can still rise to eloquence, but from a memory of experience. The attempt to present opera seria and opera buffa, not blended as in Mozart but side by side, was an impossible task ending in manufactured brilliance. It is doubtful that anyone can follow the rapid transitions from the comic to the sublime, and as the opera unfolds, despite Strauss's skill and sophistication, it is reduced more and more to a tour de force. This is perhaps most evident in the cold glitter of the unreasonably difficult part of Zerbinetta; its technical difficulties are simply unbelievable. The trouble with this opera is not so much that Strauss has substituted craftsmanship for impulse as that the impulse is dissipated by an excess of psychological reservations. He succeeds, but he loses the point of the story in the process of measuring its emotional effect.

Arabella's librettist, Hofmansthal, a devotee of art for art's sake, approached the theater as a poet and esthete. His poetic language attempted to exclude everything that savored of the ordinary world. He despised naturalism, yet his dramatic figures have not only very ordinary and realistic desires, but commit rather ordinary and even tasteless acts. The dashing officer makes love to a girl in the dark, taking her for the object of his real love, and is apparently so satisfied with this poetic experience that in the end he is perfectly willing to take the substitute for his bride. Then too, one of Arabella's beaux, Count Dominik, evidently a pragmatic nobleman, kisses the youngish Adelaide's shoulder, saying, "How enchanting you are!" To which Arabella's very practical mother replies, "Dominik—don't! Maybe later. . . ." It is always thus, for Hofmansthal is filled with a desire for the overwhelming experience, yet his only experience seems to be that he has none. These characters are supposed to be aristocrats of the old Viennese nobility, but their attitudes, problems, moral instincts—and above all, their feelings and acts—are anything but aristocratic. This would-be poetic play finishes by being tailored to the tastes of the petit bourgeois, who can be expected to appreciate such subtle naturalism as the mistaken identity of lovers in a darkened bedroom; a girl brought up as a boy and dressed, of course, in boy's garb (it worked so well in *Rosenkavalier!*); or a nice animated waltz scene in a resplendent ballroom. The libretto is full of words; they are polished and graceful, but one figure speaks while the other listens, and reality is somewhere between what is said and what is listened to.

It was around this dramatic core that Strauss spun his music. It is the music of an old man who is a sovereign craftsman, inclined to whimsical musing and still capable of occasional lyric sallies. But while the near-octogenarian who composed the profound comedy and exquisite love music of *Falstaff*, Verdi, was as fresh as ever, the Strauss of *Arabella*, at sixty-nine, was a tired man, largely bereft of original inventiveness, who had fallen back on a lavender-scented Romanticism. The conclusion one is forced to reach is that whatever is straightforward in the score is due not so much to creative power as to creative weakness. The composer is unable to hold on to the dramatic truth, which slips and is spilled, at times in a sort of subtle confusion. Whenever this happens something like Till Eulenspiegel's horn call comes to the rescue, but that device can become very annoying. Since Strauss was a most resourceful composer, he could cover up his weaknesses, and his utterances somehow acquire a certain patina which seemingly transforms the hesitations and commonplaces—in sum, the confusion—into capricious fantasy. Here and there one hears a bit of music that recalls the earlier and not yet tired Strauss, but one is saddened at the effort—quite audible and visible—of the great craftsman trying to achieve by cunning what only genuine creative ardor can accomplish.

Nevertheless, no musician can remain insensible to the immense skill of this virtuoso of the operatic métier. The *Arabella* orchestra is not the powerful instrument of *Elektra;* rather it employs a musical palette of delicate watercolors. There are few heavy accents in this score; delightful demi-tints, iridescent mixtures dominate. The vocal setting is superb and always advantageous for the singers. It is the substance of this music that is disappointing. There are a few nice lyric effusions—even arias—and some appealing ensembles, but the melodic line lacks profile. Many an old acquaintance from *Don Juan* to *Salome* makes its appearance, and, it seems to me, by design: the elderly composer reminisces. One also notices, surprisingly, a faint but recognizable Puccinian cast about some of the melodies, as well as an unmistakable quotation from *I Pagliacci*. Just what to make of this I do not know. Elderly German composers often exhibit a craving for metaphysical allusions, but since the unavoidable three-volume treatise on Strauss's symbolism and imagery is not yet written, I am without guidance on this difficult subject.

Die schweigsame Frau (The Silent Woman), composed in 1935, Strauss's seventieth year, was his first work written without the help of his faithful librettist Hofmansthal. As with Gluck before him, the change in librettist was decisive for the music.

Strauss turned to Stefan Zweig, who in turn fell back on Ben Jonson, whose *Epicoene or the Silent Woman* undoubtedly derived from the Italian improvised comedy, one of the principal sources of the opera buffa. And indeed, *The Silent Woman* is an opera buffa. Though neither a truly Shakespearean comedy like *Falstaff* nor a masterly farce like *Gianni Schicchi*, it is nevertheless a successful opera, far superior to its immediate predecessors. Strauss must have realized that *Arabella* did not recapture the aristocratic brilliance of *Der Rosenkavalier*, while the scorching eroticism of *Salome* and *Elektra* he had forsworn many years ago. He therefore drew upon the eternal source of operatic rejuvenation: pure comedy.

Some may perhaps be inclined to part company with the late music of this aging composer, but Strauss is a dangerously delusive composer. His apparent commonplace can conceal qualities that are not commonplace at all. *The Silent Woman* is bright, hypersophisticated, and inordinately clever. All of its first act is masterly in plan and execution, and though later the opera often sags, there are many other felicitous scenes. The secret of the success of this opera is, of course, that there are no pretensions; everything, or almost everything, is on the surface, and no attempt is made at profundities. But this surface is quite pleasing, for Strauss lavishes care and imaginative reality upon the details with which he surrounds his characters, and the sensitive treatment of the principal figures —the old man who hates noise and the young woman who takes pity on him—discloses unexpected qualities in this old master, who for years had been merely coasting along on his phenomenal skill and savoir-faire.

The thrice-told tale of Don Pasquale—of the amorous old guardian outwitted by a clever young couple—is repeated with skill, cunning, and a touch of almost disarming irony by a composer whose knowledge of the lyric stage was consummate. Being a true buffa, *The Silent Woman* has many ensembles, and they are devilishly difficult—so difficult, in fact, that only the most extraordinary virtuosity can do justice to them. The composer used several thousand board feet of musical lumber to panel the ensembles, which at times become breathless; a top-notch company, however, can carry them off.

Ever since Goethe many German literary men have sought to emulate the great Weimar poet by revelling in classical subjects, convinced that Aeschylus and Euripides are reborn in them. The libretto of *Daphne*, by Joseph Gregor, set to music by Strauss in 1937, is one of these classical reconstructions and imitations. The composer, urgently in need of some inspiration, was badly served by it. By reworking a lovely classical legend to include a love triangle, and vacillating between realistic sensuality and poetic metaphor, Gregor destroyed the fairy tale. And the poetic metaphor often strikes one like a wreath of roses on a skull. The tragedy, so touching and poetic in Greek legend, became distorted and pedestrian in Gregor's version.

The music, well written for the medium, nevertheless seems constantly diverted from substance to manner, and one has the impression that the composer is avoiding the implications of his own theme. There are a few arias in the vein of the *Four Last Songs*, but on the whole Strauss is merely drawing on his pension fund, on the musical annuities he had saved up for half a century.

The short prelude immediately gives away the whole musical situation. It is based on a pseudo-archaic waltz or minuet dressed up with late-nineteenth-century harmonic refinements. This sort of Mozart–Johann Strauss Viennese confection was quite pleasant in *Der Rosenkavalier*, but has now become stale. Strauss masters all the shocking audacities of the turn of the century: an embarrassingly frequent use of modulation with the aid of sudden six-four chords, garlands of augmented triads, and oh-so-wicked chromatic progressions that skate and skid, slither and dive with the aimless industry of a bluebottle fly. Here and there are some passages that catch the ear, but they are overwhelmed by others of an unreal rhetoric. Strauss was misled by the poor libretto and by his belief in the invincibility of his magnificent theatrical technique. Actually, *Daphne* is evidence of a rather mournful decline.

Fifteen

BERG

AN EVENT of extraordinary musical significance took place when *Wozzeck*, one of the masterpieces of the modern opera stage, finally reached the old boards of the Metropolitan Opera House. Alban Berg's soldier is not a glamorous hero, nor is his girl a vivacious belle; this opera is the drama of un-heroism, of senseless accident, the tragedy of a poor, harassed, common soldier who kills his woman and himself. The numerous scenes in the opera chase one another like feverish apparitions until the last bloodchilling events are reached, by which time the listener is limp and shaken. *Wozzeck* has a harsh, windbitten truth, and at times it is too tightly knitted to be comfortable. The protagonists express their feelings too nakedly to escape the censure of more self-conscious minds. At the memorable first performance there were no bravos and no noisy interruptions, for this music represents the ghastly play of human and superhuman forces which torture Wozzeck, the forces that erupt from the dull soul of the downtrodden, hopelessly trying to find expression. The fearful tension thus created appears in music of great power whose dark beauty seizes the audience. "Man is a chasm," says Wozzeck, "I'm falling downward . . . into the dizzy depths." This is the key to Georg Büchner's German drama, which, although written a century and a half ago, is a thoroughly modern work. When it was rediscovered it untied the tongues not only of the expressionist playwrights but of the musicians, too.

Alban Berg followed the poet into the bottomless chasm to give the unutterable that hovers over his words a compelling shape in music, and this music, though perhaps eclectic —deeply rooted in the Wagnerian heritage and combined with powerful impressions from Debussy and Mahler—is profoundly human and spiritual. Moreover, it is operatic stuff of the first water, handled with exemplary skill.

To Berg, a man of rare sensitivity and taste, the murder itself did not constitute the focal point of the drama. What fascinated the composer and what called forth the remarkable music he created was the librettist's revolutionary spirit and his love of humanity, which unite here in a great protest. The forlorn soldier is but a cog in the big reaper that gathers in the harvest for an unknown owner; his gradual deterioration culminates in the scene of his drowning. The whole of the man may not come out, but the unquiet element does, often with tremendous though not flamboyant pathos. The Captain, fidgety, half-hearted, and sadistic, is given extremely difficult high notes and sudden falsettos befitting his volatile nature. Already in Büchner's play, the Doctor, eccentric and malevolent, foreshadows the expressionist stage. When he listens to the moans of the drowning Wozzeck, his comments are chilling. The strutting Drum Major is just a vain and stupid male, less than a man and little more than a beast. Marie is so deeply sunk in her misery, in her endless, empty quest for existence, that she is rather animal than spiritual in her expression of rage, or tenderness, or suffering. Yet we also see her as a solicitous mother, entering passionately into the one relationship granted her that is not tainted. The scene in which she reads the Bible to her child is a rare and unforgettable moment.

Sophisticated and impeccably composed, *Wozzeck* also has a good deal of imaginative innocence, but it is the innocence that has borne the shock of death and disillusionment. It represents the spirit of loneliness, the original curse, the source of sadness among men. *Wozzeck* could have been a purely social mood-sketch, for Büchner was animated by a strong contumacious protest against political conditions, but it became a drama and an opera. Its theme is at once more modern and more ancient than Romanticism, for it is the conflict of primitive morals with the morals of civilization, the incompatibility of men of different stations. But all this is only a means—this is an opera—of obtaining lyric, irrational effects. As in *Elektra*, which was the first original breakthrough in twentieth-century opera, the real, distant master is Sophocles, for Greek drama appears here in the guise of the post-Napoleonic world as the music sings of man caught in the web of fate.

The effect of psychology on dramatic poetry, and the way it has induced a deliberate attempt to explore the world below the surface, may at first seem strange. There is of course danger in tapping the subconscious and intermingling in poetry and music thoughts which lack the original logical connotations, or which come from different levels, yet the method succeeded impressively in both *Elektra* and *Wozzeck* without resulting in meanings too multiple, too nebulous to grasp. "Atonal!" was the traditionalists' accusation, but the word is now often used less in its specific technical sense than to express a vague displeasure with perfectly logical procedures. That normal, healthy, steady, rooted, and permanent basis of music that makes possible the perpetual changes and developments in style is here in abundance. To be sure, this music is in places atonal, especially when compared to, say, Massenet's, but Berg's compassion, his asceticism, his vividness of sensation, underlying and informing the work, identify it as coming from the most profound traditional sources of music.

Our very traditionalist opera patrons were impressed but also baffled by *Wozzeck*, and their bafflement was only increased by the pronouncements of the initiated, and even more by the would-be experts. They suggest that the musical texture of *Wozzeck* is based on unheard-of revolutionary devices handled with the most abstract learning. Actually, there is nothing in *Wozzeck* that does not stem from practices well known to earlier composers. Take the "speech-song." Those

who heard a good Beckmesser in *Die Meistersinger* will realize
that Berg's speech-song is but a more general application of
the same principle that Wagner used with such good effect.
And of course all this descended from the old recitative. The
"unstable harmonic idiom" mentioned by some commentators
is fully present—and greatly relished—in *Tristan;* the average
music teacher will come a cropper right in the Prelude if he
tries to nail down its main tonality. The "advanced harmonies"
found in *Wozzeck* represent the last consequences of the
Tristan ecstasy combined with the expressive possibilities of
atonality.

On the other hand, well-meaning apologists speak with
bated breath about the hair-raising complexity of the "abstract forms" employed in this opera, immediately scaring the
wits out of the innocent operagoer. But these formidable
abstract forms, supposedly never before attempted in opera,
are among our oldest acquaintances. Did not Purcell compose
a most moving aria based on one of those "rigid" passacaglias?
And did not Verdi write "strict" fugues in *Macbeth* and *Falstaff?* There is an exceedingly subtle fugue combined with a
chorale cantus firmus in *The Magic Flute*—and I could cite
innumerable other instances of "abstract construction." There
is no good opera without logical musical construction, and
some seemingly simple ones are incredibly complex in their
structure. By mysteriously referring to these difficulties,
Berg's own champions promote vague suspicions and uncertainty in the public's mind, though *Wozzeck*, in the direct line
of descent from Wagner, should be perfectly accessible to
most of us.

Wozzeck is undoubtedly the outstanding opera of the last
half-century; once it is experienced without preconceived
prejudice, no one can shake it off. It is not the learning that
makes it great, but the suggestive force of the dramatic expression, the deep compassion and humanity it conveys. It is
great because it is elemental yet refined, theatrical yet truly
operatic, dependent on the word yet autonomous, psychological yet symbolic, affective yet constructive. These are not
just a set of contradictions: the various poles are brought to-

gether in an admirable synthesis. As I suggested above, there is a kinship between *Wozzeck* and the Attic drama: in both instances the tenseness and the struggle come from the incongruity of the great idea with the lowly concrete facts. The idea must descend from its loftly heights and be realized in the coarse ordinariness of the facts. But *Wozzeck* is not a realistic document, though it contains quite a few realistic data; it is an artistic summary and presentation of the incompatibility of the various strata of culture.

Sixteen

STRAVINSKY

STRAVINSKY'S *Oedipus Rex* had always been something of a puzzle to me until a chance double bill with Orff's *Carmina Burana*, its exact opposite in spirit and craftsmanship as well as in style, suddenly placed the Russian's work in clear relief. Neither of these is a real opera. In Stravinsky's case, however, one cannot speak of stunted melodies, harmonies, or orchestration, for, unlike Orff, Stravinsky was an incomparable master composer. His is a style of composition in which the smallest idea is amplified and transformed with immense skill and inexhaustible elegance, everything radiating in a splendor of crystalline sonority. But *Oedipus* is a curious piece. Calm, purposeful, magnificently composed, yet at times dryly stylized, this admirable specimen of the art of composing elicits from the listener something less than emotional involvement. He feels that there is something here that does not reveal itself, that the composer withholds something from him —and that is an uncomfortable feeling.

What is this coldness? What causes the distances from the listener's sympathies? *Oedipus* is deliberately cold and statuesque, both in design and execution, though it treats of the nature of man, the drama is broad and human, and the theme mighty and eternal. There is almost no trace of subjectivity in this work. Jealousy, vendetta, blood feud Stravinsky describes in brilliant music, but he places the most vivid colors on his palette seemingly without any feeling, with a light hand and a rather hard cleverness. Composing is not personal confession to him but construction and color. What interests him in his figures is only what is visible—their exterior, their gestures, their acts. The motives for their acts can only be guessed; the composer does not explore their souls. This is real *l'art pour l'art*, molded on the potter's wheel right before our eyes, the beautiful deliberately raised above every other precept as sovereign ruler. Stravinsky proclaims the immortality of art against the passing of life, a cold, scintillating, infinitely polished art. But that *impassibilité*, to quote Flaubert, is nothing but self-delusion.

Precision, elegance, even objectivity are present in Sophocles too, but in his telling of the terrible drama we taste the bitter roots of the irrationality of fate. As Matthew Arnold observed, Sophocles saw life steadily and saw it whole. The Cocteau-Stravinsky version of *Oedipus Rex* is something else. The tendency of the dramatis personae to indulge in cryptic and allusive orations makes the action slight, but one must not assume that this stylization presents no difficulties. One suspects that this superior attitude, which the cultural elite and a sizable part of the public alike admire, is not quite what it appears to be. Perhaps *Oedipus* is not so "objective" as Stravinsky claimed it to be, and perhaps his objectivity is only a gesture to hide his lyricism. He hides behind a mask because for some reason he is determined to deny the love of warm life which he so abundantly demonstrated in his "Russian" works. Such objectivity, such determined aloofness, such conscious gestures can at any minute turn into irony, into a parody of their true intentions. Time and again, when a fine melody is sung, the orchestra, that magnificent orchestra of Stravinsky's that never ceases to enchant, will lash out with mocking laughter that takes away the edge of sentiment.

It was Erik Satie who first among the rebels decided to march on the Bastille of subjectivity, years before Stravinsky and others hit upon Neoclassicism. Satie objected to the delicate musical palette of Debussy, who caused the colors and harmonies to virtually blend in the listener's ear. Satie and his followers would not agree to such latitude; they objected to such vagueness. Therefore Satie created a style of almost fearful sobriety and clarity. Everything "superfluous" is banished here; harmony, part-writing, and orchestration show an aggressive opposition to the veiled harmony and color-drenched sound of Impressionism. "Stripped of expression" was the watchword of the anti-Debussyans, and stripped their music was—but not quite, for music so devoid of expression could not live. The last scene in Satie's *Socrate*, the death of Socrates, demonstrates that the creed of anti-expression itself can become expressive. The emotional quality of the mood cannot be escaped; it invades the music. Many were influenced by the dehydrated music of Satie, whose bon mot was "music should have no sauce." Stravinsky endorsed the creed of expression-free music, but the "sauce" he would not give up; he was not a primitive composer like Satie. Though his new style had little to do with the conventions, the embers of tradition glow below the impassive musical surface as they do not in Satie and Orff.

It has been said that Classicism is yesterday's Romanticism and Romanticism tomorrow's Classicism. Perhaps in some cases the difference between apparent impassibility and subjectivity, between coolness and warmth, is merely a matter of time, of historical evolution, rather than a matter of esthetics. After all, we have seen the "mathematical counterpoint" of Bach become life itself. On the other hand, a work can be cold because its tones are too refined for many persons to hear, cold because its tragedies are no longer felt to be tragic to the average man, cold because the exquisitely carved musical lines give the impression of having been composed for the sake of their euphonic beauty rather than for lyric communication. One thing appears certain: the difference that separates Romantic from Classic, Naturalism from style, frigidity from warmth, exclusivity from popularity, impassibility from confession is not a question of value. In the case of Stravinsky we do not have to guess in which category he should be placed —he has told us in unmistakable terms where he stands and what he believes in. He is isolated not because of the content of his works but because of his esthetic convictions. To him art is serious work. He offers music that is self-centered, unconcerned with everyman's joys and sorrows, not requiring the participation of the listener beyond an intellectual satisfaction. The ancients called such an artist *doctus poeta*, the learned poet; removed from the experiences of life his works are like polished crystal chalices. Faguet, the literary critic, considered it a sign of Voltaire's merit that he has risen above popularity and is now read only by those with a superior literary culture. Is this to be Stravinsky's future? He is admired by his guild, looked upon with awe, but he is not loved by many.

Stravinsky, an innocent Russian composer, arrived in the West to find a complicated and somewhat bewildering esthetic climate. The West no longer preferred a rational sense of form and texture, both of which it considered historically ready-made and of secondary importance compared to personal sentiments expressed in their immediacy, without the benefit of deliberate elaboration. Only this situation can explain the rise and subsequent acceptance of Carl Orff's rudimentary music. Going to the other extreme, Stravinsky, to whom this attitude is offensive, rejected the expression and communication of sentiments in favor of impeccable workmanship, structure, and texture. This, in fact, is carrying to its conclusion Hanslick's esthetic thesis that music does not express anything but itself. *Oedipus* is remarkable in its relentless application of this theory. To increase the remoteness of his opera and to reduce the conceptual, sentimental meaning of the work, Stravinsky had Cocteau's French adaptation of Sophocles translated into Latin, and the stage directions enjoin the singers to resemble statues.

The works of Stravinsky's later period are the stations of a firmly plotted journey which yet does not lead anywhere. These works form a great cycle; they complement and explain one another, here fortifying, there toning down, underscoring, or refining, always with deliberation and clear intent. They are adventures without events, for they offer only reflections of experiences and not their sources. This music is full of intellectual beauties, but it bypasses human life, leading from loneliness to loneliness. From his experiences Stravinsky extracts the most general, the symbolic, thus depriving the listener of the possibility of divining intimate detail. He is the slave—we might even say victim—of his own theories. Like the Parnassiens, he proclaimed that the artist must deal with his creation impersonally, without involvement. He despised Realism and Naturalism, and his principal interest became stylistic purity, seeking for every sentence the only possible, the everlasting, form and style that can be carved into rock. He speaks of himself, of course—every creative artist does—but now he is so secretive that we are forced to delight our ears with the scintillating play of the texture of the music, to the exclusion of everything else. Suddenly we realize with a shock that the abstract pursuit of the art of composition has been carried so far that the tragic king, Oedipus, no longer means much even to his creator. The experience has become so distilled that it is detached from the creative artist's personality. From the eminence of his magnificent craftsmanship Stravinsky smiles at the stuttering of the realists, at the torrents of undisciplined music. He does not draw consequences, is neither enthusiastic nor outraged; he writes music which enables him to withdraw his own person from the game.

The ways of genius are difficult to understand, and a man of Stravinsky's rank ruled by the grace of God more than any emperor ever did. The trouble is that this music is perfect—it has little else to do but be perfect; Stravinsky, to quote Berlioz's quip, "lacks inexperience." It is a pity that, beginning with his Neoclassic period, he so completely succeeded in the art of impassibility.

Seventeen

OUT OF THE
MAIN STREAM

I F WE LEAVE the small handful of great opera houses in
the United States and enter the less exalted temples where
opera can be heard, we begin to encounter the latter-day
European composers, who have produced a surprisingly large
number of operas, thanks to the intelligent subsidy policy of
most European countries. There are some remarkable works
among these, though the majority—as has always been the
case—are mediocre at best. Few of these operas reach our
shores, but of late the university opera workshops have become interested in them because, as a rule (following Stravinsky's example) they do not require the grand opera apparatus and can be performed with modest forces. And there
is of course the valiant New York City Opera, which will
produce contemporary works even though the risk is considerable. For whereas in the old days even masterpieces like
Figaro could be forced out of the repertory in favor of a
newcomer, new operas are nowadays received with reluctance
and suspicion. During my tenure as critic, few of these operas
came within my purview, though enough of them to illustrate
the main trends.

The general characteristic of these recent operas, particularly those that come from Central Europe, is their authors' predatory grasp of the inessentials of composition. Their music is like soap bubbles—colorful, cold, and insubstantial. It floats on the intelligent surfaces of consciousness without descending into the troublesome depths of feeling. Theirs is an empty form, drained of everything that has connections with life.

I suppose it is just as legitimate to produce a lightweight *pièce d'occasion* in opera as it is to compose something like *Capriccio espagnol* or *Valse triste*, but that does not mean that the composer should ignore the requirements of the lyric stage. A case in point is Darius Milhaud's *Fiesta*, which is distressingly lacking in substance. Milhaud is a cultivated composer, but the sophistication he presents is only the vacillation of contours and the lack of conviction. He cannot get hold of a human personality; he only dangles lifeless puppets on a string. These puppets may be accounted for by either of two assumptions: that the composer knows nothing about his characters, or that he was willing to do a hack job—neither a tenable artistic point of view. But worst of all, Milhaud's musical imagination has here become sterile, and what is left works outside the theater; he can only swim laboriously in a theatrical pool. The wretched libretto of *Fiesta* is accompanied by gray, invertebrate music. The rather aimless tootling and tinkling in the orchestra is punctuated by the bleating of saxophones and various nondescript sounds made by cymbals, chimes, and so forth. One gets the impression that Milhaud, a seasoned composer, just did not care.

Rolf Liebermann's *School for Wives* starts with an overture-prelude, and before the short piece is over it is apparent that this composer writes too quickly and too slickly in an idiom that was fashionable in the late twenties. When the curtain goes up, however, we behold a typical buffa setting, the singers start their animated parlando, and everything seems shipshape in the best tradition of the genre. The orchestra sparkles and twitters, the singers execute fast repartees and flit around, while Sieur Molière, ensconced in an armchair, contributes some supposedly witty observations.

But though the orchestra glitters, it offers nothing but tricks, and the singers' movements and gestures become meaningless, because they, too, merely emit undistinguished musical platitudes. Liebermann's music recalls Burney's quip made at the expense of an Italian composer: "He was obliged to have recourse to all the arts of musical cookery, not to call it quackery." Once the composer begins these tricks who is to say where they are to stop? Well, they do stop—once—and with a suddenness that is startling: a tune appears, a very good, jolly tune, and it is completely out of Liebermann's world. I do not know who composed it, but it could not have been the author of *School for Wives;* it sounds, in spite of the harmonic salad dressing, like an eighteenth-century tune. This is an extremely risky procedure to employ, for the two idioms are poles apart, and the earlier composer's song stands out clear and cameo-like in a jumble of past and present, of the superficial and the would-be profound. The impression is unavoidable that the composer did not care what he used so long as he could scrape together enough to make an opera. He is too calculatingly rapacious in pursuit of effects and emits no gleam of a musical personality.

The fascination exerted by Shakespeare on all arts and letters is still undimmed. Every new epoch finds in him its mirror, every feeling its resonance, and every tendency the basis for the expression or transformation of its tastes. Frank Martin, a Swiss composer, is one of today's musicians who pay homage to the great dramatic poet. His opera, *The Tempest,* is a curious, even exasperating, work because while in almost every department of the lyric stage it violates the essential conventions without which music drama cannot live, there is a certain personal musical logic about it. However, this alone cannot make the lyric drama.

The Shakespearean drama, like the Greek (but unlike the French) has a certain affinity with music which was given its highest confirmation by Verdi. But Verdi, and his able librettist, Boito, knew that what makes the Shakespearean drama especially receptive to musical treatment is that the action brings out character and that, while in action, these characters grow or decline. There was no evidence of jealousy in Othello's character at the beginning; Macbeth was merely ambitious and became capable of murder only during the course of the play. Music can latch onto such human characterizations with an intensity that the spoken word alone cannot approach. But *The Tempest* is not so much dramatic as it is poetic; the projected misdeeds are abandoned at their inception; even the remorse is not genuine. The characters neither change nor develop. Prospero retires and prepares himself for death; there is neither bitterness nor elation in his attitude, and he suffers no pain. There is much in this play that sounds like the great poet's farewell and there are thoughts that are the fruit of wisdom free of illusions. No real passion disturbs its peace, and love, too, glows gently, for no obstacles have to be surmounted.

Well, then, what does Martin's music do? It talks! Martin is one of those recent composers who think that song can be replaced by declamation, by a sort of recitative which alternates between perceptible pitch and "speech-song." At times even this small concession to music is revoked and the protagonists simply converse and orate, though at other times there is a bit of song that is quite pleasant.

As a rule, composers who disregard the basic requirement of opera—song—are lavish with their orchestral commentary. Martin's orchestra does indulge in some pictorialism and "atmospherics" and is well handled, but dramatically it is neutral and without any interest. As a matter of fact, there is very little genuine musical interest in this score at any point and in any reference, though a couple of the ensembles demonstrate that the composer has talent. The device of giving the part of the airy spirit to a mime while the chorus, seated on the stage, represents his voice is theatrically fatal. His gestures should suffice; translated into concrete words, they become superfluous, a mere flailing and prancing. One more thing must be mentioned. After a long and rather dreary harmonic, melodic, and rhythmic monotony, suddenly the coarse voice of a saxophone is heard, and lo, there is rhythm—of a sort. The naive conception of some European composers concerning jazz is touching, but when this Alpine version of it appears in an opera one feels embarrassed.

Carmina Burana has not infrequently been called one of the outstanding theatrical works of modern times; it has been an international success, and many have seen in it a convincing solution of the dilemma of contemporary music. Carl Orff's work is not really an opera but a "scenic oratorio." Now, most of Handel's oratorios, too, can be staged, and to their advantage, for they are really music dramas following operatic procedures. But *Carmina Burana* is quite a different thing: it is a pantomime, a dance piece with songs and choral-orchestral accompaniment. Orff took a number of medieval lyrics, Latin and German, and strung them together, but there is neither dramatic continuity nor development, just tableaux arranged in several scenes. The first part sings of the Goddess of Love and Spring, the next takes us to the tavern, the third is what the Middle Ages called a Court of Love, while the final scene presents an invocation to the Goddess Fortuna, ruler of the world. *Carmina Burana* is an independent entity in its own right, but it also forms the first portion of a tryptich entitled *The Triumphs of Aphrodite*. Thus the work is obviously dedicated to an exaltation of love; but love, the eternal source of lyricism, here appears stylized to such a degree as to lose almost every vestige of sentiment—and it does so by design.

Orff is a man devoted to an idea which he carries out with uncompromising severity. Those of us who are accustomed to listening to traditional music are likely to be nonplussed by the sounds that emanate from this score. The strangeness is caused not by dissonance, atonality, or whatever usually bewilders the public in advanced idioms, but by the fact that there is not enough distinguishable music in *Carmina Burana*. At first the elemental simplicity of the music is stunning, but soon a certain monotony makes itself felt. This is caused not by a lack of variety but by the sameness of the procedure. Variety there is aplenty, for the composer calls in turn for whispers, shouts, lusty German folk tunes, mock Gregorian recitation, yodeling, and all sorts of other things. At times there are grunts and sighs, at others the chorus chatters like the Metropolitan Opera audience during orchestral intermezzos. Then we are transported to the German equivalent of Coney Island. But in every instance the composer drops his material without attempting the slightest manipulation of it. Yet this is no idle play with sounds; a thoroughly planned purpose is behind the well-organized score. There are few melodies; Orff prefers melismas—microscopic melodic fragments which are repeated, at times endlessly. There is no development, musical or psychological, of the kind we find even in the most advanced music—hence the feeling of not enough music—and everything is pared down to a crudely energetic primordial simplicity.

"I write for the theater in order to convey a spiritual attitude," says Orff. How is this spiritual attitude represented and conveyed in music? I quote from the analysis printed in the playbill for a performance at New York's City Center:

Orff eschews any pretense of counterpoint or any standard technique of elaboration, including even the simplest developments. . . . The harmonic progressions are simple. . . . there is virtually no chromaticism. . . . Orff does not often vary his meters. . . . there is a virtually unrelenting repetition of short phrases. . . .

This is a pretty barren picture of esthetic amoralism. When listening to this music devoid of any and all of the wondrous "standard techniques of elaboration" which have made music an art and a spiritual force, one cannot help recalling the drunken sailor in *The Tempest*. He sings a few lines, then stops: "This is a very scurvy song to sing." Then he sings another strophe: "This is a scurvy tune, too." In *Carmina Burana* he could go on repeating this judgment from the first to the last tune. Obviously, there is very little musical substance in this work, but form too is wanting; there is missing one of the most important formal requisites of the drama, cantata, or whatever *Carmina Burana* is: it has neither a beginning nor an end. The whole work consists of episodes, and this episodic quality is in reality a testimony to the absence of feeling for the whole, which no amount of theatrical realism can cure. Orff's realism is as calculated as his construction is loose and is a realism which must be expressed raw, without the intermediary artistic symbols.

There remains, then, one more factor—the rhythmic, for it is claimed that rhythm is Orff's point of departure, and that it is the vitality, the cumulative effect of his obstinate rhythm, which gives the work its "incredibly telling effect." Rhythm is a term of exceptionally elusive meaning. When one begins to examine its outwardly extended connotations one may find oneself talking loosely of instinct, cosmic force, and heaven knows what vaguely metaphysical notions. But we must not forget that the primary fact about rhythm is that it is a psycho-physiological function and that it must acquire an esthetic application before it can convey a "spiritual attitude." The ceaseless pounding of a simple, unvarying formula is certainly a poor specimen of such esthetic application and cannot remotely touch the savage grandeur—and finesse!—of the rhythmic power of a Bartók or a Stravinsky.

What then does *Carmina Burana* convey, and in what manner? According to Orff's own declaration, made after he destroyed his earlier, "conventional" works, his aim is the resuscitation of the musical theater by freeing it from all the exaggerated means of expression at which opera has arrived at the beginning of the twentieth century, and by reducing it to the elementary components from which it was first created." This sounds fine but makes little sense at either end. Besides, the device of apologizing for simplicity before committing it is a little ingenious. Orff's imagination is visual-theatrical; most of his music has no independent value as music—it is part of the decor and background. The musical motifs, subatomic, are mere allusions; they are never developed. The melody, such as it is—and it can be downright corny— is entirely diatonic. The harmony is triadic, and the principal element of construction is the ostinato. This is an altogether arbitrary, contrived, didactic art, which amuses at the beginning, bores in the middle, and irritates by the end. Orff rejects expression as one of the aims of music, rejects harmony as a soil from which melody grows, and elevates rhythm to the position of the chief progenitor of ideas. At the same time he reduces his vigorous rhythm to simple and uncomplicated patterns, dismisses counterpoint, avoids chromaticism, and discards thematic and motivic work, variation, modulation, and all formal construction that goes beyond the simplest four musical walls. In the end one realizes that Orff shows no skill in composition and unconvincingly affects a knowledge of the anatomy of music. There is no design in this work, only devices, and, amazingly enough, there is little of the pictorial either. Orff does not use a palette; he takes the colors straight from the tubes. It is unfortunate that what was probably intended as fantasy is in fact no more than ingenuity.

Now what does remain? There must be something, because Orff is a very popular composer in Germany and is acknowledged elsewhere, notably in this country, as a leading "modern" composer. His concept is hailed as a new *Gesamtkunstwerk*. At first it does seem so, because Orff demands a sort of integrated theater in which all the constituent elements have an equal share. But the Wagnerian "universal art work," whatever its claims and theoretical premises, is still opera. Orff makes the usual disclaimer of the operatic reformer: "In my work my concern is not with music but with spiritual exposition." But how can a composer forget that he is a musician? Surely neither Gluck nor Wagner, both of whom made such claims, ever ceased to be musicians, great musicians. This silly idea that operas can be created by ignoring music, which has cropped up periodically ever since Monteverdi, reminds me of what a Queen of Spain said to the King: "I can make princes of the blood without you, but what you can make without me has quite another name." In Wagner music still predominates, and on the whole absolutely so, whereas in this supposedly unified theater, music has a distinctly subordinate role; Orff's creations should not be called operas, or oratorios, or cantatas, or whatever name they go by. But then what is *Carmina Burana?* The answer is conjectural, but it acquires probability when several factors are taken into consideration: it is *Gebrauchsmusik*, "workaday music" of a particular sort. Not like Hindemith's, which never leaves the bosom of our modern Western music, but the sort that forswears the judgment and tastes of the musical elite, addressing itself to the masses in order to furnish them with an easily assimilable "contemporary" art in which all the "learned" apparatus of our millennial musical culture is sacrificed.

Orff relies on projections into the unconscious mind, a riot of upper-case rock-and-roll that sets the limbs in motion and the hips swinging. It goes without saying that the physiological-biological element should not be dismissed or even minimized. The energy issuing from the oscillations of sound communicates a certain tension whose effects are well known and have been counted upon since the beginning of recorded history. We have heard of music's erotic effects; indeed, music has been called "the greatest procurer," and Plautus gives a vivid description of the musical training given to girls preparing for the courtesan's career. Everyone is familiar with the martial feelings evoked by a military band. Though all this belongs in the realm that lies below the esthetic, what a foundation to build on it is! The whole range of the customs of life, love, religion, and everything that agitates man is involved. No wonder that music is magic, and that with it Orpheus could tame the wild beasts. Orff counts on these psycho-physiological effects and uses them with skill; the results are original and apparently exert considerable attraction upon audiences. A certain dynamism and directness of effect are indubitable, but the pleasant illusion of archaism soon fades, because all customary means of musical development are ignored. The dogged diatonicism becomes irritating, and the obstinate constancy of the primitive procedure, the enforced elemental-elementary tone make one beg for some of the "exaggerated means of expression" Orff so cavalierly dismisses. Opera was "expressive" from the moment it was born, and it was born because of the need to rise above the expressive possibilities of the spoken theater. Even a cool and meticulous classicist like Cherubini could send an audience home limp with emotional exhaustion. As to early opera, the very first full-fledged example of the species, Monteverdi's *Orfeo,* is anything but "elementary"; it contains all the essential ingredients of the genre, makes bold use of all the technical refinements of the composer's art, and is steeped in emotion.

No, Orff's is not an artistic but a social-educational concept. A glance at the list of his works will disclose a quantity of educational pieces for laymen and children, the purpose of which is to make music easily assimilable for the largest number of persons by refraining from using what he calls standard techniques of composition. *Carmina Burana* simply represents a carrying over of the socio-educational idea into the realm of art. Unfortunately, this concept originated in an era, in the 1930s, and in a country, Germany, when approved artistic efforts followed well-planned and guided formulas, and the "standard techniques of composition" of a Hindemith were proscribed. Once embarked upon this socially equalized art, there was no turning back. The sequels to *Carmina Burana* consist of the same easily assimilable hodge-podge, revealing a composer who simply does not have the sheer creative force and musical talent to convert the social concept into convincing art. As we listen to this music, the feeling cannot be dismissed that Orff is a product of the artistic doctrines promulgated during the Third Reich. For his music is a sort of instrument of mass education which carries the marching songs, work songs, and other "folk art" of that era onto a seemingly esoteric, pseudo-classical plane; but the intended and obtained mass reaction is uncomfortably familiar.

All this sounds striking to our public only because it is largely beyond the range of their ordinary musical experience, which is seldom exposed to such a crass appeal to primitive instincts. Stravinsky's *Les Noces* is a masterpiece, and being really bold and original, its recognition is restricted even at this late date. But take a watered-down imitation—*Carmina Burana* is obviously patterned after *Les Noces*—and it will be hailed everywhere, even though it cannot hold a tiny candle to the original.

Benjamin Britten is England's most prolific opera composer —in fact, one of the most prolific anywhere on the international scene. A musician of remarkable talent, he is a lyric theater man, and a courageous one. Take *The Turn of the Screw:* it took daring to make Henry James's thriller into an opera, for it is basically unsuited for the purpose, vague, full of symbolism, philosophy—and ghosts. Myfanwy Piper did a fair job of conversion, but without the particular musical structure employed by Britten this would have been a hopeless case. This structure is of great importance, and it remains to be seen whether this method of composing operas may not offer one solution to the question of contemporary opera.

For it is a system, indeed. The opera is constructed within the framework of a theme and fifteen variations. Thus Britten followed the example set by Alban Berg in *Wozzeck*, composing an opera along well-defined, "abstract" musical lines. This is not a new idea; set forms, even fugues and passacaglias, were used by earlier composers to good advantage, and complicated tonal constructions based on key relations and symbolism were used felicitously by Handel and Mozart. There was nothing artificial about this, even though the devices were used in theatrical works. Now it would seem that here we have a basic departure in Britten's own development, a complete turn of the screw in his music, too, but it is only illusion, devilishly clever illusion. Britten is a musician of stature, and his facility is legendary; therefore he has the ability to decide for himself what style to follow in any given work. He was baptized in the dodecaphonic faith on dry land, not by immersion. There is a tone row, but the faithful should not rejoice, for Britten goes his merry way paying scant attention to the doctrines; the harmonies, though very subtle, can be juicy enough to satisfy the most lecherous impressionist. As a matter of fact, the music of this opera cannot fail to satisfy all denominations. It is exceedingly well made; the continuity is smooth even though there are individual "numbers" imbedded in it, some of them of Webernesque brevity. The orchestra is handled imaginatively, though at times it does dish out pure corn, like those runs in the harp; the vocal writing is excellent, though there are some shockers. At one point one of the ghosts sings atop a tower just like an oriental snake charmer; it is a bit of exotic solfège with glockenspiel accompaniment. The work is on the whole somber, at times melodramatic, and Britten also uses folk song that suits the children's characterization. While perhaps not everyone's cup of tea, *The Turn of the Screw* is genuine opera, and it exhibits the unmistakable stamp of a musical personality.

Britten's *A Midsummer Night's Dream* is quite another story. Shakespeare's comedy, written in a glow of affection and humor, lends itself to operatic treatment in style, subject, and tone; Peter Pears and the composer adapted it for their purposes with skill. But conventional grand opera would give us only wax figures, accurately bedizened and unconvincingly posturing. With superb theatrical insight and thorough knowledge of the English musical theater, Britten made *A Midsummer Night's Dream* into what in the eighteenth century was known as a *festa* or *serenata*—a real fairy opera, vivacious, dreamy, jocular, and frisky. And he had the excellent idea of turning the little commedia dell'arte piece in the third act into a masque that breathes the spirit of the authentic comic opera.

Britten is a born opera composer. The texture of his music can be loose, but it is always dramatic in movement. His language occasionally tends to be rather enthusiastically fluent, but he can reach out impressively to genuine inventiveness and flights of imagination. He knows exactly when to turn to sustained song and when to banter, and he succeeds where most others fail—in the natural presentation of the ensembles. In this opera he established with fine judgment the right proportion of clowning and singing; the pleasant capering is never permitted to intrude on the lyricism, and the fairy-tale atmosphere is very engagingly realized. If in *The Turn of the Screw* Britten used key symbolism—white note keys against black note keys—here he employs orchestral tone-color symbolism; each group of characters is associated with certain instrumental timbres. Now we come to the role which turned out to be a most imaginative choice: Oberon, assigned to a countertenor. Ordinarily, when a countertenor is pitted against a whole batch of lusty and very personal voices, his neutral timbre stands out rather prominently. In this case the fairy king is not a bit of Elizabethan historicism but a creature as fantastic as the play.

Critics of opera are always clamoring for good and entertaining theater in a language the audience can understand— well, here it is. If the public does not take to it we may just as well throw in the sponge and admit that what we really want is mere applaudable bawling, the *Giocondas* and *Adriana Lecouvreurs*.

Before turning to the latter, I should briefly mention two works that do not fit well into any category.

Manuel de Falla is best known for the works he composed after taking up residence in Paris, where he became intimately acquainted with Dukas, Debussy, and Ravel. He soon acquired the French school's refined and sophisticated musical language and technique, which he skillfully merged with his own. *El Amor brujo*, a ballet, convincingly demonstrates this. So Falla, a profoundly Spanish musician, was at the same time an eminently European composer in the mainstream of Impressionism. But *La Vida breve*, composed at the age of twenty-nine, before Falla left his homeland, is entirely rooted in Spanish folklore; this is authentic Spanish music, far above the capabilities of Falla's immediate predecessors and contemporaries in his native country. Yet while it is based on the warm and passionate folk art of Andalusia, Falla—like Bartók—is usually his own melodist. *La Vida breve* is filled with delightful music, and there are some outstanding individual numbers, yet with all its excellent qualities it is not good music drama. The libretto deals with the thrice-told story of the jilted woman who dies of grief. While a poor libretto is a great and often fatal handicap, a musico-dramatist who is not only born to his calling but reared in a living tradition of the lyric stage can overcome it. Falla did have the dramatic instinct, but there was no real Spanish operatic tradition for him to follow. The many beautiful "set" numbers—madrigals, dances, songs—convey the working of a very attractive musical mind, but whenever the composer must reach beyond the Andalusian idiom, in the more elaborate scenes and ensembes, he seems to express himself in a somewhat foreign tongue. Also, the principal figures are not well drawn—they are not flesh-and-blood characters—so that while *La Vida breve* ends in catastrophe it is not a tragedy. Nevertheless, a good performance of this elegant and lively music offers a welcome change from the standard fare.

Few German operas of the late- and post-Wagnerian period are welcome in this country. Two fine comic operas—and both independent of Wagner—Cornelius's *The Barber of Baghdad* (contemporary with *Tristan*) and Goetz's *The Taming of the Shrew* (1874), are altogether unknown in America. Only Flotow (*Martha*), Goldmark (*The Queen of Sheba*), and Humperdinck (*Hansel and Gretel*) knew a temporary vogue. Nearer the end of the century, among the many operas of Weingartner, Ritter, Schillings, Kienzl, Pfitzner, and many others, perhaps d'Albert's *Tiefland* achieved a few performances here, but the others are not known even by name. The only work from this vintage I heard during my activity as critic was a semi-staged performance of Hugo Wolf's *Der Corregidor*.

One would expect a fine song composer to be particularly adept at writing operas, yet the history of music contradicts this notion: the greatest of them, Schubert and Schumann, failed in the theater, and Brahms never even got there. Hugo Wolf, a great song composer of mimosa-like sensitivity, was no exception to the rule; his opera, *Der Corregidor*, composed on a libretto derived from Alarcón's *The Three-Cornered Hat* (Falla's ballet goes back to the same source), is very disappointing. Here and there one encounters a little gem of a number, or a fine transplanted song, but the continuity is makeshift, the comedy often stagnates, and the *Meistersinger*

orchestra is clumsily handled. Wolf had neither stage sense
nor experience; extremely responsive to poetic values, he had
to struggle with an unpoetic and poorly constructed libretto.
Though his remarkable piano accompaniments to his songs
are minutely developed and full of variety, at times even ar-
riving at the borderland of orchestral Impressionism, his orchestral writing is laborious and heavy-handed.

Wolf was a musician for whom the "inner music" of the
poem determined the form, gait, and tone of his music to a
degree unknown to German composers and encountered only
among Frenchmen. Unlike any other musician's, his development was dictated by the poets he set to music; he had his
Mörike style, his Goethe style, and his Heyse style. Such an
ultra-refined lyricist, who hangs on every word, and hence is
a miniaturist, can never envisage an entire dramatic scene; he
can apprehend with infinite responsiveness the most delicate
verbal stimuli, but he cannot summon dramatic force. Since
in this case he dealt not with a real poet but with an amateur
dramatist, *Der Corregidor* was doomed from the outset. It is
also surprising that he should have composed a comic opera,
because his nervous concentration often gives his humorous
songs a slightly bitter taste.

Wolf's ideal was the kind of musical declamation that takes
place in the scene between Hans Sachs and Beckmesser in the
second act of *Die Meistersinger*, but he carried it too far. In
a brief song, this idiom can be charming, but in a long operatic
scene it can succeed only when the cadre and the timing are
well calculated from the theatrical point of view, as they are
in Wagner's opera. Furthermore, Wolf's vocal setting not
infrequently suggests the keyboard as its origin, which, again,
may work in a faithfully declaimed song where the poetic
meter is closely observed but fails in a dramatic vocal melody.
This opera proves the astonishing inability of harmony to
take the place of melody, which is the mainstay of opera.
Wolf was not so much a melodist as a master of weaving
motifs. The vocal line he manipulates with his fingertips, while
his hands are engaged in shaping the harmony. To be sure,
these fingertips are the most sensitive in the world, placing ac-

cents and inflections with remarkable delicacy, but the melodic line is in reality a residue of the rich chromatic-enharmonic harmony, which is constantly on the move. This creates wonderful warmth and passion in *The Italian Songbook*, but in *Der Corregidor* it is only sporadically felt. Some individual numbers taken from the opera and sung as concert pieces would make for pleasant listening, but even a superb performance could not make this work live on the stage.

Opera is a social form of art par excellence and therefore very perishable. Certain times accept certain conceptions of life which in turn permit certain forms of the theater. However, if there is a continuity of opera production, conventions develop that are well understood by the public, who therefore are never entirely at a loss when new works are added to the repertory. This explains the continuous vogue of opera in Italy, France, and Germany, and more recently in Bohemia and Russia. It also explains the fact that wherever opera is on the periphery of musical life, as in the English-speaking world, it cannot develop and is not properly understood and appreciated. Nor can it develop without active participation by native composers. It must be admitted that we have neither operatic traditions nor conventions; what we see in New York's Metropolitan Opera House or London's Covent Garden are importations from abroad, pretty well limited and localized. Yet we demand that these theaters should function as if located in Milan or Vienna.

If we look at the international scene, we see a bustling operatic life pursued in dozens of opera houses. Such operatic activity is naturally based on the solid foundation of the "classics"—Mozart, Verdi, Wagner, Puccini, Rossini, Strauss, and so forth—complemented by the local classics valid only in their own country. To this repertory must further be added contributions from living composers, as well as revivals from the nether regions of operatic history. This has been the procedure in the principal opera theaters in Europe for some time. Thus in Italy they revere their Verdi and Puccini, but they add to the repertory Dallapiccola and Paisiello; the Germans are devoted to Mozart and Wagner, but they include in their programs Henze as well as Weber. Similarly, the French are still enamored of Gounod and Massenet, but they also play Poulenc and Rameau. It is only thus that stagnation is averted and a real operatic culture maintained.

What our public does not know, and is not likely to know, is the large repertory of operas by those transition figures who bridge the gap between the favorites of the last century and our own times. Since our operagoers have never been exposed to this uninterrupted supply of home-grown opera, largely unpalatable to foreigners but nourishing fare for those conditioned by the national idiom and conventions, we have been left stranded as in no other form of art.

In Germany, although a host of composers remained engulfed in the post-Wagnerian world, a number of musicians began to realize that there must be a return to the kind of opera where music is not obscured by itself. Unfortunately, whether Schreker or Pfitzner, or dozens of others, none of this is exportable from Germany. The French post-Debussyans are just as unacceptable to foreigners as their German confreres; only Ravel's *L'Heure espagnole*, Charpentier's *Louise*, and an occasional work by Poulenc managed to cross the French borders. Bohemia is also full of opera, and for once this music is accessible to us—witness the engaging *Bartered Bride*—yet nothing else is heard; Janáček's *Jenufa*, very popular all over Central Europe, failed to establish itself in this country. And there is Polish opera, Swedish opera—all of it unexportable—and Russian opera. Some of the latter is viable anywhere if well done.

The nineteenth century, which began with Rossini and ended with Verdi, left an operatic legacy to Italy that the new century promised to continue. Puccini became as much a world conqueror as his famous forebears, but by the 1930s it was evident that while the minor masters were numerous and successful in their own country, the conquerors had disappeared. In Italy the repertory is large, but such transitional composers as Alfano or Zandonai would fare no better beyond the Alps than Pfitzner or Blech; they too depend on a public intimately acquainted with the national operatic conventions.

Every country that has produced a great deal of opera evolves an idiom that becomes part of the bloodstream of its public. Works of real stature composed in this idiom eventually make their triumphal way beyond their native boundaries, but the majority of national operas stay at home; their protagonists have a familiar likeness, an air of being figures from earlier operas disguised with new names to replay similar parts. No country has so many of these as Italy, which is quite natural since Italy is the home of opera. Besides, mediocrities are the normal and natural appendage of artistic fashions. With her many opera theaters and a large repertory, Italy can afford to maintain the operas of Cilèa, Ponchielli, Alfano, and many others because the warm vivacity and fragrance of the Italian countryside, streets, and homes usually comes through even in the poorest of these works, raising sympathetic echoes in Italian bosoms. But for the rest of the world, they are not worth a row of pins. Still, though these operas are for domestic consumption, some of them are exported—more precisely, imported for those who like musical potted plants. (Another reason is the insistence of some prima donnas on certain operas as the condition for their appearance. The opera manager, dependent on the star system, must acquiesce in this artistic blackmail.) For such an audience the Metropolitan Opera can supply some moments of agreeable artistic delusion. But what echoes can Ponchielli's *La Gioconda* raise in American bosoms? All the musical phrases are time-scarred relics, devoid of artistic personality and substance; the orchestration is routine; the melodies are held together by safety pins and the harmonies by adhesive tape. Such pernicious piffle can please only those listeners who are interested not in opera but only in spectacular singing.

In D'Annunzio's novel *Il Fuoco* (The Fire), a couple are gently rocking at dusk in a gondola. The woman closes her eyes as she listens to the gondolier's song, one of those semicommercial tunes that have displaced the ancient folksong. "This is the soul of Venice," she whispers ecstatically. "No," says her companion with feeling, "this is not the soul of Venice, only its very small image." There is indeed a great difference between the sublime and the everyday tone of a nation's artistic output; only second-rate art is willing merely to furnish accompaniment to passions, and only second-rate passions need accompaniment. The *Giocondas* are both slick and insignificant; they may possess some impromptu flavoring, but the human qualities do not shine through. The ear roller-skates along their smooth passages unchecked by any particular demand upon the attention, and their characters are as real and prosaic as one's fellow passengers on a train. *La Gioconda* is the operatic equivalent of the gondolier's song; tepid, pseudo-romantic fabrication. What do we have in common with this Cremonese opera which was born among our grandmothers' artificial flowers and stuffed canaries, in a false world forgetful that there was another Cremonese composer by the name of Monteverdi?

There are however two other varieties of this imported home-bred Italian opera: the good show, and the respectable try. Of the first of these a good example is Umberto Giordano's *Andrea Chénier*, which can be appraised from two different points of view. There are those who say that this kind of naturalistic opera is a thing of the past and should not be revived, while others aver that a good show is always justified. There is merit in this last view. Giordano, like Leoncavallo, was a one-opera man. Not that he did not compose others, but *Andrea Chénier* was his *Pagliacci*. But we should not assume that he was a lucky tyro; any opera manager who does not mount *Andrea Chénier* simply cheats his pocketbook.

All of us know how a best-selling novel is sometimes concocted. Take a good historical subject, handle it with generous license, add several grains of sex and blood, and success is assured—that is, if the ingredients are well mixed. The librettist of *Andrea Chénier* knew this business inside-out, and Giordano was a past master of operatic goings-on, of the tried and proved obsolete style and substance. He followed a pattern current at the end of the century, which consisted of a cheerful empiricism based on a sure appraisal of the feelings of the public, refractory to all definite commitments and using nothing but stock musical phrases. All the ingredients, however, are employed with skill and please the listener who simply wants a good show and good singing. Giordano had a very good sense of the stage, knowing exactly what will come off and what looks good only on paper. The courtroom scene, seething with shrieking, bloodthirsty wenches and the shouting, gesticulating mob, is a very imaginative bit of theater. If it were not for a lack of melodic profile, *Andrea Chénier* could be as much a perennial favorite as the celebrated double bill affectionately known as "Cav 'n Pag." However, that is a very big "if." As long as Giordano's vocal setting, imaginative orchestra, and colorful manipulation of principals and crowd are alive and in being, the listener is absorbed in the spectacle, though after he leaves the theater very little sticks to his musical ribs. Yet I fail to see why such expert operatics are any less justified than, say, a clever play. We do not have to invoke the name of Shakespeare or Verdi every time a play or opera is performed. If the show is good, the workmanship expert, the singing agreeable, the staging imaginative, we have a good night at the opera.

Ildebrando Pizzetti, a distinguished musician who has been in the forefront of Italian musical life for half a century, represents our third category of unexportable—or nearly so—Italian opera: the respectable try. Listening to his *Murder in the Cathedral* (libretto after T. S. Eliot's play), one feels the presence of a cultivated and elegant musical mind comfortably at home in the operatic world; yet the prevailing impression is more cultural than creative. At every turn it is evident that Pizzetti is the product of an ancient civilization of classical strength and valued ideals, but the results are not commensurate with the ideals. *Murder in the Cathedral* is a modern religious mystery play, but at the same time it is "coterie literature," like a good deal of Eliot's poetry, ultrarefined and sophisticated, and thus hardly eligible for operatic treatment. The Italian translation simplified the language and made it more suitable for musical setting. The librettist's task was to emphasize what is implied in the play, namely, what happens within Thomas à Becket rather than what happens to him—not a murder, but a spiritual struggle. Therefore, *Murder in the Cathedral* becomes a scenic oratorio consisting of a number of tableaux, some of which are impressive while others are pale and static. There is no real dramatic conflict in the theatrical sense, for the Archbishop's struggle is with himself; most of the others, notably the Women of Canterbury, are passive figures. Only the four Knights who commit the murder strike really operatic attitudes, and immediately the native Italian operatic savoir-faire appears. The music is always well bred and well written, the orchestra is handled with skill and delicacy, the choral writing is excellent; but all this is rather impersonal and unoriginal—impressionized Puccini leavened with a little Wagner.

Eighteen

AMERICAN OPERA, NATIVE AND NATURALIZED

OR THE PAST two or three decades the operatic world in the United States has shown considerable activity. I refer not to the "official" New York–Chicago–San Francisco axis of opera, for that seems to be immutable, but to the composing of operas, which, some hold, is as important as the productions themselves. Historically the English-speaking world has always regarded opera with suspicion, as a foreign importation, a plaything for the rich, and something vaguely immoral and popish at that, failing to notice that ever since Monteverdi's time, wherever opera was neglected all music declined. This was particularly true in England. Then came the spectacular regeneration of music in that country early in this century, and later the arrival of our own American composers on the international scene. Both of these movements were accompanied by a renewed interest in opera, at first sporadic and tentative, then, after the second World War, assuming vigor and considerable proportions. But as American opera proceeds at an accelerated pace, it also catches up with the problems that have beset this unique art form in those countries where it looks back upon a long past.

All operas composed by Americans are touched in one way or another by these problems.

It can be persuasively argued that the new opera, like the new literature of the advancing century, should relate to the temper of the time, its ideals, its beliefs. It was so with *The Magic Flute*, or *Fidelio*, or *La Forza del destino*. However, these ideals and beliefs must be expressed by means of the very special language and conventions of opera; topical subjects in themselves do not suffice. Wagner returned to myth and history as the favored subjects for opera, but the post-Romantic era felt that these should be abandoned for the everyday milieu. This stylistic reorientation in opera is one that seems to return periodically, almost in a natural cycle. When it reappeared toward the end of the last century, we should have expected it to embrace the bourgeois virtues of the day, but for some reason the librettists did not turn to the great dramatists of bourgeois ethics, like Ibsen, but to the extreme realists, like Sardou and Verga. And somewhat later they drew on even psychiatry and social philosophy. Exotic sensualism became one of the favorite themes, from *Salome* to *Lulu*, or the raw realism of some symptomatic phase of modern social life. Realizing the growing incompatibility of twentieth-century culture with opera, some European composers have tried new approaches to the modern lyric stage. Some employ so-called speech-song, others regulate opera by planning the music along "abstract" instrumental-formal lines. Neither of these methods has as yet furnished a lead. The first, speech-song, is a contradiction in terms—opera must be sung, or it is not opera. As to the second, though Berg's *Wozzeck*, with its intricate architectural design, is a convincing masterpiece, no one, with the exception of Britten, in *The Turn of the Screw*, has as yet successfully duplicated Berg's achievement.

Seeing the barrier in their way, many American composers reverted to the older, established operatic idiom still followed by many Europeans, trying to mine a lode that is in fact far from exhausted. They use a "conventional" musical language, and their subjects tend to be historical. Granted, the general atmosphere of many of these operas, artistically as well as dramatically, is *fin de siècle;* but an opera should not be dismissed either because it is old-fashioned or because it is in a very advanced idiom—both of which are relative notions—but only if it is badly built of poor materials. Music is by no means immune from the common tendency of each generation to become particularly impatient with and insensitive to the merits and achievements of the one before it. In the late fifties I heard some poor specimens of European avant-garde opera as well as the pleasant homespun of Samuel Barber, Douglas Moore, Robert Ward, William Bergsma, and Carlisle Floyd. These composers were immediately derogated, even by some critics of good faith and competence, because their musical language is of an older vintage, and their librettos are removed from the contemporary scene. The scornful were justified to a degree when they objected to a certain archaic grand opera quality of these operas, but only to a degree, for some of these composers simply accepted—as did Schoenberg—the musical system that was most congenial to them, and within this system they are consequent, and above all, artistically honest. Every human creation, if well realized, has validity, whatever the style or the vintage. While there are degrees of value among artistic works, the value of one does not diminish that of another. Unlike some fashionable European composers, Barber, or Moore, or Ward show no striving for effect, no self-conscious touch of modernity in manner or treatment, but an expressiveness that makes its own quiet appeal. Their works may not endure, but they have lyric talent, sincerity, and the ability to compose in an unaffected style that does not confuse the issues.

What Royal Cortissoz said about American painting, that it has "no local tradition or influence, no archaic style to be vaguely felt in advanced works," goes equally well for American music. Further, it might be questioned whether there actually is an American music, in the sense of a specifically American esthetic attitude comparable to those that distinguish French from German music. But there can be no doubt that there has been a good deal of American music with a specific character of its own, good examples being offered by Charles Ives and Aaron Copland. Still, the use of snatches of jazz, or of popular tunes, marches, and hymns, or of Negro spirituals, will not in itself make music American; if that were the case Dvořák would be one of our charter composers. After an initial trial period, reliance on such devices as a stylistic basis was largely given up. Once this stage was passed, we detect a more subtle American quality in our music. Still, the harvest of American opera is meagre, but we must recognize that its extent and measure correspond to some socio-artistic reality. The native American composers whose works I encountered during my term as critic are mostly musicians who shied away from the contemporary battlefield, obviously feeling greater affinity with the more peaceful world of the past. They have contributed to the growth of American opera; it is only regrettable that our "conservative" composers did not find new and living forces in late Romanticism.

The few American operas produced before the war were composed without any individuality, shaped on an outmoded nineteenth-century last. The little local color provided by the use of jazz or folk tunes only made this more painfully evident. Then came a young man to implant a tradition that up to that time had not found a representative in this country. Gian Carlo Menotti is an Italian composer who has become a world citizen equally at home everywhere. He brought to opera in the United States the theatrical power of catching an atmosphere, of summing up an impression. This was life, indeed, an astonished public exclaimed, and for the first time in our history an opera had a "run." It is significant, though, that Menotti's *The Consul* had its run on Broadway, and that it was given its enthusiastic reception by the drama critics and a prevailingly theater-going audience.

The pioneer has always a special meed of honor, and that honor is Menotti's for more reasons than one—he won it alike for matter and for manner. He was definitely the man of the hour, for he appeared at a moment when opera in this country was sicklied o'er with the unnatural bloom of old-fashioned grand opera; in a surprisingly new and violent tone, he shattered the world of opera-cloaks and gold-headed canes. The burgeoning opera workshops, suffering from invidious comparisons with the "legitimate" opera houses, found a model upon which to build. Since *The Medium*, first produced in 1946 by Columbia University's opera workshop, Menotti has gone all the way to the principal opera houses in the world, surely a career that is matched only by some of the famous opera composers of the past.

Gian Carlo Menotti's many-sided talents recall some of his brilliant Italian forebears. For the secret of Menotti's success is that even in America he never really strayed from the ancestral operatic faith, which in his case was the verismo of the turn of the century. He fills our ears with the jingle of Puccinian melodies that are only slightly modernized and are always on the verge of taking wing, and which, by the force of his feeling, make certain scenes almost painfully present to us. If I say that Menotti is a common-sense composer, I do not wish to be misunderstood. He has the common sense of the Italian composer who shuns the metaphysics of the Germans and the artificial nationalism of the others; he wants a dramatic tale of passion. An Italian writes Italian opera whatever the tale and the locale, for the simple reason that opera to the Italian is not an acquired medium but his natural mode of dramatic expression. Since Menotti is his own librettist, he does not have to go far to find such a tale, and if he does not vary his conflicts overmuch, his formula is a sound one for this type of opera. This is not to suggest that his characters are puppets; in his hands they come to life, at least intermittently, and speak like real people. Still, there are times when he does not succeed in persuading us that the circumstances warrant all the mental stress and pother he depicts, and in general it may be said that he seems to be striving after bigger effects than he can achieve. The music cannot take undisputed command at the decisive places, because it is unsubtle, though occasionally vivid, and the same might be said about his technique, which makes use of all the known operatic tricks.

Amelia Goes to the Ball, the earliest of Menotti's operas performed in this country, was the work of a very young Italian composer thoroughly at home with centuries-old traditions. *The Medium* is more famous, but I like *Amelia*. Not only has this work the authentic Italian opera buffa flavor, but its composer has the gift of presenting it in such a comfortably assured way that one is impelled to follow its twists and turns with interest. Nearly everything in this entertaining opera—style, subject, outlook—is traditional; Menotti has a bright and busy eye for the values of the musical theater, and though they are often mere surface values, they are used with real flair and skill. Menotti's music is very eclectic, neither conservative nor modern, but he has the true opera composer's instinct to weave text, music, and action into a believable unity. Ten years later, in *The Medium*, Menottti appears in the colors that ever since have characterized his operas: ultra-verismo. He is not fundamentally different from his ancestors—*The Medium* is still a work of realism composed by a Romantic—where he differs from the older realists is that his music is not so shapely as theirs. His writing is at times a little undisciplined; he is constantly being deflected from the straight musical line of his vision by the hurrying excitement of his theatrical imagination, anxious to get a flesh-creeping quality into his scenes. But even the untidy pages of his scores have an urgency which is often lacking in works that are closer to organized composition. The music itself is once more impersonal—even insignificant—but coming from the mouth of the heroine, as the tormented utterance of a homeless spirit, it is painfully impressive.

The Consul, a runaway international success, raised for this critic several questions. The tale of this opera is highly dramatic, eloquent, and contemporary. On first hearing, I found the work rather strenuously brilliant, reflecting admirably the youth, eagerness, and high spirits of its composer. A few years later the blend of sophistication and vigor seemed not always a happy one. Menotti writes with fervent expressiveness, yet his musical expression has a somewhat monotonous quality when not aided by the stage. The message rings with sincerity, but the musical narrative is thin and conventional, though composed with dexterity and ease by a practiced hand. The free dramatic dialogue glides into the set numbers with that natural ease only Italians or Italian-oriented composers can muster, and the ensembles, the bane of present-day composers, materialize from nowhere as if they were the easiest thing to put together. Still, in essence there is little in *The Consul* which has not been presented again and again in other operas, though most of it is done with an imaginative immediacy which justifies the work's success.

Menotti's comprehension of the spirit of our age is very real, and he confronts the issues boldly and candidly, but with a vigor that can trip over its own toes into violence, facts drawn by indignation into disproportion, trivialities magnified to become sceptres. In a word, the author-composer tends to overstate a case which has a good deal of truth in it, but which—and this is the real point of the criticism—so far as it is true may not be best served by the naturalism and sophistication of his treatment. It must be added, though, that none of his thoughts is anything but honest. One can only regret that as a musician Menotti is less inventive than as a man of the theater. There are many absorbing moments in this opera, especially in the quieter scenes, but too often the operatic cliché will spoil a dramatic picture which might have been touching, too often a rather excessive verismo will mar the effect and make the listener feel uncomfortable. He is lavish with his colors and can be crudely realistic or eloquently sentimental as the occasion seems to him to require, loth to reject any notion that promises to be theatrically effective. There is more violence than imaginative strength, more melodrama than drama; that the effect is one of power is unquestionable, but the movement is often more theatrical than human. Menotti is afraid of being dull and sacrifices lucidity to intensity. And too often the listener will be disappointed because he senses that Menotti really wanted to say

something very much more. The real merit of this work lies
in its excellent theatrical qualities—no small achievement in
contemporary opera.

A libretto shares with a play certain requirements as simple
as they are difficult to satisfy: the author must provide his
players with roles they can not only understand but feel, by
which they can express themselves through identification with
the characters as spontaneously as possible, and to which their
audience may as spontaneously respond. But the preference
in the American theater for closely chronicled ordinary lives
bedevils our fledgling opera. Librettists feel they must be
careful and realistic in detail, "true to life," and sufficiently interesting *without the music* to hold the attention. All this
librettist Menotti can achieve to a considerable degree, and
his use of the English language is felicitous, but opera demands
less of the libretto and more of the music. With the exception
of a few excellent sketches, Menotti is more successful with
incidents than with characters. He employs the musical commonplace, which is very skillfully placed at the service of the
play, and this rather wholesome commonplace is ever present,
sometimes in the foreground, generally in the background
while an absorbing theatrical action takes place on the stage.
Nevertheless, Menotti infused opera in America with a new
life, a far more valid and fruitful life than the slick Central
European products of such composers as Liebermann. Eventually our composers will learn that stagecraft and fervor, skill
and *savoir-faire*, if not supplemented by true musical inventiveness, are not enough for the creation of opera.

Nineteen

OPERA
IN ENGLISH

THE OLD controversy about opera in English is renewed
every time there is a good performance with English
text. Successful versions of *Così fan tutte* or *The Merry
Wives of Windsor* caused many members of the audience to
express delight at their ability to understand the plot; follow
the play word for word; grasp every joke, aside, and allusion.
But when we hear *Pelléas et Mélisande* in a language other
than French, as I have heard it repeatedly in Europe, another
note is added to the discussion, because it is quite obvious that
this work simply cannot be sung in translation. Those who
want every opera in English must acknowledge the fact that
Debussy's vocal line is not autonomously musical; he set to
music the French words, every one of them, and without
the natural gait of these words much of the music is meaningless. Surely no one would concede this to be true in the case
of Mozart or Verdi. But that *Pelléas* and some other operas
are untranslatable does not negate the axiom that theater without theatrical values is a contradiction in terms, nor its corollary, that theater requires understanding of what takes place
on the stage. I do not see how anyone can convincingly reject

this thesis, no matter how valid some arguments may be from the esthetic point of view, and even granting the indisputable reinforcement music gains from the original words.

Yet the problem is neither so clear-cut nor so simple as that. The fundamental divergences in grammatical structure between a Slavic, a Latin, and a Germanic language, and also between what may be called the acoustics of these respective languages, involve difficulties that not even the most skillful translator can altogether overcome. (One recalls Sheridan's protestation; "Not a translation—only taken from the French.") Furthermore, the psycho-physiological factors of voice production and projection have an important role in determining the juxtaposition of words and music, something few literary men understand.

Poets and scholars have devoted much time and energy to solving the problems of translation, for nothing permeates man's mental life more than language. It is with the aid of language that we formulate thought; in fact, we are able to express thoughts only in the measure our language permits us. In the absence of knowledge of the original tongue, such translations as compel the language to bend according to the ideas it tries to convey are the only means of a rapprochement between different cultures. The difficulty every translator faces rests on the eternal tension between form and content. The more faithful we remain to the text formally, the more chance we have to be faithful to the content—at least to what is essential in the content. Rhymed poetry offers a good example, for rhyme is like a knitted stocking: cut one stitch and the whole string unravels. Every line to be translated calls for verbal virtuosity, invention, and a new realignment of the words to fit the music's cadence. Some translators cast aside the fetters of form and use a new arrangement which they consider more suitable to the genius of their language, while others simply give up the rhyme. In the case of rhythmic poetry only a rhythmic translation can approximate the quality of the original text, for it is the rhythm that lends its particular color to the poetic idea and therewith to the musical rhythm. Those whose language can be adjusted only imperfectly to foreign rhythms have only a narrow bridge to understanding. (Perhaps this has something to do with the often uncomprehending chauvinism of the French.)

While able men of letters have created many highly satisfactory and artistic translations of poetry and prose, we must recognize that what the Italians call *poesia per musica*, a text written for the sole purpose of being set to music, constitutes a very special case requiring very special procedures. In the translation of a verse on which an aria is based, even a felicitous rendering of both form and content is not enough. The position of single words is very important, both poetically and musically; that is, the important words must be held to their original position in relation to the musical phrase. A study of the best Italian librettists will show how careful they are in placing important words. The English language is compact, more so than the Italian; it is also calmer, less musical, and slower than the freely flowing Italian. In general one might say that in their translations the French lighten the original Italian, the Germans make it heavier, while the English slow it down and bleach it a little.

I would not advocate the translation of art songs; they are usually the settings of original poems meant to be enjoyed for their own sake, though in the hands of a capable poet who also knows his music it is often feasible. If the audience is furnished with a fair poetic translation the singer should retain the original text. But when it comes to opera we are dealing with a text expressly created to be set to music and of little if any interest and value without it. Here we must judge every case on its own merits. Most librettos are the work of minor poets or dramatists, though many of them show an intimate knowledge of the requirements of the lyric stage. Here form can be slighted in favor of the best positioning of each word. As a consequence, the bulk of the operatic repertory can be translated without any loss of poetic values. As a matter of fact, skilled translation can effect a definite improvement in the works of Messrs. Illica or Meilhac. With Wagner the situation is different. His texts, with the exception of *Die Meistersinger*, are altogether unpalatable; the dogged adherence to the archaic alliterative poetic form and the heavy symbolism cannot be rendered in English without becoming ridiculous. Leave him alone and sing him in German—the substance of the music is in the magnificent orchestra anyway. But we could give *Die Meistersinger* a try. It is quite another matter when we deal with such vivid theater as *The Marriage of Figaro,* or *The Barber of Seville,* or *Wozzeck,* or *Gianni Schicchi.* Here the mood, the content, and the form of the libretto must be understood every minute, and a translation is desirable.

The Italian librettist always knew that he must use the simplest verse, because once set to music its sentimental content would be magnified tenfold. These simple lyrics can be translated very successfully, and surely the prose dialogues should not present any difficulty. But only poets with a musical background really understand these things. The mere linguist always bogs down in the interpretation of content, for he does not understand the importance of form. The translator must preserve the symbolic-pictorial associations between the music and the words, and he must observe and reconcile verbal and musical rhythm.

There are other reasons for using the singer's mother tongue which should tip the balance in favor of the opera-in-English party. The longstanding practice in Europe (though not in England), where operas are almost always sung in the country's vernacular, rests on these reasons. For the past two or three decades both press and public have been noting with pride and pleasure how many American singers are now in the forefront, holding their own in competition with some of the greatest in Europe. But the appreciative audiences scarcely realize what a handicap it is for Americans to sing in Italian, German, or French. I say "handicap" because they are forsaking their mother tongue and all that it implies in natural ease of voice production. Every language calls for a different voice production; if a native American is called upon to sing in another language, his vocal organs are compelled to function unnaturally. In Italian there are no clusters of consonants, and therefore an Italian voice, even when raw and untutored, soars freely. Other languages, especially the Germanic, are full of elements that are unfavorable to the singing voice. The Italian singer when he goes to New York or London keeps on singing in Italian and has nothing to worry about, for he is in his natural element—unless he is asked to sing in English, which can be disastrous. (There is the famous story of a lady who attended a performance of Handel's *Esther* in which one of the parts was sung by an Italian in English. Ahasuerus was singing the line "I came, my Queen, to chaste delights," but the audience heard "I comb my Queen to chase the lice.") Even though many Europeans have sung roles in an English that many of our native singers may envy, and Americans in Milan or Bayreuth have performed in Italian and German to general satisfaction, yet they were in foreign lands in more than one sense. That our singers do so well in spite of these drawbacks speaks for the dedication of the artists to the arduous study they must follow.

The phenomenal singers of the old bel canto era had only one thing in mind: the musical unfolding of the voice. This purely musical concept of singing is difficult for us to understand, for it ignores what we consider the proper interpretation of the text. No aria was sung twice the same way; the singers, usually well trained in the art of improvisation and not infrequently even in composition, considered the musical score a pretext for their own sallies into the blue yonder of vocal virtuosity. The rising opera buffa began to change things, and thenceforth the singer was expected to watch his enunciation. As a consequence, however, there was inevitably a certain loss in the esthetic quality of the vocal sound, and as we advance to still more recent times, in the wake of the great changes inaugurated by Meyerbeer and culminating in the musical declamation of Wagner, singing as an art made a complete about face. If we remember, though, that Bellini's singers were still schooled in the great Italian vocal tradition, we can understand the difficulty nowadays in finding good interpreters to take these exacting roles. It is not that great voices are absent from this world, but they are trained differently and are lacking in certain musical qualities that used to be part and parcel of a singer's equipment.

Another important change in singing styles resulted from the rise of the great literature of the Romantic song, the lied. Though we listen to song recitals in large concert halls, the lied is an intimate genre that should be sung in a room with a small audience clustered around the piano. Moritz von Schwind has a well-known etching that charmingly depicts a musicale at the home of one of Schubert's patrons, with a couple of dozen people surrounding Schubert and Vogl, the singer. The song composer's melodic curve takes cognizance of this intimacy, touching on high tones lightly. The operatically trained voices, especially those of heldentenor and dramatic soprano, favor and emphasize the high tones, and the singers have learned to make them powerful—this is what brings down the house. All Romantic opera composers exploit such voices and provide the singers with the opportunities they so desire. It is for this reason that few opera singers are good lieder singers, and vice versa. On the other hand, powerful high tones tend to be projected individually, thus momentarily leaving the context of both text and melody. The translator must watch the high notes in the score carefully because they require certain syllables that facilitate production and projection.

Italian singing instruction in the days of the bel canto was concentrated on music, but French, German, and English instruction must first of all cope with the difficulties caused by the language. Compel an Italian to sing in German or English and he will have technical difficulties and problems heretofore unknown to him; he may even hurt his voice. Now, an American singing in Italian will not hurt his voice; nevertheless, he is moving into a world that is physiologically strange to him. There is a widespread belief that the Wagnerian type of declamatory singing can ruin a naurally beautiful voice. This holds only if the singer tries to apply a bel-canto trained voice to the task. Wagner, always well informed about problems touching upon his art, was fully aware of the difficulties presented to the old-line singers by his vocal parts; what he wanted, and eventually obtained, was a singer equally well trained in singing and in declamation. With the aid of some able and learned teachers, he taught the singers how to enunciate consonants, how to eliminate the tension created by clusters of them, and how to minimize the adverse musical effects caused by the guttural sounds of the German language.

If the study of phonetics is required to enable the German singer to cope with the anti-musical qualities of his own language, how much more necessary is it for those to whom the language is foreign? Where the Germans must overcome the guttural quality of their language, the French must mitigate the nasal quality in theirs, to which must be added the special technique to deal with the pronunciation of the "mute" vowels, which in singing are anything but mute. Modern science has established the mechanical laws of phonetics, the study of which should be a mandatory subject for singers, as it is for actors. The modern singer must be well schooled in easily articulated speech before he can sing, and the modern teacher must realize that there is no such thing as a universal vocal technique; it varies from land to land, from language to language. The pianist plays on the same keyboard whether he races over a Pleyel, a Blüthner, or a Steinway, but the singer is inconvenienced the minute he abandons his mother tongue. It is for this reason, and not solely for the sake of intelligibility, that opera in English is preferable if the singers are Americans or Englishmen. But a warning is in order: The Italian librettists always knew that the vowels are the true carriers of the singing voice, and in their lyrics paid much attention to easily singable lines and words. When translating such texts, in addition to respecting musical values and rendering them in approximately faithful English (which does not happen often), translators must not fail to take into consideration the phonetic propriety of this English. It is not enough to remain faithful to the original musical line; the English version must also be faithful to the requirements of singing in English. This can be done, but again, it calls for more than routine ability to turn a neat phrase in English.

This little dissertation seems to favor—in principle, at least—opera in English; yet with all the advantages that it offers for performers and audiences alike, the problem remains largely insoluble because of the various nationalities of the great traveling stars. Opera companies with all-native personnel should by all means take advantage of good translations; if opera is to spread beyond the New York–Chicago–San Francisco axis, English-language performances are absolutely necessary. But the great opera theaters with their polyglot casts will, it appears, have to adhere to the original language of the librettos, because this is the only practical means of reconciling the diversity of background and schooling of their international celebrities.

Twenty

STAGELESS OPERA

AS OPERA becomes more popular in America and we are willing to extend both ends of the spectrum to include operas before Gluck and after Strauss, the scarcity of theaters and the unconscionably costly logistics of the lyric stage make it impossible to meet this demand. Many a good-sized and well-to-do community would be able to maintain a modest but live opera theater, but are unwilling to do so because it would unfavorably compare with the splendors of New York's Metropolitan Opera. (It is not realized that the rich operatic culture of Italy and Germany is mainly due to their many small municipal theaters which alternate repertory theater with opera.) These circumstances have led to concert or "semi-staged" performances, which, formerly an exception, now occupy entire companies expressly formed for this purpose. Unfortunately, opera without a theater is like a picnic indoors. An opera without the setting and without acting seldom satisfies even when the work is well known, but when it is totally unfamiliar much of the significance as well as the substance of the work tends to be lost. Stage music, real operatic music, often fails to exert its full power in the frozen formality of the concert platform. An opera is a play in music; it must be staged and acted, but if it is presented in concert version, then it should not offer a half-hearted gesture towards the theater. Indeed, the "partly staged" performances are even more unsatisfactory than the concert variety. The tenor is all excited, but you do not know why; the soprano is obviously dying, but she remains on her feet; a peasant in white tie and tails, his gold wrist watch flashing semaphores in true operatic fashion, is pretty odd. Nor does the stationary chorus, its members turning the pages of their scores without looking at the person they sing about, contribute to the illusion. One can of course present even Wagner in this manner by shaving the bearded gods and dressing them up in the uniform of the modern concert hall. If Wotan carries a spear, Brünnhilde a saddle, and Alberich a pail of water, everyone will understand the allusions. The performance of a long-forgotten Bellini opera in a makeshift staging at Carnegie Hall offered a scenic view that looked like a high-class funeral parlor, what with all the black-gowned and suited figures standing and sitting among the potted greenery; the scores they held could have been prayer books. What made the place really an opera house was the public, this faithful American opera public, adept at bravoing at the wrong places and smothering the ends of arias.

Different esthetic laws govern concert music and theatrical music, for they are different worlds calling for an entirely different sort of imagination from both performers and public. Opera is theater, the most involved, elaborate, and exciting form of theater. The Italian term "opera" is far more inclusive than its English interpretation, for it embraces not only the musical score but the whole theater, "the work." Well, then, how can we reduce this theatrical art work to a static, formal concert which completely disregards all other elements but the music?

In a true opera the particular charm and power of the music does not come through without staging and acting, for gesture is an expression of feeling, and the decor and costumes summarize the external aspects, providing a vision of the whole action. True, both are to a considerable degree determined by the music, but they also complement it. Musical characterization, which is the essence of opera, accounts for every step on the stage; it confronts, measures, judges. Cer-

tain scenes, parts of scenes, even single words, as well as figures and actions, have created, during the long history of
opera, definite types of musical attitudes, sentiments, and situations, which are reflected in very particular music which is
meaningless without the full theatrical picture. When listening to Haydn and Mozart one is constantly reminded that
their symphonies owe more to opera than to any other source,
but we can also see that the method of procedure is quite different when the stage is not involved, for each has its own
conventions. When the opera of the Italian schools is performed in concert form, the conventions are exchanged; we
therefore hear music of which large portions are meaningless.

Of particular interest are the passages in operatic music that
we might designate as dramatically neutral, used by the composer to connect important scenes or sections when he wants
to enhance their impact. In the theater these are not only convincing but absolutely essential for the proper relief they lend
to the development of the situation; in concert performances
they may sound like so much jog-trot music. But perhaps the
most important difference between staged and concert performances of opera is in the delineation of the characters
envisaged by the composer but slumbering in the score until
brought to life by the singers. Here too we are dealing with
long-accepted conventions, for each of various feelings and
situations (such as rage or embarrassment) has its particular
musical symbols, even forms. The protagonists are bound by
these and yet must deal with them according to the differing
dramatic character of their respective roles. To mention a
couple of examples, there is considerable resemblance between
the kind of music given to the Queen of the Night and to
Donna Anna, or between that given to Pamina and to Con-
stanze. In a concert performance we readily notice the similarity of the textures, but in a well-realized theatrical setting
we see two totally different characters, as the conventions
recede into the background. Yet these conventions are so
strong that they are in effect carried over into other musical
genres, though their original associations are eroded. The old
opera buffa cliché that illustrates the anxious heartbeats of the

rascally servant when confronted by his master reappears in Schubert's "Unfinished" Symphony in the halting syncopations that accompany that divine melody. A similar ancient operatic standby used by countless composers for two hundred years is the "fright" motif of Papageno, which appears upon the approach of Sarastro. The identical musical substance is used in the tremendous "Dies irae" in Mozart's Requiem Mass, but see the difference with which the "behavioral" element is handled in the new and different context. In most such cases the composer may not even know the origin of the symbols, but he has inherited and absorbed them.

Without the stage, paucity of musical ideas immediately becomes evident, often painfully so. Take for instance Richard Strauss, some of whose late operas are being performed here in concerts. Though he was a composer who knew every facet of the lyric stage as few have known it, what can be quite pleasant on the stage, even if not particularly inventive, appears bare and contrived when removed from its natural habitat. Even if we forget the vital role of staging, it is practically impossible, for purely musical reasons, to present such a work on the concert platform. The large orchestra belongs in the pit; when placed on the stage, together with the singers, it makes their position almost untenable, even when led by an experienced opera conductor. I might add that an opera orchestra is quite different from the concert variety; the latter cannot be turned overnight into a pit orchestra. It has been proved time and again that a good opera orchestra and a good opera conductor can do very well in the symphonic field, but the opposite is rare. From Toscanini to Reiner and Szell, the great conductors have come from the opera house.

There are still other weighty objections to performing operas in the concert hall. Because a full-length opera cannot be presented integrally in a two-hour concert, the scores are usually a bit telescoped. At times it is difficult to be sure how much of the unknown score is excluded, or even whose work it may be. I heard a performance of Pergolesi's *Il Maestro di musica*, a pleasant opera buffa, but with scarcely one number by Pergolesi in it. The work was very popular in the eighteenth century and made the rounds of Italian opera houses. Following the custom of the day, every resident maestro tampered with the score, lifting out arias and replacing them with his own or with some that his singers favored. A hundred years later the "Pergolesi" opera had become an altogether different work. Then there are the Russians, with their remarkable proclivity for altering and finishing one another's works.

Some may say, however, that the end justifies the means, and that the presence of great singers in the cast is sufficient reason for offering stageless performances. I can see merit in the concert performance of a fine opera which otherwise could not hope to be heard, or of one deficient in true theatrical qualities yet of genuine musical value. But neither Strauss, nor Bellini, nor Donizetti qualifies for such a role. Opera in concert form is a contradiction in terms and a dangerous trap for the unwary; let us have opera and let us have concerts, but let us not confuse the two.

Twenty-one

OPERETTA

T HERE ARE theaters exclusively devoted to operetta, or "light opera," but once in a while even the most august opera houses take time out from their travails to mount one or the other of these popular favorites. The public likes them, the musicians like them, and they seem to be quite at home in the opera house, especially when performed by a comely cast of good actors. Why, then, should we make such a sharp distinction between "light" and "serious" opera, operetta versus opera? Actually, it is very difficult to draw an exact line. We should not, however, use the term "operetta" as a catchall to include Broadway revues, or "musicals"; they use questionable ingredients deployed in a completely circumscribed manner, with more or less coarse accompaniment, often the work of an arranger. Neither should we include Viennese musical plays of the post-World War I period, the "commercialized" descendants of the attractive Viennese operetta of Johann Strauss's era.

"Serious" and "light" music meet in a vast borderland which they frequently cross. There is much finely wrought light music, often composed by able musicians whose work may be much more genuinely artistic than many a grave opera or ponderous symphony. Sociologically and psychologically, the domain of light music is supposed to begin where the audience does not seek artistic experience, only pastime.

But this is not a satisfactory marker, for we cannot with accuracy stake out the line between entertainment and artistic experience; perhaps it should be so. Passion and artistic will are often missing in so-called light music, but we do not find a workable criterion here either—the distinction is too complicated. Yet we can recognize that there are gifted composers who regard life, as far as their art is concerned, in the light of a limited material world and sensuous pleasure; they are full of healthy melody and rhythm, happy apostles of the old trinity of wine, women, and song. Theirs is often an excellent talent, and in their own sphere they can produce first-rate compositions because in them the quality of creative mood corresponds to the ability to shape the artistic matter. Nevertheless, their creations are still removed from the higher sphere of art, because though they may employ the same artistic means, they lack the depth of content sufficient to satisfy the demands of "high art."

Operetta, with few exceptions, is not just lighter than opera but a totally different thing, since it is lacking in the most essential features of the latter. An operetta can be perfect within its own sphere if its sentimental elements are given adequate form; it may have some of the qualities, some of the allure, of true art, may even speak its language, yet it remains within a sentimental region that is not only limited but virtually boarded up and isolated from the wholeness of human life. It can never elevate or move, nor can it "castigate mores by laughter" in the manner of Molière or Mozart.

The operetta avoids universality; it makes no effort to be a symbolic projection of life. Its aim is to refrain from touching upon life's real problems; it takes its nourishment not from genuine human passions but from manufactured, counterfeit passions whose sole aim is to create amusing or sentimental situations. But their laughter is without the conditions of any inner truth. As we look at the figures of the operetta, they all seem undeveloped and unable to develop. They are lacking in distinction between the profound and the superficial, the true and the false, for they are locked in a spiritual territory which is of a constant level, and which includes equally all in the play. The protagonists are the typical representatives of human smallness; they are pleasant, even lovable, and their quest for riches and women—usually both—is an occupation that readily evokes sympathetic understanding. Since their world is purely materialistic, eating and mating are the only worthwhile aims in life, and since this agrees with them they are in perfect harmony with themselves and with the atmosphere that surrounds them. If they are powerful, their power always comes from station or money, never from will or knowledge; if they have desires, only luck, accident, or convention can advance them, never passion or reasoning. There is no emotion to be communicated when no emotion is felt. In the operetta persons of high estate are almost always grotesque characters, for, unlike the fairy tale, the operetta seldom raises the barefoot peasant boy to a prince; such an advancement would emphasize the individual's ethical value, and such a value does not exist in the world of the operetta.

The dramatic architecture of the operetta is very simple: things can happen in any old way as long as there is at least one couple who for the time being cannot be united. There must be artificial and not-too-subtle obstacles that will delay the desired union long enough to provide an opportunity for an evening's song and dance. The presence of music, and its role in such a play, is mostly decorative. In the comic opera and the singspiel, where there is spoken dialogue, the music starts when the situation becomes lyrically charged. In the operetta it can start anywhere; the prose simply stops and the music begins. It is for this reason that the potpourri is such a favorite form with operetta composers.

Unity between text and music is achieved in the operetta by the fact that the musical numbers do not as a rule characterize a given dramatic state of mind; they merely follow the prosody. Thus it often happens that both hero and heroine sing identical music, as in the musical comedy; indeed, all of them, including the chorus, sing the same music. Unlike opera, the operetta provides no dramatic situations that are the result of character; there are only figural, choreographic situations.

A good example of the typical and genuine operetta is Lehár's *The Merry Widow*. The music is entirely justified on its own terms, for although it comes from the twilight of Viennese "light opera," it shows the hand of an accomplished musician. Unfortunately, while the music of *The Merry Widow* is still fresh, the play itself is completely faded, the story silly, and the lines too stilted to suit present-day audiences. There are many great operas with such faded librettos, but the strength of their music ennobles the silly words. Since this music is not wedded to the text to the degree it is in true opera, perhaps it could be "modernized."

There is still another category of light opera which we must designate as operetta. Here, however, the line dividing it from bona fide comic opera is very thin; in the case of real masters of the genre like Offenbach, Hervé, Lecocq, and a few others (the young Bizet also belongs in this group), it is hardly visible. A work like Offenbach's *Orpheus in Hades* presents a seriously and conscientiously worked-out score that makes high demands on all departments of the lyric theater. Offenbach's writing is consistently ingenious, witty, idiomatic, and abreast of the artistic standards of the times. Yet one thing becomes evident even in some of the best of the operettas: they are more plays *with* music than plays *in* music. The characters sing, and they may sing very good tunes, but they do not become characters *through* music, as even the most miserable concoctions of Piave's or Cammarano's books become flesh-and-blood characters in true operatic scores. In the operetta they owe their personality to the play; their character is only enhanced or colored by the music. On the other hand, there is no essential difference in the apparatus employed by these engaging French operettas and the most serious operas of its time. (I am of course speaking of "singers' opera," not of the symphonic variety.)

Looking up the date of Offenbach's *Orpheus in Hades* (newspapers prize data even more than scholars), my eye caught the closing sentence in the essay preceding the catalogue of works. While acknowledging that Offenbach's music "is the most genuinely comic ever produced by a composer in that line," grave old *Grove's Dictionary of Music and Musicians* dismisses every other merit Offenbach may have possessed. In sentiment he is judged unable to hold a candle to Johann Strauss, and in craftsmanship he is "not any way comparable to Sullivan." The surprising part of this righteous appraisal is that the date of *Grove's* new edition is 1954, but still the old British preference for the safe Victorian family entertainment as far superior to the "cynical Latin's art" is undimmed. Jacques Offenbach was the son of a German-Jewish musician and cantor who settled as a boy in Paris, but his fascinating combination of genuine lyricism and pointed parody is as French as Camembert and Beaujolais. *Grove's* comparison with Strauss and Sullivan invites reflection, as does the patronizing qualification 'in that line."

Offenbach's line is an admirable one, descending from the opéra comique of Auber, Adam, Hérold, and from Donizetti. It also has some connections with the German singspiel. His operetta is exactly what its name implies: little opera. It is a high form of entertainment music which always shows due regard for artistic responsibility. Offenbach offers light music, but by means of genuine art.

The other two paragons of the operatta were also serious and well-equipped composers. Johann Strauss *fils* was a staunch champion of contemporary music and, ironically enough, the Director of His Royal and Imperial Majesty's Court Ball Music (his official title) was the first one to acquaint the reluctant Viennese with excerpts from *Tristan und Isolde*. Arthur Sullivan, besides being the world-famous composer of Gilbertandsullivans, was a professor of composition, a church musician, and principal of the Royal College of Music. In social standing, Offenbach—the French pit musician and conductor who could not stand formal musical education at the Conservatoire for any length of time—could not match his rivals, but in other aspects all comparison ends here. Sullivan's music is very pleasant, colorful, and never fails in its effect; but his is a staid middle-class humor lacking in punch, always retaining the basic mutton-chop flavor of a sane and unventuresome English bourgeoisie. It is not the British composer who rises to Swiftian satire but the Gallicized immigrant from Cologne. Offenbach's merriment is ironical, biting, and frivolous, totally lacking in the mundane sentimentality of his Vienna and London colleagues. Strauss, in turn, represents the ravishing consolidated irresponsibility of Francis Joseph's laissez-faire empire, an anachronistic, well-fed, well-to-do, and self-centered provincial civilization in which there was little difference between archduke and a coachman. Both were apt to take discomfort for tragedy; both loved good food, wine, women, and music; and both hated to work. In the usual Strauss operetta, the waltz is the center of attention, and little attempt is made at continuous dramatic setting, whereas in Offenbach we are listening to real operatic procedures. The one significant exception in Strauss's work is *Die Fledermaus*, where he demonstrated that he could rise above the confines of his charming dance music.

What makes the Offenbachian operatta so attractive is that in this frivolous art there reigns a freedom from all conventions. This French operetta may be rollicking amusement, but it is also saturated with meaning. Here it is political, there moralizing, or just impudent and irreverent, but under the malicious sarcasm there is the very real life of the citizen of what was then the world's capital city, the laughter and tears of the boulevards. There was a good bit of Molière in Offenbach. The French called this naughty Napoleonic operetta *opéra bouffe* (not to be confused with the Italian *opera buffa*), and the theater where it was performed Bouffes Parisiennes. The *opéra bouffe* has no counterpart; it is inimitably French, and its lilting, spicy tunes often hide bitter satire. The "Napoleon" mentioned above refers to the third of the clan, whose goatee and pomaded mustache became the symbol of the Second Empire. Offenbach, with the sharp eyes of the born dramatist, saw through the glitter of this false empire, and while he presented his theatrical public with irresistibly funny entertainment, he did not spare their sensibilities. *Orpheus in Hades* is a subtle, wicked, and brilliant parody of Gluck's famous opera and a murderous satire on the Second Empire. Thus, in spite of the capital foolery, this is also criticism of a sort not lacking in philosophical humor. *La Perichole* has the usual inconsequential story, but Meilhac and Halévy, the librettists, were old hands at whittling lyrics to a fine Gallic point, and their lines are very funny. Offenbach's melodies are captivating in their piquancy and some of his arias little masterpieces, but the mordant accent is never far away. The orchestra is often very delicately handled, but at other times it is deliberately coarse, with the piccolo whistling, the cymbals clanging, and the melody carried by the cornet; and the act-ending cancans in *Orpheus* are absolutely unique in their rowdy directness. But before Offenbach died he momentarily stilled his mocking laughter and used his great theatrical gifts and sparkling musical imagination to compose a serious opera in which a good deal of the sadness of life shines through the elegant exterior. In *The Tales of Hoffmann* the jester's cap and bells are discarded; there is disillusionment and even tragedy.

Whoever wrote that piece in *Grove* ought to take a fresh look at Offenbach's scores. But he should not read them in the cozy comfort of a club in Mayfair with a glass of sherry in hand; they call for a sidewalk café and a touch of absinthe.

INDEX OF WORKS

INDEX OF NAMES